Going Home

Questions and Answers about Life After Death

Keith A. Haslem

Illumination Publishing Company
PO Box 1462
Orem, UT 84059
Illuminationpublishing.com
Illuminationpubco@gmail.com
801-358-3699

Copyright 2018 © Keith A. Haslem

All rights reserved, including the right to reproduce this book or portions thereof in any form whatsoever.
First Illumination Publishing Company paperback edition November 2018.

ISBN 978-1-7322443-0-6

Library of Congress Control Number: 2018910320

Library of Congress Cataloging-in-Publication Data is available.

Cover design by Keri Jean
Cover photo by Lilkar
Interior layout by Chelsea Holdaway

Manufactured in the United States of America

10 9 8 7 6 5 4 3 2 1

Literary permissions granted this book are listed in Appendix D.

Unless otherwise noted, scripture quotations are taken from the King James Version of the Bible.

For information about special discounts for bulk purchases, please contact 1-801-358-3699 or email Illuminationpubco@gmail.com.

This book is dedicated to my wonderful wife Sydney, whose companionship I look forward to, not only "till death do us part," but for all eternity.

And to the rest of my family, presently five fine sons, four lovely daughter-in-laws, and seventeen grandchildren who are "dividends" for first being a parent!

Last, but certainly not least, this book is dedicated to my elder Brother, who has helped me and my family beyond my ability to comprehend. I look forward to my reunion with Him with great anticipation.

Contents

CONTENTS BY KEYWORD XIII
PREFACE 1
ACKNOWLEDGMENTS 3
INTRODUCTION: MEET YOUR RESOURCES 5

PART I: BEGINNING THE JOURNEY

1—A Word to the Skeptics 25
2—Going *Back* Home—Where Did I Come From? 29
3—Who Am I? What Is My Relationship to God? 35
4—How Is Death Like a Graduation? 37
5—What Happens at the Moment of Death? 41
6—Will Someone Meet Me When I Die? 46
7—Will I See My Life Pass Before Me? 53
8—Will I Travel through a Dark Tunnel? 63

PART II: WHAT THE WITNESSES SAW

THE APPEARANCE OF THE SPIRIT WORLD 71

9—Where Is the Spirit World Located? 71
10—What Does the Spirit World Look Like? 74
11—Does the Spirit World Have an Atmosphere of Light and Love? 84
12—Are There Nights in the Spirit World? 88
13—Does the Spirit World Have a Fragrance? 90
14—Is There Music in the Spirit World? 92

THE APPEARANCE OF SPIRITS 95

15—What Does a Spirit Body Look Like? 95
16—Do Angels Have Wings? 102
17—Are There Racial Differences in the Spirit World? 104
18—What Clothing Will We Wear in the Spirit World? 106

Contents

THE ABILITIES OF SPIRITS 109
- 19—What Abilities Will We Have As Spirits?............109
- 20—How Will We Interact with Plants?...................117
- 21—What Activities Will We Engage In? 120
- 22—How Will We Travel in the Spirit World? 125
- 23—Can We Travel through Time in the Spirit World?...127
- 24—Is Technology Developed in the Spirit World?........129
- 25—Will We Eat Food in the Spirit World? 133

THE RELATIONSHIPS BETWEEN SPIRITS IN THE SPIRIT WORLD 135
- 26—Would Those in the Spirit World Like to Return to Earth? 135
- 27—Will We Be Reunited with Family and Friends? 139
- 28—Will We Be Reunited with Our Pets? 145

THE ARCHITECTURE OF THE SPIRIT WORLD 148
- 29—What Do Buildings Look Like in the Spirit World?...148
- 30—What Does a Heavenly City Look Like in the Spirit World?...150
- 31—Do Libraries Exist in the Spirit World?.........154
- 32—Do People Have Houses in the Spirit World? 158

JESUS CHRIST IN THE SPIRIT WORLD 160
- 33—What Is It Like to Meet Jesus Christ?.........160
- 34—What Does Jesus Look Like?...........................165
- 35—What Is the Best Portrayal of Jesus?...........168
- 36—Does Jesus Have a Sense of Humor? 176

PART III—WHAT THE WITNESSES LEARNED

LIFE 181
- 37—What Is the Purpose of Life? 181
- 38—Do We All Have "Missions" in Life? 187
- 39—Why Are Some Born with Disabilities?............190

Contents

   40—What Is the Purpose of Having
       Trials and Hardships in Life? 193

   41—Did We Sign Up for Our Trials in
       the Premortal World? 203

   42—How Long Is Our Mortal Life in
       Comparison to Our Immortal Life? 209

   43—Do Addictions Go with Us to the Spirit World? 211

   44—Do We All Have Guardian Angels? 213

   45—How Should We Pray? 222

   46—Why Are There So Many Churches? 225

DEATH 229

   47—Do We All Have an Appointed Time to Die? 229

   48—Why Do Some Die So Young? 236

   49—When Is Death a Blessing from God? 241

   50—How Do We "Let Go" of a Dying Loved One? 244

   51—How Long Should We Mourn the Departed? 248

   52—Are Traumatic Deaths Painful? 254

   53—Are Out-of-Body Experiences Possible? 257

   54—Do the Spirits of the Dead
       Stay with Us for Awhile? 260

   55—Can the Dead Give Us Signs
       That They Are All Right? 262

   56—Can the Spirits of the Dead Visit Us? 266

   57—Do Some Spirits Go to Neither Heaven Nor Hell? ...269

   58—What Happens to Those Who Commit Suicide? 275

SPIRITS 284

   59—When Does the Spirit Enter the Body? 284

   60—Can the Spirits of Comatose
       People Leave Their Bodies? 286

   61—Can Spirits Appear to Us During Our Dreams? 289

Contents

FAMILY 293

    62—Were Families Planned Before
    We Came to Earth? 293

    63—Will I Be Reunited with the Child I Lost? 304

    64—Are There Child Spirits in the Spirit World? 308

WOMEN 312

    65—What Is the Role of Womanhood? 312

    66—Why Did Eve Partake of the Forbidden Fruit? 315

    67—Do We Have a Mother in Heaven? 318

EMOTIONS 321

    68—Why Is It Important to Love Yourself? 321

    69—Why Is It Important to
    Forgive Yourself and Others? 324

    70—Is Repentance Possible in the Spirit World? 328

    71—Why Should We Learn to Love Unconditionally? 333

    72—How Can We Learn to Love through Service? 340

    73—Why Do We Need Humility? 346

    74—How Can Fear Stop Our Progress? 349

    75—What Are the Dangers of
    Feeling Depression and Anger? 351

    76—Why Is Materialism an Insignificant Pursuit? 354

CREATION OF LIFE 357

    77—Did We Help with the Creation of the Earth? 357

    78—Are There Other Worlds in the Universe? 359

PART IV—HELL AND EVIL SPIRITS

HELL 367

    79—What Is Hell Like? 367

    80—Does Hell Go on for Eternity? 379

EVIL SPIRITS 382

    81—Do Evil Spirits Exist? 382

    82—Is Possession by Evil Spirits Possible? 386

Contents

PART V—AFTER JESUS'S SECOND COMING
    83—What Happens After Jesus's Second Coming?........391
    84—Who Will Be Resurrected?...394
    85—What Happens After the Final Judgment?...............396

PART VI—PARTING THOUGHTS
    86—Parting Thoughts from the Researchers....................403
    87—Parting Thoughts from the Witnesses........................409
    88—Parting Thoughts from the Author..............................414

APPENDIX A: MEMORABLE QUOTES 419
APPENDIX B: INSPIRING BOOKS..424
APPENDIX C: BIBLIOGRAPHY...426
APPENDIX D: PERMISSIONS 431
INDEX..433
ABOUT THE AUTHOR 439

Contents by Keyword

KEYWORD	CHAPTER TITLE	PAGE NUMBER
Activities	21—What Activities Will We Engage In?	120
Addictions	43—Do Addictions Go with Us to the Spirit World?	211
Angels	16—Do Angels Have Wings?	102
Buildings	29—What Do Buildings Look Like in the Spirit World?	148
Child of God	3—Who Am I? What Is My Relationship to God?	35
Child Spirits	64—Are There Child Spirits in the Spirit World?	308
Churches	46—Why Are There So Many Churches?	225
Clothing	18—What Clothing Will We Wear in the Spirit World?	106
Coma Patients	60—Can the Spirits of Comatose People Leave Their Bodies?	286
Creation of Earth	77—Did We Help with the Creation of the Earth?	357
Dark Tunnel	8—Will I Travel through a Dark Tunnel?	63
Dead Stay Here	54—Do the Spirits of the Dead Stay with Us for Awhile?	260
Dead Visit Us	56—Can the Spirits of the Dead Visit Us?	266
Death—Appointed Time	47—Do We All Have an Appointed Time to Die?	229
Death—Graduation	4—How Is Death Like a Graduation?	37
Death—Traumatic	52—Are Traumatic Deaths Painful?	254

Contents by Keyword

KEYWORD	CHAPTER TITLE	PAGE NUMBER
Death As a Blessing	49—When Is Death a Blessing from God?	241
Depression and Anger	75—What Are the Dangers of Feeling Depression and Anger?	351
Disabilities	39—Why Are Some Born with Disabilities?	190
Dreams	61—Can Spirits Appear to Us During Our Dreams?	289
Dying Young	48—Why Do Some Die So Young?	236
Escort After Death	6—Will Someone Meet Me When I Die?	46
Eve	66—Why Did Eve Partake of the Forbidden Fruit?	315
Evil Spirits	81—Do Evil Spirits Exist?	382
Families	62—Were Families Planned Before We Came to Earth?	293
Fear	74—How Can Fear Stop Our Progress?	349
Final Judgment	85—What Happens After the Final Judgment?	396
Food	25—Will We Eat Food in the Spirit World?	133
Forgiveness	69—Why Is It Important to Forgive Yourself and Others?	324
Guardian Angels	44—Do We All Have Guardian Angels?	213
Heaven/Hell	57—Do Some Spirits Go to Neither Heaven Nor Hell?	269
Heavenly City	30—What Does a Heavenly City Look Like in the Spirit World?	150

Contents by Keyword

KEYWORD	CHAPTER TITLE	PAGE NUMBER
Hell	79—What Is Hell Like?	367
Hell—Duration of	80—Does Hell Go on for Eternity?	379
Houses	32—Do People Have Houses in the Spirit World?	158
Humility	73—Why Do We Need Humility?	346
Jesus—Appearance	34—What Does Jesus Look Like?	165
Jesus—Meeting Him	33—What Is It Like to Meet Jesus Christ?	160
Jesus—Painting	35—What Is the Best Portrayal of Jesus?	168
Jesus—Sense of Humor	36—Does Jesus Have a Sense of Humor?	176
Letting Go	50—How Do We "Let Go" of a Dying Loved One?	244
Libraries	31—Do Libraries Exist in the Spirit World?	154
Life Review	7—Will I See My Life Pass Before Me?	53
Love through Service	72—How Can We Learn to Love through Service?	340
Loving Unconditionally	71—Why Should We Learn to Love Unconditionally?	333
Loving Yourself	68—Why Is It Important to Love Yourself?	321
Materialism	76—Why Is Materialism an Insignificant Pursuit?	354
Missions in Life	38—Do We All Have "Missions" in Life?	187
Moment of Death	5—What Happens at the Moment of Death?	41

xv

Contents by Keyword

KEYWORD	CHAPTER TITLE	PAGE NUMBER
Mortal Life—Perspective	42—How Long Is Our Mortal Life in Comparison to Our Immortal Life?	209
Mother in Heaven	67—Do We Have a Mother in Heaven?	318
Mourning	51—How Long Should We Mourn the Departed?	248
Music	14—Is There Music in the Spirit World?	92
Nights	12—Are There Nights in the Spirit World?	88
Other Worlds	78—Are There Other Worlds in the Universe?	359
Out-of-Body Experiences	53—Are Out-of-Body Experiences Possible?	257
Parting Thoughts—Author	88—Parting Thoughts from the Author	414
Parting Thoughts—Researchers	86—Parting Thoughts from the Researchers	403
Parting Thoughts—Witnesses	87—Parting Thoughts from the Witnesses	409
Pets	28—Will We Be Reunited with Our Pets?	145
Plants	20—How Will We Interact with Plants?	117
Possession	82—Is Possession by Evil Spirits Possible?	386
Prayer	45—How Should We Pray?	222
Premortal Existence	2—Going *Back* Home—Where Did I Come From?	29
Purpose of Life	37—What Is the Purpose of Life?	181

Contents by Keyword

KEYWORD	CHAPTER TITLE	PAGE NUMBER
Racial Differences	17—Are There Racial Differences in the Spirit World?	104
Reluctant to Return	26—Would Those in the Spirit World Like to Return to Earth?	135
Repentance in the Spirit World	70—Is Repentance Possible in the Spirit World?	328
Resurrection	84—Who Will Be Resurrected?	394
Reunion with Child	63—Will I Be Reunited with the Child I Lost?	304
Reunion with Family	27—Will We Be Reunited With Family and Friends?	139
Second Coming	83—What Happens After Jesus's Second Coming?	391
Signs from the Dead	55—Can the Dead Give Us Signs That They Are All Right?	262
Skeptics	1—A Word to the Skeptics	25
Spirit Abilities	19—What Abilities Will We Have As Spirits?	109
Spirit Body—Appearance	15—What Does a Spirit Body Look Like?	95
Spirit Enters Body	59—When Does the Spirit Enter the Body?	284
Spirit World—Appearance	10—What Does the Spirit World Look Like?	74
Spirit World—Atmosphere	11—Does the Spirit World Have an Atmosphere of Light and Love?	84
Spirit World—Fragrance	13—Does the Spirit World Have a Fragrance?	90
Spirit World—Location	9—Where Is the Spirit World Located?	71
Suicide	58—What Happens to Those Who Commit Suicide?	275

Contents by Keyword

KEYWORD	CHAPTER TITLE	PAGE NUMBER
Technology	24—Is Technology Developed in the Spirit World?	129
Time Travel	23—Can We Travel through Time in the Spirit World?	127
Travel	22—How Will We Travel in the Spirit World?	125
Trials	40—What Is the Purpose of Having Trials and Hardships in Life?	193
Trials—Premortal Life	41—Did We Sign Up for Our Trials in the Premortal World?	203
Womanhood	65—What Is the Role of Womanhood?	312

PREFACE

THIS BOOK'S INTENT—TO PROVIDE COMFORT AND PEACE

This book is written first for those who have lost a loved one. The grief of separation cannot be escaped, but it may be assuaged if those left behind are confident that their loved one is in a wonderful place and wouldn't want to return even if they could.

It is also written for those close to the end of their mortal lives. If you are at this point in your life, you may be experiencing some trepidation. Hopefully, this book will alleviate most, if not all, of your concerns.

ADDRESSING IMPORTANT QUESTIONS

The majority of the world believes in a life after death, but there is remarkably little detail available, even in the Holy Bible, on what life will be like after death.

As medical technology has advanced, it has become possible to resuscitate individuals who were clinically dead. Many such individuals have outlined remarkable stories of touring a wondrous world of spirits before they were resuscitated.

Their experiences give us a glimpse of the answer to the question, "What will happen to me after I die?" These witnesses also received insight on such important questions as

"Who am I?"

"Where did I come from?"

Preface

"Why am I here on earth?"
"Why does life have to be so difficult?"

THREE PERSPECTIVES CORROBORATE EACH OTHER

Going Home draws from the following three perspectives to provide some illumination with regard to these important questions.

1. Six individuals who describe their own near-death experience (NDE) or out-of-body experience (OBE)
2. Nine individuals who have spent many years studying NDE cases
3. Doctrine of the Church of Jesus Christ of Latter-day Saints

As the reader will see, these three perspectives tend to corroborate each other and, in so doing, provide a more compelling view of life after death than any one perspective could by itself.

NOT A SCIENTIFIC STUDY

This book is not offered as proof of life after death. Nor is it meant to convince the skeptic. It is intended to illuminate the conditions of the afterlife and magnify the faith of those who already believe in life after death. In addition, this book is not research. I am merely drawing from existing sources, compiling and organizing the most illuminating information on universally relevant questions, and putting it all into a format (one question per chapter) that will facilitate the reader's inquiry on specific points of interest.

NAMING THIS BOOK

I struggled to come up with a title for this book for almost a year. The top choice on the list was *Life Is Tough,* But *Then You Die!*

Then one day the title *Going Home* just popped into my mind, and immediately I knew that should be the title. From that point on, I noted how many of the witnesses and other NDE accounts referred to the world of spirits as "home."

ACKNOWLEDGMENTS

This book was made possible by the many authors and publishing companies who granted me permission to draw from their excellent publications. (See Appendix D)

I acknowledge the exceptional help provided by Chelsea Holdaway who served as my copyeditor and vastly improved my original manuscript.

I am grateful to Dr. Matthew Baker of the Brigham Young University linguistics department who made a suggestion that improved the organization of my book.

I acknowledge the support that I always receive from my good wife Sydney, who supports me—sometimes against her better judgment—and doesn't rub it in when it turns out that she was right and I was foolish. And for being a living, breathing daily example of the type of person I should try to become.

Last but not least, I acknowledge my parents. My charitable mother enabled me to get the education I needed to support my family and brought me up in a home that focused on the spiritual matters more than the worldly ones. And to my father, who quietly set a good example for me as he spent even the last few weeks of his life focusing on personal spiritual development.

INTRODUCTION

MEET YOUR RESOURCES

AUTHOR'S NOTE

At the beginning of each chapter, I will provide a brief summary, or synopsis, of the topic or question at hand. The synopsis will be based upon the contributions of the resources introduced in this introduction.

Following the synopsis, I will quote from the resources in more detail.

SYNOPSIS

There have been more than twenty-eight books written by individuals who describe having had a near-death experience (NDE) or an out-of-body experience (OBE), where they left their bodies, visited a world of spirits, and then returned (usually reluctantly) to their bodies. I will draw primarily from the following six accounts, which I consider to be the most illuminating. Of course, I cannot guarantee the authenticity of any account but I do consider them to be highly credible. I will refer to these authors collectively as the Witnesses.

PERSONAL PERSPECTIVES OF THE WITNESSES

Book	Based on the experience of
Return from Tomorrow	George G. Ritchie, MD
Embraced by the Light: The Most Profound and Complete Near-Death Experience Ever	Betty J. Eadie

Introduction

PERSONAL PERSPECTIVES OF THE WITNESSES

Book	Based on the experience of
The Burning Within	RaNelle Wallace
I Stand All Amazed: Love and Healing from Higher Realms	Elane Durham
Flight to Heaven: A Plane Crash . . . A Lone Survivor . . . A Journey to Heaven—and Back	Captain Dale Black
There Is No Death: The Extraordinary True Experience of Sarah LaNelle Menet	Sarah LaNelle Menet

RESEARCH PERSPECTIVES

In addition, I will also draw from the work done by notable and respected researchers. These researchers have done extensive study on individuals who have had NDEs or OBEs. These researchers include:

    Elisabeth Kübler-Ross, MD
    Raymond A. Moody Jr., MD
    Kenneth Ring, PhD
    Maurice S. Rawlings, MD
    Michael Sabom, MD
    Jeffrey Long, MD
    Melvin L. Morse, MD
    Karlis Osis, PhD and Erlendur Haraldsson, PhD

RELIGIOUS PERSPECTIVE

Belief in life after death is a fundamental doctrine of The Church of Jesus Christ of Latter-day Saints.

    Their doctrine is based upon the Holy Bible and the following three books, which are also regarded as scripture:

    The Book of Mormon: Another Testament of Jesus Christ
    The Doctrine and Covenants
    The Pearl of Great Price

Introduction

Since the Church of Jesus Christ of Latter-day Saints was organized in 1830, various leaders of their faith have discoursed on elements of life after death. Therefore, the Church of Jesus Christ of Latter-day Saints Perspective is included for members of that faith and other interested individuals.

ADDITIONAL DETAILS ON THE RESOURCES OF THE WITNESSES

What follows is a more detailed background of each of the Witnesses.

GEORGE G. RITCHIE JR.

George G. Richie Jr. was born September 25, 1923. At the age of twenty, as an enlisted soldier in the army, he became acutely ill with pneumonia and was admitted to an army hospital. His condition deteriorated until his spirit finally left his body, and he embarked on an excursion into the world of spirits, escorted by Jesus Christ.

After his excursion, he was escorted back to his body and reluctantly reentered it.

Dr. Ritchie went on to become a respected physician—practicing as a psychiatrist, and holding several positions of leadership in professional medical organizations.

His experience is recounted in the book *Return from Tomorrow*, and is probably the first notable book written by someone claiming to have had a near-death experience. He later published *My Life After Dying: How 9 Minutes in Heaven Taught Me How to Live on Earth*.

Dr. Ritchie passed away of cancer in 2007 (Wikipedia, s.v. "George G. Ritchie," last modified 11 November 2017, en.wikipedia.org/wiki/George_G._Ritchie).

BETTY J. EADIE

Betty J. Eadie was born in 1942 in Valentine, Nebraska.

During a 1973 hysterectomy, complications arose and led to Betty's clinical death and her experience in the world of spirits. While there, she was informed that she must return to her body to fulfill her intended mission.

Introduction

Her book, *Embraced by the Light: The Most Profound and Complete Near-Death Experience Ever,* chronicles her experience. It was a No. 1 *New York Times* best seller.

Five years after her NDE, Betty visited the doctor who performed her hysterectomy. She told the doctor

> I wasn't interested in seeking a lawsuit; I just wanted to know what went wrong—that it meant a lot to me to know.... Yes, he said, there were complications that night; they had lost me for a while but had felt that it was best not to mention anything to me. Then he went on to explain what had happened. I had hemorrhaged during the operation, and it appeared that the hemorrhage occurred again later night. At the time of my death, I had been left alone during the nurses' shift change, and because I was unattended, they didn't know exactly how long I had been dead. (Eadie, *Embraced by the Light*, pp. 133–34)

Since her near-death experience, Betty has spent more than thirty-seven years speaking to groups regarding the afterlife. She has also published *The Awakening Heart* (also a best seller), *The Ripple Effect,* and *Embraced by the Light: Prayers and Devotions for Daily Living.*

Betty also sponsors a website: www.embracedbythelight.com.

Betty's husband, Joe, died in 2011. She is the mother of eight children, and as of 2011, fifteen grandchildren and seven great-grandchildren (Wikipedia, s.v. "Betty Eadie," last modified 15 January 2018, en.wikipedia.org/wiki/Betty_Eadie).

RANELLE WALLACE

RaNelle Wallace and her husband crashed in a single-engine airplane on October 9, 1985, in the mountains of central Utah. She was badly burned, but she and her husband managed to hike to the freeway where they were able to get help. An ambulance transported them to a hospital. While en route to the hospital, RaNelle's heart stopped. In her

Introduction

account, RaNelle's spirit left her body, and she was met by her deceased grandmother who escorted her on a visit to the world of spirits.

After her excursion, her grandmother told her that she needed to return to her body. "Your children need you, RaNelle," and "It's not just your children, RaNelle. You have things to do—things that aren't finished yet . . . your mission isn't complete" (Wallace, *The Burning Within*, p. 115). RaNelle was resistant until she met a spirit who she learned was intended to be her future son. (See Chapter 62: "Were Families Planned Before We Came to Earth?")

I have had several conversations with RaNelle; two things stand out in my memory. After meeting me for the first time, rather than doing the customary thing and simply shaking my hand as she was leaving, she gave me a hug—an act consistent with the primary theme of her book: We need to learn how to love one another.

The second thing I remember is that, during our conversation, she longingly said something to the effect, "I'm just anxiously waiting for the day I can go home again!"

RaNelle's book, *The Burning Within*, is a fascinating glimpse of the spirit world, and the story of her recovery from the plane crash is inspiring.

Since her recovery, RaNelle has been actively giving community service and has been a professional speaker. After helping a family escape from a burning home, RaNelle was named Woman of the Year by the state of California and received a letter of commendation from President Ronald Reagan.

RaNelle is the mother of four children and lives in Utah (Wallace, *The Burning Within*, inside flap).

Introduction

ELANE DURHAM

Elane Durham died at the Mercy Hospital in Chicago, Illinois, on October 20, 1976, of cardiac arrest, which was attendant to a rupture of an arteriovenous malformation—a brain tumor. She was pronounced dead by the emergency-room physician. A Catholic deacon came to administer her last rites and also witnessed that Elane was dead. Elane spent approximately one hour in the world of spirits. She refers to her experience not as a "near-death experience," but as a "death vision" because she knows she was dead, not near-death.

Sometime after her death vision, Elane's family physician obtained her records from Mercy Hospital regarding her treatment there. After reviewing the records, he confirmed that for a brief period of time Elane "had not made it" (Durham, *I Stand All Amazed*, p. 94).

Two weeks after her near-death experience, while still in her hospital room, Elane recognized the voice of the deacon who had administered her last rites. As she tells it:

> "Pardon me," I said as he looked at the foot of my bed for the red cross that would denote that I was Catholic. "Could you have been in the emergency room two weeks ago?"
>
> "Well, I might have been," he answered, still not looking at me. "Why, were you there?" It was then that he finally looked up, and as he focused on me, his eyes grew wide with surprise.
>
> "Yes," I responded while he stared, "they brought me in on what they thought was a drug overdose."
>
> By this time he had hold of my foot. "You died!" he exclaimed. "You died!"
>
> I did my best to smile. "I know. But I'm here, and I'd like to talk to you. Something happened to me, and I'd like to talk to you about it. Do you have time to visit?"
>
> ... "But you died," he repeated with amazement. "I can't believe this.... They were prepping you for the morgue when I got here! You couldn't have seen me! You had already died!" (*I Stand All Amazed*, pp. 94–96)

Elane struck up a friendship with the Catholic deacon, Stanley Cebrzynski, that has continued for more than twenty years. His own account of administering last rites to her is included in her book on pages 96–98.

Introduction

She recounts her story in her book *I Stand All Amazed: Love and Healing from Higher Realms*, which was published in August 1998.

CAPTAIN DALE BLACK

On July 18, 1969, Dale Black, then nineteen years old, boarded a twin-engine Piper Navajo. Problems developed moments after takeoff and the plane lost power and crashed into a concrete building at the speed of 135 miles per hour, then fell 70 feet to the ground. The pilot, Gene Bain, died at the scene. The other passenger, Chuck Burns, died later at the hospital.

For three days, Dale was in a coma. When he came out of the coma, in addition to the physical trauma, he had amnesia regarding the crash and the events leading up to the crash. But he immediately realized that he was a changed person. He felt great compassion and concern for everyone, including total strangers.

The story of his physical rehabilitation is amazing, and it includes events that would seem to be obvious miracles—resultant from his fervent faith that God would heal him and enable him to pursue his lifelong dream of becoming a professional aviator.

Several months into his recovery, his amnesia began to resolve and he began to remember the details of the crash. He also remembered an out-of-body experience he had during the three days his body was in a coma, during which time he visited a world of spirits.

Although he was never clinically dead, his account is very similar to other NDE accounts.

It was almost forty years before Captain Black decided to go public with his story, feeling that the time had finally come and that there was good purpose for doing so.

It could be argued by skeptics and cynics that because a clinical death was never documented, that his story could be a creative fabrication, coinciding with other NDE accounts. The greatest evidence of its veracity is the type of life Dale Black lived for the almost forty years *prior to* the publication of his account.

He has taken the opportunity to talk to many people, including complete strangers, about Jesus Christ, and has urged them to make Christ the focus of their lives.

Introduction

He is the founder of Eagle International Ministries, where he "led scores of teams on short-term Christian missionary projects to over fifty counties since 1981" (Black, *Flight to Heaven*, p. 186). He notes that he has "volunteered on almost a thousand flights to more than fifty countries, building churches, orphanages, and medical clinics . . . and [he has] trained lay ministers and medical personnel to help the needy worldwide, usually at [his] own expense" (*Flight to Heaven*, pp. 11–12).

His fervor is at least partially motivated by what he learned during his out-of-body experience.

Dale also has a PhD in business with an emphasis in airline management and marketing. As of 2010, he and his wife were owners of a real estate company and lived in Southern California.

His book *Flight to Heaven: A Plane Crash . . . A Lone Survivor . . . A Journey to Heaven—and Back*, published in 2010, is a remarkable story of faith—particularly with respect to the events that transpired after his accident.

SARAH LANELLE MENET

Sarah endured a horrific childhood with an abusive father. Her first marriage ended in divorce, and she was beset with a number of medical problems. Her second husband was much like her abusive father and the marriage ended in a bitter divorce. In 1979, she took an entire bottle of Tylenol with codeine in an attempt to take her own life.

Prior to taking the pills, Sarah called her sister, who then called the police. Because of this, Sarah received medical care in time. Although the paramedics initially pronounced her dead, she was eventually resuscitated.

Introduction

Sarah's book, *There Is No Death: The Extraordinary True Experience of Sarah LaNelle Menet*, was published in 2002.

AUTHOR'S NOTE AND RECOMMENDATION

I should note that all six of the Witnesses are Christians, and four of them write about meeting or seeing Christ during their experience. I cannot be sure that non-Christians would have similar experiences. For one thing, they may see a being of light, but not recognize that it is Christ because they don't believe in Christ.

I highly recommend that you read the entirety of these authors' accounts. Their accounts are not only fascinating because they recount the Witnesses' experiences in the spirit world, but they are also inspirational because you read of the challenges the Witnesses endured after their return to their bodies.

The following table gives some comparative information on the six Witnesses.

	George G. Ritchie Jr.	Betty J. Eadie	RaNelle Wallace	Elane Durham	Dale Black	Sarah Lanelle Menet
Date of NDE/OBE	12/20/1943	11/18/1973	10/9/1985	10/22/1996	7/18/1969	1979
Cause of NDE	Double lobar pneumonia	Hysterectomy complications	Small plane crash	Cardiac arrest	Small plane crash	Suicide attempt
Year account was published	1978	1992	1994	1998	2010	2002
Did they meet Jesus?	Yes	Yes	No	Yes	No	Yes

PERSONAL INFORMATION ON THE SIX NEAR-DEATH-EXPERIENCE WITNESSES

Introduction

I will also reference from the following books, whose authors wrote of their own near-death experiences.

Proof of Heaven: A Neurosurgeon's Journey into the Afterlife	Eben Alexander, MD
To Heaven and Back: A Doctor's Extraordinary Account of Her Death, Angels, and Life Again	Mary C. Neal, MD
The Message	Lance Richardson

The following is a list of additional books written by or about individuals who describe near-death experiences.

I Saw Heaven: A Remarkable Visit to the Spirit World	Lawrence E. Tooley
Heaven Is for Real: A Little Boy's Astounding Story of His Trip to Heaven and Back	Todd Burpo
Saved by the Light: The True Story of a Man Who Died Twice and the Profound Revelations He Received	Dannion Brinkley
Caught Up Into Paradise	Richard E. Eby, DO
Full Circle: The Near-Death Experience and Beyond	Barbara Harris and Lionel C. Bascom
God's Heavenly Answers: Near-Death Experience Revealed	Joyce H. Brown, PhD, ND, EFT
A Place Called Heaven	Dr. Gary L. Wood
Visions of Glory: One Man's Astonishing Account of the Last Days	John Pontius
My Descent into Death: A Second Chance at Life	Howard Storm

Introduction

A Glimpse of Eternity: One Man's Story of Life Beyond Death	Ian MacCormack
90 Minutes in Heaven: A True Story of Death and Life	Don Piper
My Journey to Heaven: What I Saw and How It Changed My Life	Marvin J. Besteman
Fast Lane to Heaven: A Life-After-Death Journey	Ned Dougherty
My Glimpse of Eternity	Betty Malz
Afterlife: What Really Happens on the Other Side	Barry R. Strohm
40 Days in Heaven: The True Testimony of Seneca Sodi's Visitation to Paradise, the Holy City, the Glory of God's Throne	Reverand Elwood Scott
Face to Face with Jesus: A Former Muslim's Extraordinary Journey to Heaven and Encounter with the God of Love	Samaa Habib
I Knew Their Hearts	Jeff Olsen

Introduction

RESEARCHERS OF NEAR-DEATH EXPERIENCES

In addition to the NDEs of the above-mentioned individuals, I will also cite the works of the following prominent NDE researchers.

DR. ELISABETH KÜBLER-ROSS

Until her death in 2004, Elisabeth Kübler-Ross, a Swiss-American psychiatrist, was widely regarded as the world's leading authority on the issue of death and dying. Dr. Kübler-Ross worked with an estimated twenty thousand terminally ill patients over the course of twenty years. She authored many publications. Her most renowned book, *On Death and Dying: What the Dying Have to Teach Doctors, Nurses, Clergy and Their Own Families*, first published in 1970, discusses her theory on the five stages of psychological reaction experienced by individuals facing death. During her life, she was awarded twenty honorary doctorate degrees from various universities.

She is also regarded as a pioneer of the hospice movement. Her work inspired others to pursue near-death studies.

Although she described herself as a "skeptical semi-believer" early in her career, she became convinced, as a result of her research, that life continues after death.

DR. RAYMOND A. MOODY JR.

Dr. Moody outlines his research of NDEs in *Life After Life: The Bestselling Original Investigation that Revealed "Near-Death Experiences."* First published in November 1975, it has since sold more than thirteen million copies worldwide. Over the course of his career, extending for more than twenty years, Dr. Moody has interviewed more than three hundred individuals who describe out-of-body experiences that have elements that are consistent with each other and with those of the Witnesses previously introduced in this chapter.

I will also refer to Dr. Moody's later publications *Reflections on Life After Life* and *The Light Beyond*.

Introduction

DR. KENNETH RING

Dr. Ring is a professor emeritus of psychology at the University of Connecticut. He did extensive research in the field of near-death studies. He published a number of books regarding his studies including, *Life at Death: A Scientific Investigation of the Near-Death Experience* and *Heading Toward Omega: In Search of the Meaning of the Near-Death Experience*. Raymond A. Moody has been quoted saying that Dr. Ring's research validated his own book, *Life After Life*.

DR. MICHAEL B. SABOM

Dr. Sabom, a cardiologist, started investigating near-death experiences after reading Dr. Moody's book *Life After Life*. His initial skepticism turned into a five-year study in which he considered the ten separate elements of a near-death experience as outlined in Dr. Moody's book.

DR. MAURICE RAWLINGS

Dr. Rawlings, also a cardiologist, resuscitated a patient who died while taking a stress test. In the process of the resuscitation, the patient regained consciousness and told Dr. Rawlings that he was in hell and asked him to not stop trying to bring him back. He also asked Dr. Rawlings to pray for him. As a result of this experience, Dr. Rawlings became interested in studying bad NDE accounts. The majority of NDE accounts are very pleasant. Dr. Rawlings's opinion is that bad NDE accounts may be as frequent as good accounts, but the conscious minds of people who have had such experiences repress them because of their horror. The bad NDE is usually only remembered if the information is gained immediately after the experience.

His book *Beyond Death's Door* was published in 1978.

DR. JEFFREY LONG

Dr. Long is a radiation oncologist practicing in Houma, Louisiana. He encountered the phrase near-death experience (NDE) in 1984. A few years later, the wife of one of his friends told him of her own NDE and his interest grew. In 1998, he founded the Near-Death Experience Research Foundation and its associated website, NDERF.org.

Introduction

The purpose of the website is to invite people who have had near-death experiences to respond to more than a hundred questions regarding their experience. During the first ten years of the website's operation, more than 1,300 people visited the site and responded to the questions. After studying their responses, Dr. Long identified "nine lines of evidence . . . [that] converge on one central point: *There is life after death*" (Long, *Evidence of the Afterlife*, p. 4).

His book *Evidence of the Afterlife: The Science of Near-Death Experiences* was published in 2010 and became a *New York Times* best seller.

DR. MELVIN MORSE

With the underlying confidence that "children don't lie"—as expressed by one of Dr. Morse's university professors—Dr. Morse, a renowned pediatrician, undertook a study of young children who had had near-death experiences (Morse, *Closer to the Light*, p. 14).

His study spanned more than eight years and produced many fascinating case histories. Ten years after their NDEs, some of these children were revisited to see what effect their experience had had on their subsequent lives.

His book, *Closer to the Light: Learning from the Near-Death Experiences of Children* was on the *New York Times* best-seller list.

DR. KARLIS OSIS and
DR. ERLENDUR HARALDSSON

In their book *At the Hour of Death: A New Look at Evidence for Life After Death*, Dr. Osis and Dr. Haraldsson detail an extensive scientific study of the experiences of individuals just prior to their deaths. Drs. Osis and Haraldsson surveyed more than a thousand doctors and nurses who had interaction with patients just prior to their deaths.

RELIGIOUS RESOURCES CITED

HOLY BIBLE

The Holy Bible contains remarkably few references to the conditions of life after death. The most notable is in Luke 16 where the story of

Introduction

Lazarus and the rich man is told. Lazarus went to "Abraham's bosom" (Luke 16:22)—obviously a paradisaical realm—while the rich man went to "a place of torment" (Luke 16:28).

While Jesus was on the cross, He spoke of His imminent departure into paradise (See Luke 23:43).

THE CHURCH OF JESUS CHRIST OF LATTER-DAY SAINTS' SCRIPTURES

In addition to the Holy Bible, members of the Church of Jesus Christ of Latter-day Saint, regard three additional books as scripture.

The Book of Mormon

The Book of Mormon: Another Testament of Jesus Christ contains the accounts of three peoples who came over from the Old World to the American continent.

The Jaredites came over at the time of the Tower of Babel. This civilization annihilated itself through civil war several hundred years before Christ was born, with the exception of two survivors: one of which came across a people called the Mulekites and lived with them for nine months before dying.

This second group, the Mulekites, came over from Jerusalem during the reign of King Zedekiah, and eventually combined with descendants of the third group: the Nephites.

The Nephites came over from Jerusalem about 600 BC. This group divided into two nations—the Nephites and the Lamanites—that had many periods of wars. About the year AD 421, the Lamanites entirely annihilated the Nephites, with the exception of a prophet named Moroni. The descendants of the Lamanites are the American Indians.

The Book of Mormon is made up of the writings of various prophets who lived among these peoples. Some of these prophets include: Nephi, Mosiah, Alma, Mormon, and Moroni.

Doctrine and Covenants

The Doctrine and Covenants, as stated in the introduction to the book, is "a collection of divine revelations and inspired declarations."

Introduction

While most of the revelations were received through the prophet Joseph Smith Jr., the final section of the book records a vision given to Joseph F. Smith—the prophet of the Church of Jesus Christ of Latter-day Saints in 1918 and a nephew of Joseph Smith Jr. This vision offers notable information regarding activities in the world of spirits.

The Pearl of Great Price

The subtitle of the Pearl of Great Price reads, "a selection from the revelations, translations, and narrations of Joseph Smith—first prophet, seer, and revelator to the Church of Jesus Christ of Latter-day Saints."

Two of the books within this volume—the book of Moses and the book of Abraham—contain information related to the world of spirits and the afterlife.

Also included in this volume is a document written by Joseph Smith Jr. called the "Articles of Faith," which outlines thirteen fundamental beliefs of the Church of Jesus Christ of Latter-day Saints.

LEADERS OF THE CHURCH OF JESUS CHRIST OF LATTER-DAY SAINTS

Since the martyrdom of Joseph Smith Jr. in 1844, the presidents of the Church of Jesus Christ of Latter-day Saints and the Quorum of the Twelve Apostles have always been regarded as prophets, seers, and revelators. Consequently, I will refer to the teachings of some of these men in the course of inserting religious perspective. The leaders of the Church of Jesus Christ of Latter-day Saints to be quoted are:

Name	Position	Born and Died
Joseph Smith Jr.	First prophet and president	1805–1844
Brigham Young	Second prophet and president	1801–1877
Wilford Woodruff	Fourth prophet and president	1807–1898
Joseph F. Smith	Sixth prophet and president	1838–1918
Heber J. Grant	Seventh prophet and president	1856–1945

Introduction

Name	Position	Born and Died
David O. McKay	Ninth prophet and president	1873–1970
Spencer W. Kimball	Twelfth prophet and president	1895–1985
Ezra Taft Benson	Thirteenth prophet and president	1899–1994
Gordon B. Hinckley	Fifteenth prophet and president	1910–2008
Thomas S. Monson	Sixteenth prophet and president	1927–2018
Russell M. Nelson	Seventeenth prophet and president	1924–
Parley P. Pratt	Apostle	1807–1857
Orson Pratt	Apostle	1811–1881
Bruce R. McConkie	Apostle	1915–1985
Dallin H. Oaks	Apostle	1932–
Henry B. Eyring	Apostle	1933–
Dieter F. Uchtdorf	Apostle	1940–
Jeffrey R. Holland	Apostle	1940–
Jose L. Alonso	General Authority Seventy	1958–
Stirling W. Sill	Assistant to the Quorum of the Twelve Apostles	1903–1994

MISCELLANEOUS REFERENCES

CHILDREN'S SONGBOOK

In the Church of Jesus Christ of Latter-day Saints, children ages three to eleven attend what is called "Primary" on Sundays. Here, they learn the gospel, in part, through the songs they sing. Some of these songs will be referenced.

ANONYMOUS RESOURCES

On occasion, I will cite anonymous resources. Some of these resources are members of my own family, but I will not identify them in order to protect their privacy.

PART I
Beginning the Journey

1

A WORD TO THE SKEPTICS

SKEPTICISM OF LIFE AFTER DEATH IS INDEFENSIBLE

Nobody *knows* that there is no life after death. They have only their opinion. On the other hand, voluminous research has been done by respected professionals such as Dr. Raymond A. Moody, Dr. Kenneth Ring, Dr. Elisabeth Kübler-Ross, Dr. Michael B. Sabom, Dr. Maurice Rawlings, Dr. Jeffrey Long, Dr. Karlis Osis, Dr. Erlendur Haraldsson, and many others, all of whom have compiled thousands of case histories of individuals who have witnessed another realm of living.

With the advancement of resuscitation techniques, many people who were clinically dead have been brought back to life. It is likely that any cardiologist could tell you about some of his own patients who have described having an out-of-body experience just prior to being resuscitated.

In 1981, Dr. George Gallup conducted a poll determining that there were approximately thirteen million people, or 5 percent of the population, who had had a near-death or out-of-body experience ("How Common Are Near-Death Experiences? NDEs by the Numbers," Tara MacIsaac, *The Epoch Times*, accessed March 30, 2018, www.theepochtimes.com/how-common-are-near-death-experiences-ndes-by-the-numbers_757401.html. See also "How Many NDEs Occur in the United States Every Day," Dr. Jeff, *NDERF*, www.nderf.org/NDERF/Research/number_nde_usa.htm).

Keith A. Haslem

ELISABETH KÜBLER-ROSS

Perhaps Dr. Elisabeth Kübler-Ross—who studied more than twenty thousand NDE cases—said it best:

"One shouldn't try to convince other people. When they die they will know it anyway."

"If someone doesn't like a certain truth, he will come up with a thousand arguments against it. However, again, this is his problem. One shouldn't try to convince other people. When they die, they will know it anyway" (*On Life After Death*, p. 7–8).

RAYMOND A. MOODY JR.

One of the questions occasionally asked of Dr. Moody was: "How do you know that all these people aren't just lying to you?"

"The notion that these accounts might be fabrications is utterly untenable."

> It is quite easy for persons who have not listened and watched as others have related near-death experiences intellectually to entertain the hypothesis that these stories are lies. However, I have witnessed mature, emotionally stable adults—both men and women—break down and weep while telling me of events that happened up to three decades before. I have detected in their voices sincerity, warmth, and feeling which cannot really be conveyed in a written recounting. So to me, in a way that is unfortunately impossible for many others to share, the notion that these accounts might be fabrications is utterly untenable.
>
> In addition to the weight of my own opinion, there are some strong considerations which should rule heavily against the fabrication hypothesis. The most obvious is the difficulty of explaining the similarity of so many of the accounts. How is it that many people just happen to have come up with the same lie to tell me over a period of eight years. Collusion remains a theoretical possibility here. It is certainly conceivable that a nice elderly lady from eastern North Carolina, a medical student from New Jersey, a Georgia veterinarian, and many others several years ago banded together and conspired to carry out an elaborate hoax against me. However, I don't regard this to be a very likely possibility! (*Life After Life*, p. 137–38)

Going Home

EBEN ALEXANDER

Dr. Eben Alexander, a neurosurgeon who had a near-death experience, quotes Albert Einstein:

"Everything is [a miracle]."

"There are only two ways to live your life. One is as though nothing is a miracle. The other is as if everything is" (*Proof of Heaven*, p. 147).

Dr. Alexander tells of returning to a church service after his near-death experience. (Prior to his experience he would typically only attend church on Easter and Christmas.)

Religion at least tries to bring us to God.

> My memory of my time out of my body was still naked and raw, and everywhere I turned in this place that had failed to move me much before, I saw art and heard music that brought it all right back. The pulsing bass note of a hymn echoed the rough misery of the Realm of the Earthworm's-Eye View. The stained glass windows with their clouds and angels brought to mind the celestial beauty of the Gateway. A painting of Jesus breaking bread with his disciples evoked the communion of the Core. I shuddered as I recalled the bliss of infinite unconditional love I had known there.
>
> At last, I understood what religion was really all about. Or at least was supposed to be about. I didn't just believe in God; I knew God. As I hobbled to the alter to take Communion, tears streamed down my cheeks. (*Proof of Heaven*, pp. 147–48)

"The scientific community . . . [says that] science and spirituality cannot coexist. They are mistaken."

> Science—the science to which I've devoted so much of my life—doesn't contradict what I learned up there. But far, far too many people believe it does, because certain members of the scientific community, who are pledged to the materialistic worldview, have insisted again and again that science and spirituality cannot coexist.
>
> They are mistaken. (*Proof of Heaven*, pp. 72–73)

Keith A. Haslem

MARK TWAIN

"It ain't what you don't know that gets you into trouble. It's what you know for sure that just ain't so" (As quoted in Dyer, *Memories of Heaven*, p. 32).

THE CHURCH OF JESUS CHRIST OF LATTER-DAY SAINTS PERSPECTIVE

The first line of a beloved Primary children's hymn—"A Child's Prayer"—reads: "Heavenly Father, are you really there?"

(I suggest watching a rendition of this song on YouTube.)

AUTHOR'S PERSPECTIVE

Happiness is better than any other option.

Leaving behind all the overwhelming evidence of life after death, I would ask the skeptic: does it make you *happy* to believe that you will be "annihilated" at your death?

On the other hand, consider the countless people who *do* believe in life after death and are happy with that hope. If they are wrong, well, at least they were happy in their delusions!

2

GOING *BACK* HOME—WHERE DID I COME FROM?

SYNOPSIS

During their experiences in the spirit world, Betty Eadie, RaNelle Wallace, Elane Durham, and Sarah LaNelle Menet all make reference to remembering or learning that we all lived as spirits in a spirit world before coming to earth.

Scriptures in the Holy Bible in the books of Job, Jeremiah, Ecclesiastes, and Acts allude to a premortal existence.

The concept of a premortal existence is a fundamental belief in the theology of the Church of Jesus Christ of Latter-day Saints.

BETTY J. EADIE

"I knew that I had been there before . . ."

"During this view of the pre-mortal existence, I was impressed by the beauty and glory of each spirit. I knew that I had been there before, that each of us had, and that we had been filled with light and beauty. Then the thought came to me, referring to us all: 'If you could see yourself before you were born, you would be amazed at your intelligence and glory'" (*Embraced by the Light*, p. 97).

Keith A. Haslem

RANELLE WALLACE

"Before coming to earth . . . brothers and sisters in eternity . . ."

I saw that we all stood before our Father before coming to earth, brothers and sisters in eternity. I experienced this anew, just as I had experienced it in my own pre-mortal life. I saw that we chose to come here, to face trials and to gain the experiences of this earth. I saw that we elected to follow a Savior who would redeem us from the sins of our mortal lives and bring us back to our Father. . . .

I saw that our God knew each of us individually. He knew our hearts, our souls, and he loved us unconditionally. It was as though he spent unmeasured time with each of us, counseling us, loving us. Time did not exist; each of us had always had a relationship with him. (*The Burning Within*, pp. 106–9)

ELANE DURHAM

Elane was given foreknowledge that her life on earth would be very difficult.

I saw that the choice of my mortal family had already been made, and that I was quite anxious to join them. I knew that I would be entering mortality as the oldest of a family of several children, and I knew that our family would have problems, even severe ones. Yet I had agreed to these conditions willingly for the purpose of soul growth we would all experience.

. . . I was able to see a number of children that were to be "mine." They had helped choose to have me in their world either as a birth mother, grandmother, or foster mother, and I had willingly agreed.

. . . One of the other spirit beings asked if I was sure that I could deal with so many trials and difficulties. Apparently he thought I was taking on a pretty heavy load.

"Yes," I told him.

"Are you sure?" he asked again.

"Yes," I responded firmly. (*I Stand All Amazed*, pp. 83–84)

Going Home

SARAH LANELLE MENET

A "block" to prevent us from remembering our lives before

> We spent thousands of years as spirits before coming to earth, and we will spend millions more in the spirit world and beyond after we leave this existence. We are only here on earth for a relatively short span, which seems like a few minutes to everyone in the spirit world.
>
> We are all connected to and have known each other in a very real way for eons. . . . We don't remember this because shortly after we are born, a block is put on a part of our "spiritual DNA" to prevent us from remembering our lives before coming to earth. However, every once in a while some small memory will leak through the block, and we will have a vague recognition of people or places. That is why many of us may have at some time in our lives met someone that we immediately "clicked" with, someone that we felt we had known "forever." Indeed, it may be so. (*There Is No Death*, p. 96)
>
> When it came time for us to come here, we were given the choice, once again, as to whether we wanted to live as mortals for a time on earth or to remain in God's presence. No one was ever forced to do anything. It was all a matter of agency. After our choice was made to become mortal, we formed groups and were organized with those spirits we wanted to have as part of our earthly family. Usually we chose to be with those spirits to whom we were closest, the spirit friends we loved the most from whom we could learn the most. (*There Is No Death*, pp. 104–5)

BIBLICAL PERSPECTIVE

Although the concept of a premortal existence is not common in Christian religions, several scriptures in the Bible allude to it.

Job refers to several meetings in heaven when the sons of God "came to present themselves before the Lord . . ." (Job 1:6 & Job 2:1).

In His conversation with Job, the Lord asked

> Where wast thou when I laid the foundations of the earth?
>   When the morning stars sang together, and all the sons of God shouted for joy? (Job 38:4, 7)

Keith A. Haslem

The Lord told the prophet Jeremiah, "Before I formed thee in the belly I knew thee; and before thou camest forth out of the womb I sanctified thee, and I ordained thee a prophet unto the nations" (Jeremiah 1:5).

The disciples of the New Testament apparently believed in a premortal existence because they asked Jesus, as they passed by a man who had been born blind, "Master, who did sin, this man, or his parents that he was born blind?" (John 9:2). If the man was born blind as a result of his sins, they must have been committed prior to his mortal life.

The Apostle Paul taught the Athenians "we are the offspring of God . . ." (Acts 17:29; see also Acts 17:24–29).

Ecclesiastes, speaking of death, said, "Then shall the dust return to the earth as it was: and the spirit shall return to God who gave it" (Ecclesiastes 12:7).

THE CHURCH OF JESUS CHRIST OF LATTER-DAY SAINTS PERSPECTIVE

"Each [human being] is a beloved son or daughter of heavenly parents."

In September 1995, the presidency of the Church of Jesus Christ of Latter-day Saints issued an official pronouncement intended to represent the church's view on the importance of the family unit. It includes reference to a "premortal realm."

"THE FAMILY: A PROCLAMATION TO THE WORLD"

WE THE FIRST PRESIDENCY and the Council of the Twelve Apostles of The Church of Jesus Christ of Latter-day Saints, solemnly proclaim that marriage between a man and a woman is ordained of God and that the family is central to the Creator's plan for the eternal destiny of His children.

ALL HUMAN BEINGS—male and female—are created in the image of God. Each is a beloved son or daughter of heavenly parents, and as such, each has a divine nature and destiny. Gender is an essential characteristic of individual premortal, mortal, and eternal identity and purpose.

IN THE PREMORTAL REALM, spirit sons and daughters knew and worshipped God as their Eternal Father and accepted His plan by which His children could obtain a physical body and gain earthly experience to progress toward perfection and ultimately realize his or her divine destiny as an heir of eternal life. The divine plan of happiness enables family relationships to be perpetuated beyond the grave. Sacred ordinances and covenants available in holy temples make it possible for individuals to return to the presence of God and for families to be united eternally.

JOSEPH F. SMITH
(sixth president of the Church of Jesus Christ of Latter-day Saints)

"Our spirits existed long before they took upon them this tabernacle . . ."

> It is true, all of us are clothed with mortality, but our spirits existed long before they took upon them this tabernacle we now inhabit. When this body dies, the spirit does not die. The spirit is an immortal being, and when separated from the body takes its flight to the place prepared for it, and there awaits the resurrection of the body, when the spirit will return again and re-occupy this tabernacle which it occupied in this world. (*Gospel Doctrine*, p. 444)

PEARL OF GREAT PRICE

All living things were created spiritually first.

One of the books in the Pearl of Great Price—the book of Moses—teaches that all living things were created spiritually first.

> And every plant of the field before it was in the earth, and every herb of the field before it grew. For I, the Lord God, created all things, of which I have spoken, spiritually, before they were naturally upon the face of the earth. (Moses 3:5)

Keith A. Haslem

CHILDREN'S SONGBOOK

In the Church of Jesus Christ of Latter-day Saints, children sing a song that talks about their premortal existence during their Sunday meetings. The first verse reads:

> I lived in Heaven a long time ago it is true;
> Lived there and loved there with people I know. So did you.
> Then Heav'nly Father presented a beautiful plan,
> All about earth and eternal salvation for man.

(You can search "I Lived in Heaven Mormon Tabernacle Choir" on YouTube to hear a full production of this song.)

AUTHOR'S PERSPECTIVE

Having been a parent and a grandparent, I've noted, with interest, that the personalities and aptitudes of children are manifest very early in their development. One child is shy, another totally fearless and outgoing, even as a toddler. Is it possible that our personalities, interests, and aptitudes were developed during what could have been eons of time prior to mortality?

Without an existence before mortality, the conscious decision to come here, and the hope of life hereafter, wouldn't life be a pointless exercise?

3

WHO AM I? WHAT IS MY RELATIONSHIP TO GOD?

SYNOPSIS

Our resources reinforce the concept introduced in Chapter 2: "Going *Back* Home"—that we are all sons and daughters of God and, thereby, are also spiritual siblings.

SARAH LANELLE MENET

"We are literally sons and daughters (of God)."

"God is our Father in Heaven and we are literally sons and daughters of this deity. I learned that He and Jesus Christ are two separate, glorified beings" (*There Is No Death*, p. 38).

ELANE DURHAM

"We are all children of our Father in Heaven, sisters and brothers."

"I came to understand that we are all children of our Father in Heaven, sisters and brothers, and because of that relationship I hold a responsibility for everyone else" (*I Stand All Amazed*, p. 46).

BIBLICAL PERSPECTIVE

References in the Holy Bible support this concept.

"We are the offspring of God."

Keith A. Haslem

"Forasmuch then as we are the offspring of God, we ought not to think that the Godhead is like unto gold, or silver, or stone, graven by art and man's device" (Acts 17:29).

"The Father of spirits"

"Furthermore we have had fathers of our flesh which corrected us, and we gave them reverence: shall we not much rather be in subjection to the Father of spirits, and live?" (Hebrews 12:9).

THE CHURCH OF JESUS CHRIST OF LATTER-DAY SAINTS PERSPECTIVE

As referenced in the previous chapter, in "The Family: A Proclamation to the World," members of the Church of Jesus Christ of Latter-day Saints believe,

"ALL HUMAN BEINGS—male and female—are created in the image of God. *Each is a beloved son or daughter of heavenly parents . . .*" (emphasis added).

AUTHOR'S PERSPECTIVE

The significance of the concept that we are the "offspring of God" cannot be overstated. Doesn't any son or daughter have the capacity to become like his or her parents? The Apostle John alludes to this potential in 1 John 3:2, "Beloved, now are we the sons of God, and it doth not yet appear what we shall be: but we know that, when he shall appear, we shall be like him."

We have the potential (not during this life I'm sure) to become perfect, like God, else why would Jesus have commanded His disciples to "Be ye therefore perfect, even as your Father which is in heaven is perfect" (Matthew 5:48).

How many people struggle with low self-esteem because of how they are treated by others, including their own family or spouse? A clear understanding of our heavenly heritage and potential can alleviate all personal insecurities.

I believe, as expressed by what is probably *the* favorite children's hymn in the Church of Jesus Christ of Latter-day Saints, that "I am a child of God." (You can search on YouTube for "I Am a Child of God Mormon Tabernacle Choir" to hear a rendition.)

4

HOW IS DEATH LIKE A GRADUATION?

SYNOPSIS

According to our resources, death is nothing to be feared. Several of our resources liken it to a "graduation" (Eadie, *Embraced by the Light*, p. 82), such as "from grammar school to high school or college" (Moody, *Life After Life*, p. 97). Another comparison made is that death is like the emergence of a "butterfly from a cocoon" (Durham, *I Stand All Amazed*, p. 30). It is also likened to a "new birth" (Menet, *There Is No Death*, p. 1), or "the most important event in life" (Sill, "To Die Well").

BETTY J. EADIE

"A sort of graduation party"

> Into the garden came a group of spiritual beings.... They surrounded me, and I felt that they were gathering to celebrate a sort of graduation party for me. I had died (or graduated, as their term seemed to indicate), and they were there to greet me. Their faces were beaming with delight as though they were looking at a child who had just experienced something incredibly delicious for the first time. I realized that I remembered them all from before my earth life, and I ran to them and hugged and kissed each one. My ministering angels—my dear monks—were there again and I kissed them....
>
> My escorts ... now told me that I had died prematurely and that this wasn't really a graduation party, but a time to show me what I would receive when I returned at the right time. They were very

Keith A. Haslem

happy to see me and to support me, but they knew I had to go back. (*Embraced by the Light*, pp. 82–83)

DR. RAYMOND A. MOODY JR.

One of Dr. Raymond Moody's subjects also compared death to a graduation.

"You just graduate from one thing to another"

"After you've once had the experience that I had, you know in your heart there's no such thing as death. You just graduate from one thing to another—like from grammar school to high school or college" (*Life After Life*, p. 97).

SARAH LANELLE MENET

"The new birth"

"Those on the other side refer to it [death] as the 'new birth'" (*There Is No Death*, p. 1).

ELANE DURHAM

"Like butterflies from a cocoon"

"Truly, I now knew, there was no such thing as death. We only change forms. Like butterflies from a cocoon, our spirits leave our bodies and soar to a higher realm. And through the power of Christ I had soared to be with Him" (*I Stand All Amazed*, p. 30).

DR. ELISABETH KÜBLER-ROSS

"Death is 'shedding a cocoon.'"

"Dying is only moving from one house into a more beautiful one—if I may make a symbolic comparison" (*On Life After Death*, p. 3).

"Death is simply a shedding of the physical body like the butterfly shedding its cocoon. . . . It's like putting away your winter coat when spring comes. You know that the coat is shabby and you don't want to wear it anymore. That's virtually what death is all about" (*On Life After Death*, p. 26).

"Many people are beginning to be aware that the physical body is only the house or the temple, or as we call it the cocoon, which we inhabit for a certain number of months or years until we make the transition called death. Then, at the time of death we shed this cocoon and are once again as free as a butterfly to use the symbolic language that we use when talking to dying children and their siblings" (*On Life After Death*, p. 43).

"As soon as you have finished . . . you are allowed to go home, to graduate!"

"You will come to know that all your life on earth was nothing but a school that you had to go through in order to pass certain tests and learn special lessons. As soon as you have finished this school and mastered your lessons, you are allowed to go home, to graduate!" (*On Life After Death*, p. 11).

THE CHURCH OF JESUS CHRIST OF LATTER-DAY SAINTS PERSPECTIVE

DAVID O. MCKAY
(ninth prophet and president of the Church of Jesus Christ of Latter-day Saints)

"There is no cause to fear death."

"There is no cause to fear death; it is but an incident in life. It is as natural as birth. Why should we fear it? Some fear it because they think it is the end of life, and life often is the dearest thing we have. Eternal life is man's greatest blessing. . . . With all my soul I know that death is conquered by Jesus Christ" (Burton, *For They Shall Be Comforted*, p. 45).

Keith A. Haslem

STIRLING W. SILL
(an Assistant to the Twelve)

"Death is a kind of graduation day for life."

"The most important event in life is death. We live to die and then we die to live. Death is a kind of graduation day for life. It is our only means of entrance to our eternal lives" ("To Die Well").

Members of the Church of Jesus Christ of Latter-day Saints believe that transition to the afterlife will be quite pleasant. Their confidence is based in part on the following scripture: "And it shall come to pass that those that die in me shall not taste of death, for it shall be sweet unto them" (D&C 42:46).

POETIC PERSPECTIVE

An unknown poet offers this perspective:

> When God sends forth a tiny soul
> To learn the ways of earth
> A mother's love is waiting there—
> We call this wonder—birth.
> When God calls home a tired soul
> And stills a fleeting breath
> A Father's love is waiting there
> This too is birth—not death.
> (As quoted in Sorenson, *The Journey Beyond Life*, p. 12)

AUTHOR'S PERSPECTIVE

Graduating college was a happy day for me. Little did I know then how difficult life would continue to be. But knowing what I know now about life after death, I look forward to my final graduation, and hope that I will feel as the Apostle Paul expressed: "I have fought a good fight, I have finished my course, I have kept the faith" (2 Timothy 4:7).

5

WHAT HAPPENS AT THE MOMENT OF DEATH?

Having laid the important groundwork of who we are, where we came from, and what death is, we can now proceed with what happens when the physical body dies.

SYNOPSIS

According to our resources, at the moment of death, your spirit—sometimes referred to as your soul—will separate from your physical body. By almost all accounts, your spirit will rise a few feet to a point where you can look down on your physical body, whether it's in a hospital room, the scene of an accident, etc. You may see medical personnel working feverishly to resuscitate you. If family members are present, you will see them and sense their emotions as they realize you have died. Yet you will feel quite calm and peaceful, and any pain you have been experiencing will be gone. Initially, you may not realize you are dead, as was the case with George G. Ritchie.

GEORGE G. RITCHIE

"Someone was lying in that bed . . . impossible! I . . . had just gotten out of that bed!"

> The train! I'd miss the train! I jumped out of bed in alarm, looking for my clothes. The X-ray people didn't know, of course, about the train; that's why they had put me in here instead of sending me back where the jeep was waiting.

Keith A. Haslem

> My uniform wasn't on the chair. I looked beneath it. Behind it. No duffel bag either. Where else in this little closet of a room could they have put them? Under the bed maybe? I turned around, then froze.
>
> Someone was lying in that bed.
>
> I took a step closer. He was quite a young man, with short brown hair, lying very still. But... the thing was impossible! I myself had just gotten out of that bed! For a moment I wrestled with the mystery of it. It was too strange to think about—and anyway I didn't have time. (*Return from Tomorrow*, pp. 36–37)

ELANE DURHAM

Elane recalls looking at her body from inside the ambulance as she was being transported to the hospital after a series of massive seizures. She also remembers

"Watching it all as though I were walking beside myself."

"My next memory is of being wheeled into the emergency room, only for some reason I was watching it all as though I were walking beside myself, on the right side of the gurney, and not lying down on the gurney looking up" (*I Stand All Amazed*, p. 18).

DALE BLACK

Dale Black, badly injured in a small plane crash, saw his body as it was treated in an emergency room.

"I had a bird's-eye view of the entire ER."

> As we burst through the doors of the ER, something inexplicable happened, sending me into uncharted territory.
>
> Suddenly I found myself suspended in midair, hovering over the wreckage of my body. My gray pants and short sleeve shirt were torn to shreds and soaked in blood and fuel.
>
> I had a bird's-eye view of the entire ER and watched the flurry of activity like a bystander. They wheeled the blue gurney I was on into a room about thirty-five feet square.
>
> They undid the red straps that held me and moved me onto a metal table. I hovered above the end of the table, near my feet, and just below the acoustical tile ceiling.

Going Home

> A thick-boned, gray-headed doctor approached my body, standing near my left shoulder, and began inspecting me. He gently turned my head to the left, focusing on the damage to my face. He went about his work professionally and unemotionally.
>
> What happened to me? I wondered. Where am I?
>
> Three nurses were in the room, the shortest of which stood to the doctor's left. The other two were on the opposite side of the table, cutting off what remained of my clothes, working furiously. . . .
>
> As the trauma team worked feverishly, I felt surprisingly detached. I recognized myself on the table, but felt no anxiety, no sense of urgency, no pain, no sadness, nothing.
>
> It was a schizophrenic feeling, being two places at once, your body on the table below, another very real part of you floating near the ceiling above. That may be my body, I thought, but I'm up here. I can't be dead because I feel so alive. Amazingly, I wasn't shocked by all this, just curious, still wondering what had happened (*Flight to Heaven*, pp. 28–30).

After a few minutes in the ER, Captain Black recounts

> I began moving higher, slowly but steadily. I noticed details in the light fixtures as I approached them. I saw into the air-conditioning ducts in the ceiling. I was moving away from my body, slowly . . . out of the room . . . down the hallway.
>
> I began picking up speed. The movement was effortless, and I had no sensation of self-movement. I didn't know where I was going, but I was distinctly aware that some irresistible force was drawing me there.
>
> The speed of the movement increased. I couldn't stop it, couldn't steer it.
>
> I moved faster, faster, and faster still.
>
> Then suddenly . . .
>
> I was gone. (*Flight to Heaven*, pp. 31–32)

RAYMOND A. MOODY JR.

In his book *The Light Beyond*, Dr. Moody writes of people who see medical personnel or relatives anxiously waiting in the hospital.

"Out of their body but watching the doctors work on them."

Keith A. Haslem

The boundaries imposed by space in our every day lives are often broken in NDEs. During the experience, if NDEers want to go somewhere they can often just think themselves there. People say that while they were out of their body but watching the doctors work on them in the operating room, they could simply wish their way into the waiting room to see their relatives. . . .

I have several examples of people who had out-of-body experiences during their resuscitations and were able to leave the operating room to observe relatives in other parts of the hospital.

One woman who left her body went into the waiting room and saw that her daughter was wearing mismatched plaids.

What had happened was that the maid had brought the child to the hospital and in her haste had just grabbed the first two things off the laundry pile.

Later, when she told her family about her experience and the fact that she had seen the girl in these mismatched clothes, they knew that she must have been in that waiting room with them.

Another woman had an out-of-body experience and left the room where her body was being resuscitated. From across the hospital lobby, she watched her brother-in-law as some business associate approached him and asked what he was doing in the hospital.

"Well, I was going out of town on a business trip," said the brother-in-law. "But it looks like June is going to kick the bucket, so I better stay around and be a pallbearer."

A few days later when she was recovering, the brother-in-law came to visit. She told him that she was in the room as he spoke to his friend, and erased any doubt by saying, "Next time I die, you go off on your business trip because I'll be just fine." He turned so pale that she thought he was about to have a near-death experience himself.

Another of these experiences happened to an elderly woman I was resuscitating. I was giving her closed heart massage on an emergency room examining table and the nurse assisting me ran into another room to get a vial of medication that we needed.

It was a glass-necked vial that you're supposed to hold in a paper towel while breaking off the top so you don't cut yourself. When the nurse returned, the neck was broken so I could use the medicine right away.

When the old woman came to, she looked very sweetly at the nurse and said, "Honey, I saw what you did in that room, and you're going to cut yourself doing that." The nurse was shocked. She admitted that in her haste to open the medicine, she had broken the glass neck with her bare fingers.

The woman told us that while we were resuscitating her, she had followed the nurse back to the room to watch what she was doing. (*The Light Beyond*, pp. 18–20)

AUTHOR'S PERSPECTIVE

Upon leaving the body, many accounts infer that the spirit remains for a short time in the immediate vicinity. However, fairly soon thereafter, the graduate will be met by one or more spirits who will serve as an escort in the transition into the spirit world. Most accounts state that these escorts are deceased members of the graduate's own family. Grandparents often serve in this capacity.

6

WILL SOMEONE MEET ME WHEN I DIE?

SYNOPSIS

The accounts from individuals who have had near-death experiences almost universally say they were met after a few moments by another spirit. You may not recognize the person immediately because they will look to be about twenty-five to thirty years old, and if that spirit is your grandparent or some other deceased family member, they may look quite different from the way you remember them. You might also be met by a group of spirits, all of who are happy to escort you into the spirit world. Or you may be met by Jesus Christ Himself, as was the case with three of the six Witnesses I have used as resources for this book.

Regardless of who comes to be your escort, you will likely feel a great love emanating from them. If you don't recognize your escort and feel their love for you, that's not a good sign.

GEORGE G. RITCHIE

"You are in the presence of the Son of God."

> I stared in astonishment as the brightness increased, coming from nowhere, seeming to shine everywhere at once.... It was impossibly bright: it was like a million welders' lamps all blazing at once.... For now I saw that it was not light but a Man who had entered the room....
>
> The instant I perceived Him, a command formed itself in my mind. "Stand up!" The words came from inside me, yet they had an

Going Home

authority my mere thoughts had never had. I got to my feet, and as I did came the stupendous certainty: "You are in the presence of the Son of God." (*Return from Tomorrow*, pp. 48–49)

Jesus then proceeded to take George on what might be described as a tour of the spirit world, visiting regions that varied between paradisaical and hellish.

BETTY EADIE

"I'm home. I'm home. I'm finally home."

I saw a pinpoint of light in the distance. . . . As I approached it, I noticed the figure of a man standing in it, with the light radiating all around him. As I got closer the light became brilliant—brilliant beyond any description, far more brilliant than the sun—and I knew that no earthly eyes in their natural state could look upon this light without being destroyed. . . . And as our lights merged, I felt as if I had stepped into his countenance, and I felt an utter explosion of love.

It was the most unconditional love I have ever felt, and as I saw his arms open to receive me. I went to him and received his complete embrace and said over and over, "I'm home. I'm home. I'm finally home."

There was no questioning who he was. I knew that he was my Savior, and friend, and God. He was Jesus Christ, who had always loved me, even when I thought he hated me. (*Embraced by the Light*, pp. 40–42)

Jesus then introduced Betty to two female spirits. He told her:

"Go learn of things."

Jesus instructed the first two women to escort me, and I felt their happiness at being with me. As I looked at them, I remembered them; they were my friends! They had been two of my close friends before I came to earth, and their excitement at being with me again was as great as my own. As Jesus was about to leave me with them, I felt his amusement again, and he seemed to whisper to my spirit, "Go learn of things," and I understood that I was free to see and experience all that I wanted. . . . The Savior left us then, and my two friends embraced me. The love here encompassed all; everybody had it. Everybody was happy . . . their love was unconditional. They loved me with all of their hearts. (*Embraced by the Light*, pp. 73–74)

ELANE DURHAM

"I absolutely recognized him . . . the Lord Jesus Christ."

I saw in the light's core the outline of a man—a glorious being apparently made of light that seemed more golden in color than the radiance that shown all about him. And though I thought of Him as light, He certainly had all the physical aspects and substance of a man. I saw His hands, His arms, His body, His neck, His head—I even noted His facial characteristics, though I am at a loss to describe them now. Yet withal He was a being of power and glorious light so incredible that I could not really comprehend Him.

But I do remember His eyes! The were so clear and bright—yet there was color to them—a beautiful blue color outlined in deeper blue that made me think of the color of the distant ocean on a clear day. But it wasn't so much the color of His eyes as it was the power in them, that awed me. Those fathomless eyes penetrated my very soul. They knew me beyond anything I was ever capable of knowing about myself—and to my absolute and dumbfounded amazement, still He loved me. In fact, the love I had felt from the moment of seeing the light had grown steadily stronger, and now it somehow reached out and literally began to encircle me and draw me closer. . . .

I knew then that I had been with Him before, for I absolutely recognized him . . . the Lord Jesus Christ. (*I Stand All Amazed*, pp. 30–31)

RANELLE WALLACE

"RaNelle . . . it's Grandma."

A woman walked toward me dressed in white. Her hair was white, and her face shown with light. I had no fear of her; the love I felt allowed no fear. She came forward and stood immediately before me. Then she smiled . . . [and] spoke my name.

"RaNelle."

But her lips didn't move. Her smile never changed and my first thought was, "Wow, what a trick! Her lips didn't move."

Going Home

> "RaNelle," she said again, and I realized her voice sounded in my mind and not in my ears. How could this be?
>
> "RaNelle . . . it's Grandma."
>
> And the moment she said this, I recognized her. She was my mother's mother. But she looked different than I had remembered. She was full and rounded and vibrant. She appeared to be about twenty-five years old but her hair was glorious white, and everything about her was radiantly beautiful. Her body was glorious, and I began to understand why I hadn't recognized her. She had been frail and sick all the years I had known her. Then the realization hit me.
>
> Grandma was dead; she had died a couple of years before. And I thought, if she's dead, then what am I doing here?
>
> Oh, I'm dead. (*The Burning Within*, pp. 95–96)

DALE BLACK

"Accompanying me were two angelic escorts."

After leaving the hospital, Dale Black recounts that he traveled along a narrow pathway of light, and realized he was not alone.

> At this time, I became aware that I was not traveling alone. Accompanying me were two angelic escorts dressed in seamless white garments woven with silver threads.
>
> They . . . appeared masculine and larger than I. Their skin tone was light golden brown and their hair fairly short. I could see their emotions, clearly delighted to be ushering me through this wonderland. They moved just behind me, one to the left of me, one to the right. Remarkably, my peripheral vision was enhanced, and I could see both of their glowing faces at the same time. I could even see behind me while hardly moving my head. (*Flight to Heaven*, pp. 98–99)

SARAH LANELLE MENET

"I did not recognize her, though she seemed somewhat familiar."

> Out the back of my head I could see a beautiful woman coming up a path behind me.
>
> I recognized powerfully at this time that I could see with every part of my body, not just with my eyes. I was aware of what was happening all around me. I could even see out of my fingertips. It was

strange and wonderful to have that remarkable spirit body, a thing of light and substance beyond earthly description and capable of doing so much more than our bodies of flesh.

As this angelic woman approached nearer, I turned around to face her. Her hair was a dark blond and swirled up on her head in the style of what we call a "French twist." She had on a peach-colored robe with a turquoise cummerbund around her waist and a cream-colored shawl draped over her shoulder and hanging down to the ground. She was wearing no shoes. Her robe had a soft, glimmering sheerness to it that seemed to be transparent yet was actually opaque.

I did not recognize her, though she seemed somewhat familiar. I felt I should know her but had no idea who she was. As I looked at her I was somehow able to determine that she was an older woman, even thought she looked to be about thirty years old. Another wonderful thing I understood about spirit bodies was that they all looked to be about the same age. They were all absolutely beautiful and perfect, and while it was easy to tell them apart by their individual physical features, it was also possible to recognize each other spirit to spirit.

Upon reaching me, she said with surprise, "LaNelle, what are you doing here?" I questioned how she knew who I was. I understood in the intuitive way I had come to expect by now that there was something like a kind of signal that alerts family members in the spirit world when a relative on earth is about to die or "cross over." This provides the opportunity for them to be there and dress the new arrival, sometimes even before he or she leaves their body. This woman, whom I did not know, was a relative of mine. She had been caught by surprise, somehow knowing that it wasn't my time to cross over, so she had hurried to reach me. . . .

She continued, "You cannot stay here. You have to go back. . . ." I protested, "I don't want to go back. I don't want to go back." (*There Is No Death*, pp. 49–50)

Several years after her return, Sarah found a photograph of her grandmother Sarah, who had died when Sarah was a baby.

"When I saw the photograph, I immediately recognized her as the beautiful lady in the spirit world who sent me back" (*There Is No Death*, p. 128).

Going Home

DR. ELISABETH KÜBLER-ROSS

No one dies alone.

> The biggest fear of children is to be alone, to be lonely, to not be with someone. At the moment of this transition, you are never, ever alone. You are never alone now, but you don't know it. But at the time of transition, your guides, your guardian angel, people whom you have loved and who have passed on before you, will be there to help you. We have verified this beyond a shadow of a doubt, and I say this as a scientist. There will always be someone to help you with this transition. Most of the time it is a mother or father, a grandparent, or a child if you have lost a child. (*On Life After Death*, p. 27–28)

"In general, the people who are waiting for us on the other side are the ones who loved us the most" (*On Life After Death*, p. 9).

DR. RAYMOND A. MOODY JR.

"All these people were there."

In his book *The Light Beyond*, Dr. Moody quotes the following account:

> I had this experience when I was giving birth to a child. The delivery was very difficult, and I lost a lot of blood. The doctor gave up, and told my relatives I was dying. However, I was quite alert through the whole thing, and even as I heard him say this I felt myself coming to. As I did, I realized that all these people were there, almost multitudes it seems, hovering around the ceiling of the room. They were all people I had known in my past life, but who had passed on before. I recognized my grandmother and a girl I had known when I was in school, and many other relatives and friends. It seems that I mainly saw their faces and felt their presence. They all seemed pleased. It was a very happy occasion, and I felt that they had come to protect or to guide me. It was almost as if I were coming home, and they were there to greet or to welcome me. All the time, I had the feeling of everything light and beautiful. It was a beautiful and glorious moment. (*Life After Life*, pp. 55–56)

Keith A. Haslem

DRS. KARLIS OSIS and ERLENDUR HARALDSSON

Karlis Osis, PhD and Erlendur Haraldsson, PhD published the book *At the Hour of Death* in 1977. It details an extensive scientific study of individuals' experiences just prior to their deaths as reported by more than a thousand doctors and nurses who interacted with these patients.

Doctors Osis and Haraldsson wrote that a common occurrence among these dying individuals was the recognition of deceased family members who had come to meet them as they were close to passing away.

AUTHOR'S PERSPECTIVE

Being omniscient, Jesus knew that George G. Ritchie, Betty J. Eadie, and Elane Durham would return to their bodies. Perhaps His decision to meet them was so they could become witnesses of His reality and His unconditional love.

It's only logical that a loving God would send someone to our alleviate fears and anxieties in order to make the transition to the next world comfortable.

7

WILL I SEE MY LIFE PASS BEFORE ME?

SYNOPSIS

According to the Witnesses, usually very soon after leaving the body you will experience what is commonly called a "Life Review"—something akin to the expression of having your life pass before your eyes—but it will be much more comprehensive.

Incomprehensibly, this experience seemingly happens within a few moments, as somehow the scenes of your life are viewed not individually but simultaneously. Another element is that you appear as a participant in what might be compared to a hologram. You won't just view the events, you'll relive them; feeling the impact you had on others.

It seems that the primary purpose of this review is so that you are in the position to judge yourself. Perhaps the most disturbing element of this review is that you will *feel* how you affected others with the things you did or didn't do, or the things you said or didn't say. In essence, all the pain you caused for others will boomerang back on you.

ELANE DURHAM

Upon meeting Jesus Christ, Elane recalls that the first words He said to her were a question:

"What have you done for your fellow man?"

> He asked me then with His wordless communication, and instantly my entire life was before my eyes. It wasn't like I was seeing a movie, with scenes laid out in sequence. Instead it was somehow all at once,

so that many different aspects of my life were laid out for me to see and contemplate all in the same instant. And in that same instant I chose, because of all the trauma and abuse I had experienced, to focus on every incident for which I felt guilt and shame. These, I was certain, would cause Him to release me and turn away from me.

But no, that didn't happen. Instead he told me that every single aspect of my guilt and shame had either been forgiven by Him already because of my repentance, or had come about because of how I had been raised or treated, and had not, therefore, been of my choice. As I struggled to understand this He reminded me that I had never turned my back on God, but had daily sought Him, begging for forgiveness for the sins I had committed, and pleading for His presence in my life. Now, I realized abruptly, those prayers and pleadings were being answered. (*I Stand All Amazed*, pp. 31–32)

In her review, Elane also viewed an incident from her childhood.

In my "review" I was shown all the times when I had acted indifferently or even cruelly toward my younger brother—the times I had let him take the blame for my childhood mischief, or the times I had hurt him in some other way. For instance, I remembered once when I had thrown a small block of wood off a stair railing and hit him, and had felt quite indifferent to his pain. Now I found myself experiencing his pain, his feelings of intimidation and all the insecurities he felt in having me as an older sister, and I suddenly understood him better, probably, than he had ever understood himself. (*I Stand All Amazed*, p. 33)

BETTY J. EADIE

"Well-defined holograms"

My life appeared before me in the form of what we might consider extremely well defined holograms, but at tremendous speed. . . . I was astonished that I could understand so much information at such a speed. My comprehension included much more than what I remember happening during each event in my life. I not only re-experienced my own emotions at each moment, but also what others around me had felt. I experienced their thoughts and feelings about me. . . . Then I saw the disappointment that I had caused others, and I cringed as their feelings of disappointment filled me, compounded by my own

Going Home

> guilt. I understood all the suffering I had caused, and I felt it.... I saw how much grief my bad temper had caused.... I saw my selfishness, and my heart cried for relief. How had I been so uncaring?
>
> Then in the midst of my pain, I felt the love of the council come over me ... and I realized that the council was not judging me. I was judging myself....
>
> The Savior stepped toward me, full of concern and love. His spirit gave me strength, and he said that I was judging myself too critically. "You're being too harsh on yourself" he said.

Then [Betty] also saw the effects of her kind acts. And she learned a significant lesson.

> A powerful thought hit me, and I repeated it over and over in my mind: Love is really the only thing that matters. Love is really the only thing that matters, and love is joy!
>
> It all seemed so simple. If we're kind, we'll have joy. (*Embraced by the Light*, pp. 112–14)

"My sins and shortcomings . . . were tools for me to learn by."

> So the review quickly changed from a negative experience to a very positive one.... I saw my sins and shortcomings in a multi-dimensional light. Yes, they were grievous to me and others, but they were tools for me to learn by, to correct my thinking and behavior. I understood that forgiven sins are blotted out. It is as if they are overlaid by new understanding, by a new direction in life. This new understanding then leads me to naturally abandon the sin. Although the sin is blotted out, however, the educational part of the experience remains. Thus the forgiven sin helps me to grow and increases my ability to help others. (*Embraced by the Light*, pp. 115–16)

RANELLE WALLACE

"I didn't just understand the events; I relived them."

> A brief scene flashed before me. A series of pictures, words, ideas, and understanding. It was a scene from my life. It flashed before me with incredible rapidity, and I understood it completely and learned from it. Another scene came, and another, and another, and I was seeing my entire life, every second of it. And I didn't just understand the events; I relived them. I was that person again, doing those things

Keith A. Haslem

to my mother, or saying those words to my father or brothers or sisters, and I knew why, for the first time, I had done them or said them. Entirety does not describe the fullness of this review . . . and I understood the impact I had on others.

A part of me began to anticipate certain events, things in my life I would dread seeing again. But most of them didn't show up, and I understood that I had taken responsibility for these actions and had repented of them. I saw myself repenting of them, sincerely wanting God to remove the weight and guilt of those terrible actions. And he had. I marveled at his sublime love and that my misdeeds could be forgiven and removed so easily. But then I saw other scenes that I hadn't anticipated, things that were just as awful. I saw them in horrible detail and watched the impact they had on others. I saw that I had let many people down in my life . . . people had depended on me . . . and I had said, I'm too busy or it's not my problem. . . . My cavalier attitude had caused real pain and heartache in others, pain I had never known about. . . .

Until that moment I had never realized that ignoring responsibilities was a sin.

I re-experienced myself doing good things. . . .

As the review of my life came to an end I was in agony. I saw everything I had ever done in vivid, immediate detail—the bad things, haunting and terrifying in their finality, and the good things, ringing with greater reward and happiness than I had ever imagined. But in the end I was found wanting. I found myself wanting. Nobody was there to judge me. Nobody had to be. I wanted to melt in the agony of self-indictment. The fires of remorse began to consume me, but there was nothing I could do. (*The Burning Within*, pp. 91–94)

GEORGE G. RITCHIE

In George Ritchie's account, he is met by a being of light and receives the impression that he is in the presence of Jesus Himself. Jesus asks him:

"What did you do with your life?"

"It seemed to be a question about values, not facts: what did you accomplish with the precious time you were allotted?" (*Return from Tomorrow*, p. 52).

Going Home

"Every single episode of my entire life."

When I say He knew everything about me, this was simply an observable fact. For into that room along with his radiant presence—simultaneously, though in telling about it I have to describe them one by one—had also entered every single episode of my entire life. Everything that had ever happened to me was simply there, in full view, contemporary and current, all seemingly taking place at that moment.

How this was possible I didn't know. (*Return from Tomorrow*, pp. 49–50)

SARAH LANELLE MENET

"The worst parts . . . were when I had intentionally hurt someone else."

I started thinking about all the things I had done in my life. As the thoughts formed in my mind, a window seemed to open before me and my life's review began. . . . It was if someone had a video that ran at fast-forward, showing my entire life from my birth until the moment I arrived in the spirit world. It only took a few seconds, and yet I was doing more than just watching the events of my life pass by. With each event I not only saw my actions, but I heard the thoughts I was thinking and felt what I was feeling at the time. I was reliving each experience, only this time I could see all that was happening around me as well. I could see and feel what those I interacted with were seeing and feeling. I could actually feel their pain or joy and understand what they were thinking as they reacted to my actions. For me, this was not a pleasant experience.

. . . The worst parts of the review were when I had intentionally hurt someone else. Somehow the emotions of the moment combined, and I felt not only my anguish but also the pain felt by others. I was in misery.

Quickly I came to understand two very important concepts: The first was that I alone am responsible for my actions. . . .

The second was that our thoughts, words, and actions are extremely powerful and have an effect upon more people than we realize. . . . The ripples or effects of our life's actions also come back to us, for good or bad. If we have had good thoughts and actions that helped and lifted others, we will feel the benefits as they ripple back to us. Unfortunately, the opposite is also true. Acts of unkindness and cruelty will have their negative impact upon us as well.

As I watched the actions of my life in review, I became ashamed of many of the things I had done and began to feel the pain personally that I inflicted upon others during the course of my life.

. . . I saw incidents and events in that review that I had completely forgotten, including those so small that they seemed insignificant, yet there they were—every detail, good or bad. (*There Is No Death*, pp. 43–47)

. . . Everything that a person says, does, or thinks from the time they are born to the day they die is recorded in their own soul, not written down by some heavenly being as we may have thought.

I now grasped the concept that because of these recordings in our spiritual DNA, when we pass from this life we will be able to look at another being in the spirit world and "read" their life . . . and I understood that if I concentrated a little harder I could read the entire life history of each person focused on. . . .

. . . As these thoughts and explanations came into my mind, I became frightened. There were parts of my life I definitely did not want others to see, and now, in dismay, I realized I could not hide anything from anyone.

. . . [However] A person having repented may still remember [things repented of] . . . but those details would be kept from others. I also realized that there was no casual interest in "looking into" people's lives. (*There Is No Death*, pp. 42–43)

RAYMOND A. MOODY JR.

From his research, Dr. Moody comments on the commonly experienced Life Review:

"Everything appeared at once, and they could take it all in."

The initial appearance of the being of light and his probing, non-verbal questions are the prelude to a moment of startling intensity during which the being presents to the person a panoramic review of his life. It is often obvious that the being can see the individual's whole life displayed and that he doesn't need information. His only intention is [to] provoke reflection.

Going Home

> This review can only be described in terms of memory, since that is the closest familiar phenomenon to it, but it has characteristics which set it apart from any normal type of remembering. First of all, it is extraordinarily rapid. . . . The remembrance was instantaneous; everything appeared at once, and they could take it all in with one mental glance. However it is expressed, all seem in agreement that the experience was over in an instant of earthly time.
>
> Yet, despite its rapidity, my informants agree that the review, almost always described as a display of visual imagery, is incredibly vivid and real. In some cases, the images are reported to be in vibrant color, three-dimensional, and even moving. . . . Even the emotions and feelings associated with the images may be re-experienced as one is viewing them.
>
> Some of those I interviewed claim that, while they cannot adequately explain it, everything they had ever done was there in this review—from the most insignificant to the most meaningful. Others explain that what they saw were mainly the highlights of their lives. Some have stated to me that even for a period of time following their experience of the review they could recall the events of their lives in incredible detail. (*Life After Life*, pp. 64–65)

One of Dr. Moody's subjects made the following observations regarding his life review:

"Other things I regretted that I had left undone."

> I knew I was dying, and I remember thinking that I wanted to provide for my family. I was distraught that I was dying and yet that there were certain things that I had done in my life that I regretted, and other things that I regretted that I had left undone.
>
> This flashback was in the form of mental pictures, I would say, but they were much more vivid than normal ones. I saw only the high points, but it was so rapid it was like looking through a volume of my entire life and being able to do it within seconds. It just flashed before me like a motion picture that goes tremendously fast, yet I was fully able to see it, and able to comprehend it. . . . I definitely felt the presence of a very powerful, completely loving being there with me through this experience.
>
> It is really interesting. When I recovered, I could tell everyone about every part of my life, in great detail, because of what I had been through. It's quite an experience, but it's difficult to put into

words, because it happens so rapidly, yet it's so clear. (*Life After Life*, pp. 69–70)

In his book *The Light Beyond*, Dr. Moody describes the Life Review as follows:

"I feel their sadness, hurt, and regret."

When the life review occurs, there are no more physical surroundings. In their place is a full-color, three-dimensional, panoramic review of every single thing the NDEers have done in their lives.

This usually takes place in a third-person perspective and doesn't occur in time as we know it. The closest description I've heard of it is that the person's whole life is there at once.

In this situation, you not only see every action that you have ever done, but you also perceive immediately the effects of every single one of your actions upon the people in your life.

So for instance, if I see myself doing an unloving act, then immediately I am in the consciousness of the person I did that act to, so that I feel their sadness, hurt, and regret.

On the other hand, if I do a loving act to someone, then I am immediately in their place and I can feel the kind and happy feelings.

Through all of this, the Being is with those people, asking them what good they have done with their lives. He helps them through this review and helps them put all the events of their life in perspective.

All of the people who go through this come away believing that the most important thing in their life is love.

For most of them, the second most important thing in life is knowledge. As they see life scenes in which they are learning things, the Being points out that one of the things they can take with them at death is knowledge. The other is love.

When people come back they have a thirst for knowledge. Frequently, NDEers become avid readers, even if they weren't very fond of books before, or they enroll in school to study a different field than the one they are in. (*The Light Beyond*, pp. 14–15)

Based upon his many interviews, Dr. Raymond Moody makes the following observation about purpose of the life reviews:

The importance of learning to love and gain knowledge.

Going Home

"As they witness the display, the being [of light] seems to stress the importance of two things in life: Learning to love other people and acquiring knowledge" (*Life After Life*, p. 65).

Dr. Moody quotes from the near-death experience of one man who said:

"There will always be a quest for knowledge . . . it goes on after death."

> All through this, he [the being of light] kept stressing the importance of love. . . . He pointed out to me that I should try to do things for other people. . . . There wasn't any accusation in any of this, though. When he came across times when I had been selfish, his attitude was only that I had been learning from them too.
>
> He seemed very interested in things concerning knowledge, too. He kept on pointing out things that had to do with learning, and he did say that I was going to continue learning, and he said that even when he comes back for me (because by this time he had told me that I was going back) that there will always be a quest for knowledge. He said that it is a continuous process, so I got the feeling that it goes on after death. (*Life After Life*, pp. 67–68)

In *Life After Life*, Dr. Moody speaks of subjects who, as they are in the presence of the "being of light," are asked if they are ready to die.

"What have you done with your life?"

> The being almost immediately directs a certain thought to the person into whose presence it has come so dramatically. Usually the persons with whom I talked try to formulate the thought into a question. Among the translations I have heard are: "Are you prepared to die?", "Are you ready to die?", "What have you done with your life to show me?", and "What have you done with your life that is sufficient?"
>
> . . . Incidentally, all insist that this question, ultimate and profound as it may be in its emotional impact, is not at all asked in condemnation. The being, all seem to agree, does not direct the questions to them to accuse or to threaten them, for they still feel the total love and acceptance coming from the light, no matter what their answer may be. Rather, the point of the question seems to be to make them think about their lives. (*Life After Life*, pp. 60–61)

Keith A. Haslem

DR. ELISABETH KÜBLER-ROSS

"You will remember every deed, and know every word that you ever spoke."

> In this light, in the presence of God, Christ, or whatever you want to name it, you have to look back on your entire life from the first day until the last. . . . You know in minute detail every thought you had at any time during your life on earth. You will remember every deed, and know every word that you ever spoke . . . at this moment you know all consequences from your thoughts, and from every one of your words and deeds. (*On Life After Death*, pp. 11–12)

> What we hear from our friends who have passed over, people who came back to share with us, is that every human being, after this transition, is going to have to face something that looks very much like a television screen. You will be given an opportunity—not to be judged by a judgmental God—but to judge yourself, by having to review every single action, every word, and every thought of your life. You make your own hell or your own heaven by the way you lived. (*On Life After Death*, p. 35)

AUTHOR'S PERSPECTIVE

Hurtful acts will boomerang back on us.

It might be supposed that this life review was given to these individuals *because* they were returning to mortality and they needed this new perspective of what is truly important.

Whether *everyone* who dies will immediately have this experience cannot be known. But the fact that this experience is possible argues that it will happen, sooner or later. The possibility of such an experience makes me think about the wisdom of the Boy Scout slogan, "Do a good turn daily."

The possibility of a "life review" in the presence of Jesus has had, perhaps, a greater impact on me personally than any other concept in this book. Am I a more considerate person now that I am aware of this potential event in my future? I believe so.

I've found myself doing "good turns" that I would not have considered previously. It's been said, "the proof is in the pudding."

8

WILL I TRAVEL THROUGH A DARK TUNNEL?

SYNOPSIS

It is commonly reported that travel to the spirit world consists of moving through a dark tunnel. Although common, this experience is not universal. Some rise to a position in space, with the view an astronaut might have.

In the case of the tunnel, you may see bright, vivid, colorful flashing lights as you fly feet first, at tremendous speed, through the tunnel. It may seem as though you are traveling a great distance. Eventually, you will see a dot of light that will become larger as you approach it. The light will appear to be brighter than the sun, and you may be somewhat fearful of the effect it might have upon you.

In some NDE accounts, the escort is not met until the graduate emerges from this tunnel into the spirit world. In other accounts, the escort was met prior to the tunnel and then accompanied the graduate through the tunnel, almost as if their presence offered some sort of protection.

The emergence into the world of spirits is a dazzling experience and will be discussed in the next chapter.

RANELLE WALLACE

"Into a narrow tube . . . flying feet first"

> Suddenly I began to be afraid. Immense blackness flooded over me like a rapid, dense fog. The darkness was so absolute that nothing was

Keith A. Haslem

> visible, and it seemed like nothing ever could be visible in it. Then, just as suddenly, bright, vivid lights began flashing around me, psychedelic lights that were brighter and more colorful than anything I had ever seen before. I looked down at myself, and in the brilliance of the lights saw that my body looked perfectly well again. No burns, no bleeding, my hands and feet were whole. I stood in the midst of a spectacular light show, feeling absolutely whole and complete. . . .
>
> . . . I was sucked into a narrow tube and I began flying through it feet first. The tube was extremely tight, and I became more frightened because it almost felt like my body was being sucked inside out. My speed was tremendous—indescribable. Nothing on earth has ever gone that fast, nothing could. It felt as if I were whizzing past galaxies, but the colors and lights were right next to me, almost brushing against me, and my fears mounted.

RaNelle describes hearing the voices of two men traveling beside her. They were talking in a language that seemed familiar to her, but that she could not understand. After a period of time, she describes:

> A dot of light appeared far off in front of me. . . . Emanating from it was a love and hope and peace that my soul hungered for. I wanted, I needed this brilliant, radiant light. The black tube took the shape of a tunnel now, opening up as I neared its end. The light burst before me, filling everything with brightness, and I was coming upon it impossibly fast. Oh, my gosh, I thought, it's brighter than the sun. It'll blind me! It'll kill me!
>
> I remembered my burns from the plane crash and was afraid they would ignite again in this radiance. But I couldn't stop myself. I was drawn to the light by forces I could not control, so I shut my eyes against my impending destruction. But my eyes wouldn't shut. They felt shut—but somehow I could still see. And then I was in the light.
>
> Like a nuclear explosion, the light pierced me. Every particle of me was shot through with blinding, brilliant light, and I had a feeling of transparency.
>
> My skin didn't burn. My eyes still saw. I floated in this light, bathed in it, and the love that surrounded me and filled me was sweeter and finer than anything I had ever felt. I was changed by it, refined, rarified, made pure. I basked in its sweetness, and the traumas of the past were far behind me, forgotten and transformed by peace. Then an image appeared in the distance. (*The Burning Within*, pp. 90–95)

At this point, RaNelle was met by her grandmother, who served as her escort while in the world of spirits.

ELANE DURHAM

After leaving her body in the hospital, Elane Durham reports:

"I realized that the light was traveling toward me just as I was moving toward it, and it was moving at a great speed."

There came within my being a soft pop—like a bubble breaking. Then my spirit was free of my body, and I felt myself lifting.

Abruptly aware that I could see clearly again I rose upward, passing within about ten inches of the side of the priest's face [who was administering last rites to her]. I saw that he had dark hair and dark-rimmed glasses, as well as a voice that I knew I would never forget. I next saw the little nurse who had been praying for me. . . .

[I] knew a "part of me" was being left on the gurney, but at that moment I felt a great indifference toward it. Instead I found myself luxuriating in my new freedom.

In fact, I felt more alive than I could ever remember feeling. I now had expanded senses, and I could see things so very clearly! I found myself in a dense, foggy area with light like might be seen near dusk or dawn. I had no fear, and I was filled with the knowledge that I wasn't alone.

. . . Upon turning to my right I saw a bright light in the distance, slightly above the horizon. It was like a large star or close planet might appear, and a halo of light surrounded it. My spirit lifted and somehow rose toward this beacon, which was emanating rays through its halos, though I had no idea of how I was moving. . . .

. . . I realized that the light was traveling toward me just as I was moving toward it, and it was moving at a great speed. As we came closer together, I saw rays of light filter out through the halos, and I realized that there was a personality to this light. I also felt an immense amount of love from it, a different kind of love than I had ever felt before, love that was completely overwhelming. . . . I knew I was being welcomed to come closer. (*I Stand All Amazed*, pp. 25–26)

As I got closer to the light I heard a voice—but again as in the beautiful meadow, not with my ears alone. It was as if every thing that I was, every particle of my being, was absorbing what I heard. I not only

Keith A. Haslem

heard the voice, but I felt it as He spoke to me, saying, "Through me you have Eternal Life." (*I Stand All Amazed*, p. 29)

DALE BLACK

"A path in the darkness delineated by the light."

Leaving the hospital, I sped through what appeared to be a narrow pathway. An incandescent-like beam of light, almost like a searchlight, originated from me and illuminated my path. It wasn't a tunnel of light that I was traveling through. It was a path in the darkness that was delineated by the light. Outside of this pathway was total darkness....

The speed at which I traveled was blinding, and the path narrowed to twice the width of my body. I had no pain, no discomfort whatsoever....

At this time, I became aware that I was not traveling alone. Accompanying me were two angelic escorts dressed in seamless white garments woven with silver threads.... (*Flight to Heaven*, pp. 98–100)

RAYMOND A. MOODY JR.

In his book *Life After Life*, Raymond A. Moody writes:

"Pulled very rapidly through a dark space of some kind."

"People have the sensation of being pulled very rapidly through a dark space of some kind. Many different words are used to describe this space. I have heard this space described as a cave, a well, a trough, an enclosure, a tunnel, a funnel, a vacuum, a void . . . , a valley, and a cylinder" (*Life After Life*, p. 21).

Dr. Moody quotes a gentleman he interviewed:

"You could compare it to a tunnel."

"I had a very bad allergic reaction to a local anesthetic, and I just quit breathing—I had a respiratory arrest. The first thing that happened—it was real quick—was that I went through this dark, black vacuum at super speed. You could compare it to a tunnel, I guess" (*Life After Life*, pp. 31–32).

Going Home

He also quotes a woman who "drew a parallel from a television show":

"A tunnel of concentric circles."

"There was a feeling of utter peace and quiet, no fear at all, and I found myself in a tunnel—a tunnel of concentric circles. Shortly after that, I saw a T.V. program called The Time Tunnel, where people go back in time through this spiraling tunnel. Well, that's the closest thing to it that I can think of" (*Life After Life*, p. 33).

"A very dark, very deep valley."

Another man who talked to Dr. Moody "drew a somewhat different parallel, one from his religious background." He says:

"Suddenly, I was in a very dark, very deep valley. It was as though there was a pathway, almost a road, through a valley, and I was going down the path. . . . Later, after I was well, the thought came to me, 'Well, now I know what the Bible means by the "valley of the shadow of death," because I've been there'" (*Life After Life*, pp. 33–34).

Dr. Moody reports that not every case study involves a tunnel.

"Up stairways"

> Some people go up stairways instead of through a tunnel. One woman said she was with her son as he was dying of lung cancer. One of the last things he said was that he saw a beautiful spiral staircase going upward. He put his mother's mind at peace when he told her that he thought he was going up those stairs.
>
> Some people have described going through beautiful, ornate doors, which seems very symbolic of a passage into another realm. (*The Light Beyond*, p. 11)

Dr. Moody comments:

> I should point out that not all NDEers have a tunnel experience. Some report a "floating experience" in which they rise rapidly into the heavens, seeing the universe from a perspective reserved for satellites and astronauts.

Keith A. Haslem

The psychotherapist C. G. Jung had an experience like this in 1944 when he had a heart attack. He said that he felt himself rise rapidly to a point far above the earth.

One child I talked to said that he felt himself rise far above the earth, passing through the stars and finding himself up with the angels. Another NDEer described himself as zooming up and seeing the planets all around him and the earth below like a blue marble. (*The Light Beyond*, p. 15)

AUTHOR'S PERSPECTIVE

The fact that not all accounts are the same actually reinforces the likelihood of their authenticity. If the accounts were fabricated they would probably be identical in order to corroborate each other.

PART II
WHAT THE WITNESSES SAW

The Appearance of the Spirit World 71

The Appearance of Spirits 95

The Abilities of Spirits 109

The Relationships between
Spirits in the Spirit World................................ 135

The Architecture of the Spirit World 148

Jesus Christ in the Spirit World........................ 160

WHERE IS THE SPIRIT WORLD LOCATED?

SYNOPSIS

Sarah LaNelle Menet, George Ritchie, and leaders of the Church of Jesus Christ of Latter-day Saints assert that the spirit world is on this planet, occupying an unseen dimension.

SARAH LANELLE MENET

"Occupying the same space"

> I was impressed that the spirit world is actually occupying the same space as the earth but in a different dimension. That is why departed family members know much of what is going on in our lives and are concerned with our progress or lack thereof. In reality, they are very near to us. If the "film" were removed from our eyes, we would see them all around us. (*There Is No Death*, p. 109)

GEORGE G. RITCHIE

A spiritual city "superimposed" on a physical city.

> When we first came down into the city I could see the physical city that any of us would see if we were landing at night by a jet airliner. What made me feel as though my vision was out of focus was seeing another city superimposed on our physical city. I came to understand this belonged to these astral [spirit] beings. In the deepest sense, most

of the beings of one realm weren't aware of the existence of the other. (*My Life After Dying*, p. 25)

THE CHURCH OF JESUS CHRIST OF LATTER-DAY SAINTS PERSPECTIVE

BRIGHAM YOUNG
(second prophet and president of the Church of Jesus Christ of Latter-day Saints)

The spirit world is "right here."

"'Where is the spirit world?' Brigham Young asked. He then answered his own question: 'It is right here. . . . If the Lord would permit it, and it was His will that it should be done, you could see the spirits that have departed from this world, as plainly as you now see bodies with your natural eyes'" (*Journal of Discourses*, 3:369).

EZRA TAFT BENSON
(thirteenth prophet and president of the Church of Jesus Christ of Latter-day Saints)

"Not far from us."

"The spirit world is not far away. . . . Our loved ones who have passed on are not far from us" ("*Life is Eternal*," *Ensign*, June 1971, p. 33).

PARLEY P. PRATT
(a member of the first Quorum of the Twelve Apostles)

"On the very planet where we were born."

As to its location, it is here on the very planet where we were born, or in other words, the earth and other planets of life sphere, have their inward or spiritual spheres, as well as their outward, or temporal. The one is peopled by temporal tabernacles, and the other by spirits. A veil is drawn between the one sphere and the other, whereby all the objects in the spiritual sphere are rendered invisible to those in the temporal. (*Key to the Science of Theology*, p. 76)

JOSEPH SMITH JR.
(first prophet and president of the Church of Jesus Christ of Latter-day Saints)

"Not far from us."

"The spirits of the just are exalted to a greater and more glorious work: hence they are blessed in their departure to the world of spirits . . . they are not far from us." (*History of the Church*, 6:52)

AUTHOR'S PERSPECTIVE

Is it difficult for you to believe in something that cannot be seen?

Have you ever seen radio waves, microwaves, TV waves, or the stream of data going in and out of your smart phone? No. Only scientific evidence that they exist. Have you ever seen the wind? No. Only *evidence* of it as you see plant life move and feel the breeze against your skin. Obviously, there is much that you believe in that cannot be seen.

10

WHAT DOES THE SPIRIT WORLD LOOK LIKE?

SYNOPSIS

According to our resources, the most succinct way to describe the paradisaical region of the spirit world is "indescribably beautiful."

You will see incredible gardens, the likes of which you have never seen on earth, with flowers more vibrant and colorful than you've ever imagined: towering trees, picturesque shrubbery, sparkling streams, shimmering lakes, cascading waterfalls, beautiful valleys, majestic mountains, immaculate meadows of grass, and a beautiful sky. You will sense an intelligence in all these creations and understand that they enjoy meeting you.

In the midst of it all there will be an exquisite fragrance. You will hear peaceful music, something akin to background music, that is more beautiful than anything you've ever heard. And you will feel a warm, gentle breeze. You may even sense a delicious flavor in your mouth.

In the midst of this sensory feast, you will feel the love of God more intensely than you've ever felt before—even though you may not be in His presence.

RANELLE WALLACE

"We simply don't have the language [to describe] the beauty of that world."

A garden cannot exist on earth like the one I saw. I had been in gardens in California that had taken my breath away, but they were struck

Going Home

> into insignificance by the scene before me now. Here was an endless vista of grass rolling away into shining, radiant hills. We have never seen green in our world like the deep shimmering green of the grass that grew there. Every blade was crisp, strong, and charged with light. Every blade was unique and perfect and seemed to welcome me into this miraculous place.
>
> Profusions of flowers were splashed on the hills in colors I had never imagined. Flowers of all sizes and forms—living, radiating, and glorying in their beauty—-erupted from the hills and valleys without end. The colors were indescribable. We may have fifty or a hundred tints of orange in this world. In that one there are millions. I saw tints of orange that defy comprehension. Shades of roses and hints of pink stretched on forever, every subtle shade a unique color, every color connecting in perfect harmony with other colors, and every arrangement a miracle. Our colors all seem to be grays and browns and blacks in comparison—dead, drab, everything a muddle of the same staid tints. Even our brightest colors are artificial. There, colors vibrated with life, creating subtle shades of mood and atmosphere. The colors did more than please me, they infused me with happiness in their completion, in their wholeness. It was as if every blade of grass, every flower, every tree, had a unique prism from which light and spirit exploded.
>
> And the whole garden was singing. The flowers, grass, trees, and other plants filled this place with glorious tones and rhythms and melodies; yet I didn't hear the music myself. I could feel it somehow on a level beyond my hearing. As my grandmother and I stopped a moment to marvel at this magnificent scene, I said to myself, "Everything here seems to be singing," which was woefully inadequate to describe what I felt. We simply don't have language that adequately communicates the beauty of that world. (*The Burning Within*, pp. 101–2)

At this point in her narrative, RaNelle has a remarkable experience with a flower. I've elected to put it in Chapter 20: How Will We Interact with Plants?

"Large powerful trees [with intelligence]"

> I saw large powerful trees . . . . The trees were similar to Palmyra trees that grow in the tropics—only much larger. . . . I sensed their intelligence . . . and I knew that reaching their full height and width and firmness actually gave meaning to their existence. Their trunks

were their foundation, and their leaf spread and total size was, in effect, their glory. The trees produced a scent that reminded me of something bouquetish, very flowery. Then I smelled another scent, a mixture between sweet pine and lilac. It came from a large stately tree that reminded me of a pine tree but was fuller.

The sky above the trees had a lavender hue that seemed to turn blue in places where the light was greater. As I stood reflecting on all this, letting the entire scene permeate my being, my grandmother spoke again.

"All this comes from God, and the power to sustain it comes from him. It is the power of his love. Just as the plant life on earth needs soil, water, and light for nourishment, spiritual life needs love. All creation springs from God's love, and everything he creates has the capacity to love in turn. Light, truth, and life is all created in love and is sustained by love. God gives it love. We give it love. And thus creation grows." (*The Burning Within*, pp. 103–4)

BETTY J. EADIE

"Mountains . . . valleys . . . rivers . . . cascading waterfall"

As we went outdoors into the garden I saw mountains, spectacular valleys, and rivers in the distance. My escorts left me, and I was allowed to proceed alone, perhaps to experience the full beauty of the garden unencumbered by the presence of others. . . . I walked on the grass for a time. It was crisp, cool and a brilliant green, and it felt alive under my feet. But what filled me with awe in the garden more than anything were the intense colors. We have nothing like them.

When light strikes an object here, the light reflects off that object a certain color. Thousands of shades are possible. Light in the spirit world doesn't necessarily reflect off anything. It comes from within and appears to be a living essence. A million, a billion colors are possible. . . .

A beautiful river ran through the garden not far from me, and I was immediately drawn to it. I saw that the river was fed by a large cascading waterfall of the purest water, and from there the river fed into a pond. The water dazzled with its clarity and life. (*Embraced by the Light*, pp. 78–80)

ELANE DURHAM

"A taste . . . absolutely delicious . . . a soft wafting melody"

Suddenly I was alive and free, running across a most beautiful field. Down by the winding river. . . . As far as the eye could see there were white daisies, millions of them, scattered all through the grasses that rolled off to my right toward the river and the people. And though the daisies were white there were colors everywhere, incredible and subtle colors that I cannot even begin to describe.

To my left a low hill rose with trees and shrubbery scattered across it. The trees, as well as the grasses and flowers, had a spiritual life force all their own, and again, colors that were unbelievable. I savored a taste in my mouth that I can't begin to describe, though it was absolutely delicious. Music flowed lightly, a harmonious sound that is so hard to describe. It was like everything that existed, from the blades of grass to the water of the river, the trees and the earth; the life forces of all these . . . was somehow blended into a soft wafting melody that was not being played, exactly, but truly existed. Surely it was the most beautiful peaceful music I had ever heard. (*I Stand All Amazed*, pp. 18–19)

SARAH LANELLE MENET

"A large and beautiful lake . . . and varieties of fish"

While one paramedic was talking on the phone, the other was still working on me. When the one hung up the receiver, the other said, "Let's try to revive her. Get the paddles out." All this interaction took place within a moment of time. When they said this, I became upset and tried talking to them. I said, "Leave it alone." I did not want to go back into that clump of clay. I think I said it twice, and when they ignored me, I lost interest. Instantly, I was no longer floating in the air above them. I was standing at the edge of a beautiful silver lake. (*There Is No Death*, p. 25)

The move from the previous location was instantaneous. In less than the blink of an eye I found myself in an entirely different world from the one I had inhabited since birth—a world unlike anything I had ever seen or imagined. I stood by a large and beautiful lake located to the right of me....

It was overwhelmingly beautiful. The water glistened like diamonds and had the appearance of liquid silver. As I leaned over the edge, the water was crystal clear, and I found that I could see for miles, clear down to the bottom. I don't know how deep it was, but it was very, very, deep. There were tremendous numbers and varieties of fish swimming through the underwater foliage that was everywhere waving in the currents. The fish and the foliage were of the most vivid colors—very bright and not of our world.

The only way to describe the colors I saw there would be to explain that the spectrum as we know it in this world is muted and dulled, as though seen through some sort of glass that makes colors subdued and somehow less vibrant. To state that our vision in this life is vastly limited would be an understatement. Here we are able to see only a tiny fraction of what I could see there. Not only are the colors like nothing we can imagine, but the words do not exist in our vocabulary to adequately describe them.

As I stood at the edge of this magnificently beautiful shimmering lake, I was enticed by the water and wanted to fall into it and allow it to surround or envelop me. Instinctively I knew that the water was alive in its own way with a spirit about itself, and that it would not harm me. I wasn't aware of how this knowledge came to me, just that it did. The curiosity lasted only for a moment, and then my attention turned to the rest of my surroundings. (*There Is No Death*, pp. 27–29)

As I looked around, drinking it all in, a tremendous feeling of peace came over me. Here I was, separated from everything that I had known before and there were no feelings of loss for the possessions I had left behind. My material treasures, my dear children, or anyone else that might have loved me were not on my mind. All I could think of was how very wonderful it was to be in this place. (*There Is No Death*, pp. 30–31)

"Like being wrapped in a blanket of love"

Regarding the sense of smell, there is a fragrance that exists there which is incredible and unlike anything that I have ever smelled before. This scent is not like any perfume, spice or earthly flower.... It made me feel peaceful, restful, and calm. This fragrance made me feel alive and wonderful, just as everything else did. Every sense is accentuated and contributes to the feeling of well-being that permeates that amazing world, like being wrapped in a blanket of love (*There Is No Death*, p. 32).

I looked up away from the water to the setting surrounding the lake. It was simply breathtaking. Everywhere there were wonderful flowers and vegetation unknown to our world. The flowers were so different in color and so vibrant that I can still see them clearly in my mind today but again cannot begin to describe them. I have no names for them and to try and describe the colors would be like explaining red or blue to a person blind from birth. (*There Is No Death*, p. 29)

"A gentle warm breeze"

"The grass was a bright, vivid green and felt like soft, lush velvet. There was a gentle warm breeze that caused ripple patterns in the grass. The trees were of various shades and their branches moved similar to the swaying grass. Never in my life had I seen anything in nature to match the beauty of what I saw in that realm" (*There Is No Death*, p. 29).

"The sky was a wonderful deep rich blue and there were objects floating in it which at first appeared to be clouds. As I looked closer, I could see that they were actually formations of swirling light with a cloudlike appearance. It was unusual and breathtaking, yet it felt perfectly normal" (*There Is No Death*, p. 30).

"My newly acquired senses soon made me aware that the grove of trees I stood in and the plants and the grass around me were alive and communicating to me that they not only knew who I was but were happy that I was there with them. While not thinking like we do, they nonetheless seemed to have feelings and a form of intelligence that, though different from our own, was still very real. I stood there for a while feeling the love for me that radiated from these forms of life that I now viewed from a completely different perspective" (*There Is No Death*, p. 31).

DALE BLACK

In his account, Dale Black describes a beautiful heavenly city.

Keith A. Haslem

I was fast approaching a magnificent city, golden and gleaming among a myriad of resplendent colors. The light I saw was the purest I had ever seen. And the music was the most majestic, enchanting, and glorious I had ever heard.

I was still approaching the city, but now I was slowing down. Like a plane making its final approach for landing. I knew instantly that this place was entirely and utterly holy. Don't ask me how I knew, I just knew. I was overwhelmed by its beauty. It was breathtaking. And a strong sense of belonging filled my heart; I never wanted to leave. Somehow I knew I was made for this place and this place was made for me. Never had I felt so "right" anywhere. For the first time in my life, I was completely "whole."

The entire city was bathed in light, an opaque whiteness in which the light was intense but diffused. In that dazzling light every color imaginable seemed to exist and—what's the right word?—played. If joy could be given colors, they would be these colors. The colors were pure and innocent, like children playing in a fountain, splashing, chasing each other, gurgling with laughter. Water everywhere sparked in the sunshine.

The colors seemed to be alive, dancing in the air. I had never seen so many different colors. If the brightest light on earth could shine through the most magnificent chandelier with tens of thousands of flawless crystals, it would appear as dirty glass in comparison to the amazing brightness and colors that entranced me.

It was breathtaking to watch. And I could have spent forever doing just that. The closer I got to the city, the more distinct the illumination became. The magnificent light I was experiencing emanated from about forty or fifty miles within the city wall.

I saw a great phosphorescent display of light that narrowed to a focal point that was brighter than the sun. Oddly, it didn't make me squint to look at it. And all I wanted to do was to look at it. The light was palpable. It had substance to it, weight and thickness, like nothing I had ever seen before or since.

The light from a hydrogen bomb is the closest I can come to describing it. Just after the bomb is detonated—but before the fireball that forms the mushroom cloud—there is a millisecond of light that flashes as the bomb releases its energy. It was something like that but much larger.

The glow and energy of this light radiated in all directions, upward and outward. It wasn't something you shielded your eyes from; it wasn't something you even flinched at. Just the opposite. It was warm and inviting. Almost hypnotic in its ability to draw you in to it.

Somehow I knew that light and life and love were connected and interrelated. It was as if the very heart of God lay open for everyone in heaven to bask in its glory, to warm themselves in its presence, to bathe in its almost liquid properties so they could be restored, renewed, refreshed.

Remarkably, the light didn't shine on things but through them. Through the grass. Through the trees. Through the wall. And through the people who were gathered there.

There was a huge gathering of angels and people, millions.... They were gathered in a central area that seemed over ten miles in diameter. The expanse of people was closer to an ocean than a concert hall. Waves of people, moving in the light, swaying to the music, worshiping God (*Flight to Heaven*, pp. 98–100).

"Mountains you wanted to revere"

I was outside the city, slowly moving toward its wall, suspended a few hundred feet above the ground. I'm not sure how I knew directions there, but I had a strong, almost magnetic sense, that it was northwest. Which meant I was approaching the city from the southeast.

A narrow road led to an entrance in the wall, which led into the city. I moved effortlessly along the road, escorted by my two angelic guides, on what seemed to be a divine schedule. Below me lay the purest, most perfect grass, precisely the right length and not a blade that was bent or even out of place. It was the most vibrant green I had ever seen. If a color can be said to be alive, the green I saw was alive, slightly transparent and emitting light and life from within each blade.

The iridescent grass stretched endlessly over gently rolling hills upon which were sprinkled the most colorful wild flowers, lifting their soft petaled beauty skyward, almost as if they were a chorus of flowers caught up in their own way of praising God. The fragrance that permeated heaven was so gentle and sweet, I almost didn't notice it amid all there was to see and hear. But as I looked at the delicate, perfect flowers and grass, I wanted to smell them. Instantly, I was aware of a gentle aroma. As I focused, I could tell the difference between the grass and the flowers, the trees, and even the air. It was all so pure and intoxicating and blended together in a sweet and satisfying scent.

Keith A. Haslem

> In the distance stood a range of mountains, majestic in appearance, as if they reigned over the entire landscape. They were not mountains you wanted to conquer; these were mountains you wanted to revere.
>
> It seemed that my vision had been extremely enhanced. How otherwise could I see the colors I was seeing or the light that was in everything? It was something like being in a 3-D movie and then putting on the 3-D glasses. Or being in the darkest night and putting on night goggles. Suddenly everything has more dimensions, more richness. But that is an understatement. Multiply that by ten thousand and it would be like what I was experiencing. There are no words that captures the scenes that were before me. Utterly breathtaking. (*Flight to Heaven*, pp. 101–2)

BIBLICAL PERSPECTIVE

"Paradise"

As he hung on the cross between the two thieves, Jesus told one of them: "To day shalt thou be with me in paradise" (Luke 23:43).

THE CHURCH OF JESUS CHRIST OF LATTER-DAY SAINTS PERSPECTIVE

The righteous dead go to "paradise."

> Now, concerning the state of the soul between death and the resurrection—Behold, it has been made know unto me by an angel, that the spirits of all men, as soon as they are departed from this mortal body, yea, the spirits of all men, whether they be good or evil, are taken home to that God who gave them life.
>
> And then it shall come to pass, that the spirits of those who are righteous are received into a state of happiness, which is called paradise, a state of rest, a state of peace, where they shall rest from all their troubles and from all care, and sorrow. (Alma 40:11–12)

Going Home

AUTHOR'S PERSPECTIVE

One might expect that paradise would be beautiful and wonderful. By all accounts, it is fantastic beyond our ability to imagine it. Not surprising, unless God used *all* of His creative abilities creating the earth.

"DISCLAIMER"

Does everyone who does *not* go to hell go to this paradisaical area in the spirit world? From the many NDE accounts I've read it seems obvious there are many different regions in the spirit world. More than just paradise or hell (See Chapter 57: Do Some Spirits Go to Neither Heaven Nor Hell?).

The five Witnesses quoted above are, to the best of my knowledge, devout Christians, which, I believe, qualified them to enter this paradisaical region.

11

DOES THE SPIRIT WORLD HAVE AN ATMOSPHERE OF LIGHT AND LOVE?

SYNOPSIS

According to our resources, the light in the paradise realm of the spirit world emanates from God, instead of emanating from the sun. Remarkably, this same light also carries the love of God with it, so that to be in paradise is also to feel the love of God at the same time, even though His actual presence is elsewhere.

Those in "hell" find themselves in a place of darkness and therefore do not feel the love of God.

RANELLE WALLACE

"I floated in this light . . . and the love that surrounded me."

And then I was in the light.

Like a nuclear explosion, the light pierced me. Every particle of me was shot through with blinding, brilliant light, and I had a feeling of transparency.

My skin didn't burn. My eyes still saw. I floated in this light, bathed in it, and the love that surrounded me and filled me was sweeter and finer than anything I had ever felt. I was changed by it, refined, rarified, made pure. I basked in its sweetness, and the traumas of the past were far behind me, forgotten and transformed by peace. (*The Burning Within*, p. 95)

DALE BLACK

During his experience, Dale Black approached a heavenly city and recalls a "magnificent light."

"Somehow I knew that light and love were connected and interrelated."

> The magnificent light I was experiencing emanated from about forty or fifty miles within the city wall.
>
> I saw a great phosphorescent display of light that narrowed to a focal point that was brighter than the sun. Oddly, it didn't make me squint to look at it. And all I wanted to do was to look at it. The light was palpable. It had substance to it, weight and thickness, like nothing I had ever seen before or since.
>
> The light from a hydrogen bomb is the closest I can come to describing it. Just after the bomb is detonated—but before the fireball that forms the mushroom cloud—there is a millisecond of light that flashes as the bomb releases its energy. It was something like that but much larger.
>
> The glow and energy of this light radiated in all directions, upward and outward. It wasn't something you shielded your eyes from; it wasn't something you even flinched at. Just the opposite. It was warm and inviting. Almost hypnotic in its ability to draw you in to it.
>
> Somehow I knew that light and life and love were connected and interrelated. It was as if the very heart of God lay open for everyone in heaven to bask in its glory, to warm themselves in its presence, to bathe in its *almost liquid properties* so they could be restored, renewed, refreshed. (*Flight to Heaven*, pp. 99–100; emphasis added)

RAYMOND A. MOODY JR.

From his research, Dr. Moody notes that many NDErs encounter a being of light.

"The love and warmth that emanates from this being [of light]... are utterly beyond words."

> What is perhaps the most incredible common element in the accounts I have studied, and is certainly the element which has the most profound effect upon the individual, is the encounter with a very bright

light. Typically, at its first appearance this light is dim, but it rapidly gets brighter until it reaches an unearthly brilliance. Yet, even though this light (usually said to be white or "clear") is of an indescribable brilliance, many make the specific point that it does not in any way hurt their eyes, or dazzle them, or keep them from seeing other things around them (perhaps because at this point they don't have physical "eyes" to be dazzled).

Despite the light's unusual manifestation, however, not one person has expressed any doubt whatsoever that it was a being, a being of light. Not only that, it is a personal being. It has a very definite personality. The love and warmth which emanate from this being to the dying person are utterly beyond words, and he feels completely surrounded by it and taken up in it, completely at ease and accepted in the presence of this being. He senses an irresistible magnetic attraction to this light. He is ineluctably drawn to it. (*Life After Life*, pp. 58–59)

THE CHURCH OF JESUS CHRIST OF LATTER-DAY SAINTS PERSPECTIVE

Members of the Church of Jesus Christ of Latter-day Saints believe that *all* light emanates from God.

"Light proceedeth forth from the presence of God to fill the immensity of space."

This is the light of Christ. As also he is in the sun, and the light of the sun, and the power thereof by which it was made.

As also he is in the moon, and is the light of the moon, and the power thereof by which it was made:

As also the light of the stars, and the power thereof by which they were made. . . .

And the light which shineth, which giveth you light, is through him who enlighteneth your eyes. . . .

Which light proceedeth forth from the presence of God to fill the immensity of space—

The light which is in all things, which giveth life to all things. (Doctrine and Covenants 88:7–9, 11–13)

AUTHOR'S PERSPECTIVE

By all accounts, feeling God's love in the spirit world is the most satisfying aspect of being there. It seems only logical that this element would be present everywhere, inasmuch as we can't expect that we will always be in God's actual presence.

12

ARE THERE NIGHTS IN THE SPIRIT WORLD?

SYNOPSIS

Will we sleep in the spirit world? We do that now due to the frailties of our physical bodies, to which we will not be subject in the spirit world.

Several of our resources state that there are no nights in the spirit world, and we will not require sleep.

SARAH LANELLE MENET

"No nights [in the spirit world]"

"I learned that time does not exist there as we think of it on earth. Again, I must say that this is all very difficult to explain with our limited vocabulary to those who have not experienced it. Suffice it to say that in this spirit world there are no seconds, minutes, hours, or days. There are no nights either" (*There Is No Death*, p. 32).

BIBLICAL REFERENCE

"No night there"

"And there shall be no night there; and they need no candle, neither light of the sun; for the Lord God giveth them light" (Revelation 22:5).

THE CHURCH OF JESUS CHRIST OF LATTER-DAY SAINTS PERSPECTIVE

BRIGHAM YOUNG
(second prophet and president of the Church of Jesus Christ of Latter-day Saints)

Brigham Young taught on several occasions that those in the spirit world do not sleep.

While teaching at the funeral of Thomas Williams—regarding conditions in the spirit world—he said:

"I want to sleep no more."

"My spirit is set free, I thirst no more, I want to sleep no more, I hunger no more, I tire no more, I run, I walk, I labor, I go, I come, I do this, I do that, whatever is required of me, nothing like pain or weariness. I am full of life, full of vigor, and I enjoy the presence of my heavenly Father by the power of his Spirit" (*Journal of Discourses*, 17:142).

Brigham Young also taught:

"[Spirits] sleep not."

"When you are in the spirit world, everything there will appear as natural as things now do. Spirits will be familiar with spirits in the spirit world—will converse. . . . You will there see that those spirits we are speaking of are active; they sleep not" (*Discourses of Brigham Young*, p. 380).

AUTHOR'S PERSPECTIVE

I'm going to hold out hope that we can occasionally take a nap even if we don't need it. However, I suspect we will be so enthralled with our new environment and opportunities that we won't want to sleep.

13

DOES THE SPIRIT WORLD HAVE A FRAGRANCE?

SYNOPSIS

Several of the Witnesses mentioned the wonderful fragrance of the spirit world.

SARAH LANELLE MENET

"Made me feel peaceful, restful, calm . . . alive and wonderful"

> Regarding the sense of smell, there is a fragrance that exists there which is incredible and unlike anything earthly that I have ever smelled before. This scent is not like any perfume, spice, or earthly flower. If I concentrate, I can still remember it clearly. It made me feel peaceful, restful, and calm. This fragrance made me feel alive and wonderful, just as everything else did. Every sense is accentuated and contributes to the feeling of well-being that permeates that amazing world, like being wrapped in a blanket of love. (*There Is No Death*, p. 32)

DALE BLACK

"Pure and intoxicating"

> The fragrance that permeated heaven was so gentle and sweet, I almost didn't notice it amid all there was to see and hear. But as I looked at the delicate, perfect flowers and grass, I wanted to smell them. Instantly, I was aware of a gentle aroma. As I focused, I could tell the difference between the grass and the flowers, the trees, and

Going Home

even the air. It was all so pure and intoxicating and blended together in a sweet and satisfying scent. (*Flight to Heaven*, p. 101)

AUTHOR'S PERSPECTIVE

If paradise, or heaven, is to be a perfection of all things pleasant, then it is only logical that it would also include a pleasing aroma.

14

IS THERE MUSIC IN THE SPIRIT WORLD?

SYNOPSIS

By all accounts, the music of the spirit world is more beautiful than anything we've heard on earth. It flows seemingly nonstop, akin to background music.

ELANE DURHAM

"The most beautiful, peaceful music I had ever heard"

> Music flowed lightly, a harmonious sound that is so hard to describe. It was like everything that existed, from the blades of grass to the water of the river, the trees and the earth; the life forces of all these . . . was somehow blended into a soft wafting melody that was not being played, exactly, but truly existed. Surely it was the most beautiful, peaceful music I had ever heard (*I Stand All Amazed*, p. 19).
>
> There is music that I can't even begin to describe, and neither can I tell where it comes from. (*I Stand All Amazed*, p. 28)

BETTY J. EADIE

"Beyond the ability of any symphony or composer here.... Our best music here would sound like a child playing on a tin drum."

> Every drop from the waterfall had its own intelligence and purpose. A melody of majestic beauty carried from the waterfall and filled the garden, eventually merging with other melodies that I was now only faintly aware of. The music came from the water itself, from its intelligence, and each drop produced its own tone and melody which mingled and interacted with every other sound and strain around it. The water was praising God for its life and joy. The overall effect seemed beyond the ability of any symphony or composer here. In comparison, our best music here would sound like a child playing on a tin drum. We simply don't have the capacity to comprehend the vastness and strength of the music there, let alone begin to create it. (*Embraced by the Light*, p. 80)

Betty wrote about music she heard in the spirit world that acted like a "spiritual salve," that possessed "the power to heal" broken spirits (*Embraced by the Light*, p. 87).

DALE BLACK

"Music was everywhere . . . [and] it never stopped. . . . Beautiful beyond belief"

> Next I heard the faint sound of water rushing in the distance. I couldn't see the water, but it sounded as if it were rivers cascading over a series of small waterfalls, creating music that was ever-changing.
>
> Music was everywhere. The worship of God was the heart and focus of the music, and everywhere the joy of the music could be felt. The deepest part of my heart resonated with it, made me want to be a part of it forever. I never wanted it to stop. It swelled within me and without me as if it were inviting me into some divine dance.
>
> The music was a seamless blend of vocals and instrumentals, the voices enhancing the instruments, and the instruments enhancing the vocals. Neither diminished the other but rather enriched the other. There was no competition, only cooperation. Perfect harmonic order. I had the feeling—and it was the most satisfying of feelings—that I was made for the music, as if each muscle in my body were a taut string of some finely tuned instrument, created to play the most beautiful music ever composed. I felt part of the music. One with it. Full of joy and wonder and worship. Perhaps this is what love sounds like when put to music. It felt so. And every part of me felt it.

Keith A. Haslem

I was in complete harmony with it, and it accompanied me, beguiling me onward throughout my journey. I thought I would burst with exuberance as I found myself included in such sacred and joyous melodies. I wanted to pause and let the music resonate so I could savor the glorious experience. But it never stopped. It just kept on playing.

The music of praise seemed to be alive and it passed through me, permeating every cell. My being seemed to vibrate like a divine tuning fork. I felt all this, every ecstatic moment of it. And I never wanted it to end. The music there, like the light that was there, existed in everything, and everything felt in perfect harmony. There was not a note of discord. Not a trace of someone playing his own music. Not a bit of competition anywhere. This was perfect unity. Expressed toward one focus—God.

It was as if all of heaven knew the beat, the tempo, the words, the pitch, the tone, and all participated in their unique way but in a way that all was united into one song. There were not different songs played together; it was all one song, sung by everyone, simultaneously.

It was beautiful beyond belief. And it was blissful beyond belief. I never felt such overwhelming peace. (*Flight to Heaven*, pp. 102–3)

SARAH LANELLE MENET

Harps in the spirit world?

"I should mention that as I was looking down this corridor and into the rooms, I hear music playing. I am reluctant to describe the instruments that made the music as harps; however, that is exactly what they sounded like. The music was heavenly and offered a soothing or comforting background to the many activities in which people took part" (*There Is No Death*, pp. 40–41).

AUTHOR'S PERSPECTIVE

In my contemplations I've wondered, how dull would life be without music and sports? Could paradise be paradise without music?

(I still have hope for sports.)

15

WHAT DOES A SPIRIT BODY LOOK LIKE?

SYNOPSIS

Several of the witnesses indicate that a spirit body looks like a physical body. However, a spirit body will have no defects or handicaps. Appendages not present in mortality will be restored. Any pain felt during mortality will be gone.

Instead of blood, you will see light coursing through your body like clear blood. You will not be overweight and will appear to be in the range of twenty-five to thirty-five years old. You will retain your gender. You will give off your own light, which may be more or less than those around you.

RANELLE WALLACE

RaNelle Wallace described her own hand while in the spirit world.

"My hand was clear . . . light coursing through it like clear blood."

> My grandmother held out her hand and said, "Come quickly."
> I reached out to take it and stopped.
> "Wow," I said. "Look at my hand."
> My hand was clear, like transparent gel, but there was light coursing through it like clear blood. But, the light didn't run in irregular patterns as it would in veins; rather, the light shot through my hands like rays or beams. My whole hand sparkled with light. I looked down and saw that my feet also sparkled with light. And I noticed

again that they weren't burned. My feet and hands were perfect and whole. They radiated this glistening, beaming light, and I looked at my grandmother and saw that her light was brighter than mine. Every part of her was more brilliant. (*The Burning Within*, pp. 99–100)

SARAH LANELLE MENET

"No weight problems . . . or any type of physical defect"

"Another thing that I noticed was that the people gave off their own light. The glow varied from person to person, and a few were of a more distinctive golden hue. When I asked about the difference in illumination between the people, I learned that their light was in direct proportion to how each individual had lived their life while on earth. This answer seemed to satisfy my curiosity for the time being" (*There Is No Death*, p. 39).

"There will be no weight problems, no scars, or any type of physical defect" (*There Is No Death*, p. 129).

"Another wonderful thing I understood about spirit bodies was that they all looked to be about the same age. They were all absolutely beautiful and perfect" (*There Is No Death*, p. 50).

DALE BLACK

"Male and female . . . none overweight"

For some reason I clearly understood that I should not be touched, at least not yet. No one tried to touch me, and I didn't have a need to be embraced. The love I received from my spiritual family was so fulfilling and satisfying that no human touch could rival how loved I felt.

As I gazed into the radiant faces of these precious people, I looked into eyes that were more colorful than any on earth. Their smiles were brighter. Their countenances more alive. Each person was a living, vibrant, eternal being, exuding the very life of God.

I didn't think about whether they were male or female, although there were both. I saw them for who they were. None were skinny, none overweight. None were crippled, none were bent or broken. None were old, none were young. If I had to guess, I would say they appeared to be around thirty years old. They had no wrinkles, no signs of shifting or sagging, no signs of aging at all. I somehow understood that time was not an enemy here. Although some form of time does seem to exist in heaven, no one aged. No one died. Nothing decayed. (*Flight to Heaven*, p. 108)

RANELLE WALLACE

"About twenty five years old"

The reader will remember that RaNelle's grandmother had the appearance of being about twenty-five years old.

As RaNelle visited with spirits who had been her friends prior to her earthly existence, she observed that "We all looked the same age, somewhere in our twenties" (*The Burning Within*, p. 109).

SARAH LANELLE MENET

During her experience, Sarah met a "beautiful woman" who she later learned was her grandmother who had died when she was a baby. She observed that her grandmother appeared to be "about thirty years old" (*There Is No Death*, p. 50).

RAYMOND A. MOODY JR.

Dr. Moody commented on his subjects' description of spiritual beings.

Spirit beings have shape, density, and energy.

> Despite its lack of perceptibility to people in physical bodies, all who have experienced it are in agreement that the spiritual body is nonetheless something, impossible to describe though it may be. It is agreed that the spiritual body has a form or shape (sometimes a globular or an amorphous cloud, but also sometimes essentially the same shape as the physical body) and even parts (projections or surfaces analogous to arms, legs, a head, etc.). (*Life After Life*, p. 46)

In his book *Life After Life*, Dr. Moody quotes from several subjects:

"[The subject's "being"] felt as if it had a density to it, almost, but not a physical density—kind of like, I don't know, waves or something, I guess: Nothing really physical, almost as if it were charged, if you'd

Keith A. Haslem

like to call it that. But it felt as if it had something to it" (*Life After Life*, p. 48).

Another subject said:

> "[When I came out of the physical body] it was like I did come out of my body and go into something else. I didn't think I was just nothing. It was another body . . . but not another regular human body. It's a little bit different. . . . And I know I still had something you could call hands" (*Life After Life*, p. 49).

One subject remarked:

> I remember being wheeled into the operating room and the next few hours were the critical period. During that time, I kept getting in and out of my physical body, and I could see it from directly above. But, while I did, I was still in a body—not a physical body, but something I can best describe as an energy pattern. If I had to put it into words, I would say it was transparent, a spiritual as opposed to a material being. Yet it definitely had different parts. (*Life After Life*, p. 49)

Another subject reported:

> "I was out of my body looking at it from about ten yards away, but I was still thinking, just like in physical life. . . . I wasn't in a body, as such. I could feel something, like a clear form. I couldn't really see it; it was like it was transparent, but not really. It was like I was just there—an energy, maybe, sort of like just a little ball of energy" (*Life After Life*, p. 50).

In *The Light Beyond*, Dr. Moody tells the experience of one of his patients whom he resuscitated.

> At this point, they [people, immediately after leaving their bodies] may try to attract the attention of the people present by touching them. But when they do, their hands go right through the person's arm as though nothing was there.
>
> This was described to me by a woman I personally resuscitated. I saw her have a cardiac arrest and immediately started chest massage. She told me later that while I was working on restarting her heart, she was going up above her body and looking down. She was standing behind me, trying to tell me to stop, that she was fine where she was. When I didn't hear her, she tried to grab my arm to keep me from inserting a needle in her arm for intravenous fluid. Her hand passed

right through my arm. But when she did that, she later claimed that she felt something that was the consistency of "very rarified gelatin" that seemed to have an electric current running through it.

I have heard similar descriptions from other patients. (*Life After Life*, pp. 8–9)

In the same book, Dr. Moody reported on some of the interviews he has done with NDEers.

"Tubes of light up his arms"

They still seem to be in some kind of body, even though they are out of their physical bodies. . . . It has arms and a shape although most are at a loss to describe what it looks like. Some people describe it as a cloud of colors, or an energy field.

One NDEer I spoke to several years ago said he studied his hands while he was in this state and saw them to be composed of light with tiny structures in them. He could see the delicate whorls of his fingerprints and tubes of light up his arms. (*Life After Life*, p. 10)

Spirit bodies don't have handicaps.

Dr. Raymond Moody writes about a man who "fell from a billboard onto some high-voltage wires." He lost his legs and part of one arm from the burns. He had an out-of-body experience in the operating room. While looking down at his own body, the first thought that came to his mind was, "Look at that poor man." He didn't even recognize the body on the table as being his own. When he finally realized that the badly damaged body was his, he noticed something else peculiar: his spiritual body was not handicapped in any way (*Life After Life*, p. 86).

ELISABETH KÜBLER-ROSS

Dr. Kübler-Ross also writes that spirit entities are not subject to previous physical handicaps:

"We have no pain and no handicaps."

We experience a total wholeness. . . . If we have been amputees, we will have our legs again. If we have been deaf mutes, we can hear and talk and sing. If we have been a multiple-sclerosis patient in a wheelchair with blurred vision, blurred speech and unable to move our legs, we are able to sing and dance again.

It is understandable that many of our patients who have been successfully resuscitated are not always grateful when their butterfly is squashed back into the cocoon. . . . In the state of the ethereal body, we have no pain and no handicaps. (*On Life After Death*, p. 49)

Dr. Kübler-Ross cites working with several blind people who "were not only able to tell us who came into the room first and who worked on the resuscitation, but they were able to give minute details of the attire and the clothing of all the people present, something a totally blind person would never be able to do" (*On Life After Death*, p. 50).

THE CHURCH OF JESUS CHRIST OF LATTER-DAY SAINTS PERSPECTIVE

Members of the Church of Jesus Christ of Latter-day Saints believe that when we are resurrected our bodies will look as if we were in the prime of our lives. The appearance of the spirit, prior to the physical resurrection, would likely be the same.

JOSEPH SMITH JR.
(first prophet and president of the
Church of Jesus Christ of Latter-day Saints)

"The spirit is a substance . . . it is material, . . . it is more pure, elastic, and refined matter than the body . . . it existed before the body, can exist in the body; and will exist separate from the body" (*Teachings of the Prophet Joseph Smith*, p. 207).

BRIGHAM YOUNG
(second prophet and president of the
Church of Jesus Christ of Latter-day Saints)

Brigham Young taught "Spirits are composed of matter so refined as not to be tangible to this coarser organization" (*Journal of Discourses*, 3:371–72).

AUTHOR'S PERSPECTIVE

Certainly, transformation to a spirit body will be wonderful for those whose bodies have been riddled with deformities or pain during mortality.

Will it feel strange to have everyone look like they are approximately thirty years old, to look about the same age as your parents, grandparents, or great-grandparents? Or will it feel natural, like we are all just friends again, which is probably what we were in the premortal world.

16

DO ANGELS HAVE WINGS?

SYNOPSIS

It is an old secular notion that angels have wings. Elane Durham and Joseph Smith Jr. dispel that myth.

ELANE DURHAM

"Laughable... when their powers were actually so much greater than that"

> With the same wordless, mental communication He had been using, Christ informed me that one of these men—whom I knew were some of His holiest angels—would soon be with me to show me things what would make my return to my body better understood.
>
> None of these men I was viewing had wings, and as I realized that they were angels as well as former mortals, the understanding filled my mind that angels are simply individuals who had been selected... because of their righteousness—both men and women, I "knew"—to labor in God's work in that spirit realm. These particular angels had advanced to such a state of purity that they radiated the same sort of light and glory that Christ radiated, though to a milder degree, and they accomplished things with the same sort of power. In fact, it seems almost laughable in retrospect to think that these angels even needed wings to fly, when their powers were actually so much greater than that. (*I Stand All Amazed*, p. 51)

THE CHURCH OF JESUS CHRIST OF LATTER-DAY SAINTS PERSPECTIVE

JOSEPH SMITH JR.
(first prophet and president of the Church of Jesus Christ of Latter-day Saints)

The prophet Joseph Smith Jr. also refutes the notion that angels have wings:

"An angel of God never has wings" (*History of the Church*, 3:392).

AUTHOR'S PERSPECTIVE

The purpose of wings on any creature is to enable them to move more rapidly than they can with their feet alone. If angels are able to move at the speed of thought (as will be discussed in Chapter 22), wings would be nothing more than a cumbersome appendage.

17

ARE THERE RACIAL DIFFERENCES IN THE SPIRIT WORLD?

SYNOPSIS

Neither Elane Durham nor Dale Black noticed any racial differences in the spirit world.

ELANE DURHAM

After discovering that during our premortal life we'd all been a part of one big family, with a Heavenly Father and Mother, Elane noticed that there were no races in the spirit world.

"No races" in the premortal realm.

> Of course this [premortal family] meant that there were no races in that premortal realm, in fact, my memory of my experience is that the only skin color in that realm is "light" for every being I saw was somehow made up, to one degree or another out of light. . . . I am at a loss to explain . . . the purposes of the various races here in mortality, save my assumption that they are all part of the divine plan to teach us how to love one another. (*I Stand All Amazed*, p. 41)

DALE BLACK

No "racial differences"

Dale Black visited a heavenly city and was received by many spirits who had come to welcome him:

"Their skin tones were different but blended together so that no single person stood out. I did not notice any racial differences, but I was aware that they had come from many tribes and nations" (*Flight to Heaven*, p. 108).

AUTHOR'S PERSPECTIVE

If we are all descendants of Adam and Eve, then we are all of one race. How or why racial differences evolved is a mystery which I'm confident we will someday understand.

I expect it is as Elane Durham speculates, "part of the divine plan to teach us how to love one another" (*I Stand All Amazed*, p. 41).

18

WHAT CLOTHING WILL WE WEAR IN THE SPIRIT WORLD?

SYNOPSIS

Many of our resources refer to the inhabitants of the spirit world wearing white robes. However, several of the witnesses suggest that we will be able to wear *whatever we feel most comfortable in.*

RANELLE WALLACE

RaNelle noted that her grandmother was wearing the dress that she had been buried in—bought by RaNelle's mother—probably to help RaNelle recognize her more easily (*The Burning Within*, p. 100).

Jim, a friend of RaNelle's who had been a drug dealer on earth was dressed in "jeans and a blue shirt that was unbuttoned to mid-chest. This was how he normally wore his shirts on earth" (*The Burning Within*, p. 97).

Later, RaNelle saw a group of millions of people who had previously lived on the earth and noted, "I saw that each person wore clothing from his or her own time period on earth. As with my friend Jim, they wore what they were comfortable in" (*The Burning Within*, p. 113).

BETTY J. EADIE

Clothing is provided for new arrivals into the spirit world.

Betty observed "ancient looking looms" being used to weave cloth that would be made into clothing for spirits coming into the spirit world from earth.

> I went closer and picked up a piece of the cloth they were weaving. Its appearance was like a mixture of spun glass and spun sugar. As I moved the cloth back and forth, it shimmered and sparkled, almost as though it were *alive* (emphasis added). The effect was startling. . . . The workers explained that the material would be made into clothing for those coming into the spirit world from earth. (*Embraced by the Light*, pp. 74–75)

ELANE DURHAM

"I was dressed in a simple long gown of white material that shimmered with soft, pastel glimmers of more colors than I could begin to comprehend. It was as if the white were *alive* (emphasis added), and the light about my own being was reflected off it" (*I Stand All Amazed*, p. 19).

SARAH LANELLE MENET

"New-spirit-entrant robe"

> As I remained on the top of the hill surveying the city before me, I became aware that I was not clothed. I was completely naked, and yet my state of undress did not concern me in the least. I had no thoughts of being seen by others, even though I could see that there were thousands down below in the city. When I thought about clothing, I immediately understood that I had not passed through the barrier, or "film" that separates this spirit world from the mortal world.
>
> I also understood that whenever anyone passes from mortality, no matter what their status or behavior on earth, they are greeted by a loved-one almost instantly and given a robe to wear. The clothing given identifies the wearer as a new arrival and is called a "new-spirit-entrant robe." These robes differ from the ones worn by other spirits that have been in the spirit world for a longer time. In that way, when a new arrival is greeted, they are recognized and received with a warm welcome. (*There Is No Death*, pp. 34–35)

Keith A. Haslem

While some apparently do choose white, many of the people wore beautiful pastel robes. Both men and women wore the same style of clothing, made of shimmering fabric similar to silk but much finer. The fabric glowed and appeared like spun light. The robes were long, down to the ankle, and slit a little up the side almost to the knee. They wore cummerbunds around their waists and long shawls of various pastel colors over their shoulders. (*There Is No Death*, pp. 38–39)

GEORGE G. RITCHIE

George, in a visit to one of many "enormous buildings," mentions seeing people who "were covered from head to foot in loose-flowing hooded cloaks which made me think vaguely of monks" (*Return from Tomorrow*, p. 69).

BIBLICAL REFERENCE

Many NDE accounts mention people wearing a white robe. In the Bible, the book of Revelation makes a mention of such a heavenly garment:

"And one of the elders answered, saying unto me, What are these which are arrayed in white robes? and whence came they?" (Revelation 7:13).

AUTHOR'S PERSPECTIVE

Perhaps I could get used to wearing a robe, but I'm glad to hear from RaNelle that we can wear what we're most comfortable in. This is consistent and predictable. I can't think of anything that God has compelled us to do against our own will.

19

WHAT ABILITIES WILL WE HAVE AS SPIRITS?

SYNOPSIS

We discussed previously that the spiritual body looks like the physical body, but with no defects or handicaps. But according to the Witnesses, the spirit body also has amazing abilities, such as

- the ability to see in all directions at the same time and see great distances
- the ability to communicate telepathically
- the ability to learn extremely rapidly and entertain multiple thoughts simultaneously
- the ability to travel at the speed of thought

360-degree vision

SARAH LANELLE MENET

"I could see with every part of my body."

> Out of the back of my head I could see a beautiful woman coming up the path behind me.
> I recognized powerfully at this time that I could see with every part of my body, not just with my eyes. (*There Is No Death*, pp. 49–50)

Keith A. Haslem

Heightened vision

RAYMOND A. MOODY JR.

In his book *Life After Life*, Dr. Raymond Moody quotes an individual who experienced heightened abilities during his near-death experiences.

> Another man reported that while he was "dead" his vision seemed incredibly powerful and, in his words, "*I just can't understand how I could see so far*" (*Life After Life*, p. 51; emphasis added).

Mental telepathic powers

RANELLE WALLACE

The reader will remember that RaNelle Wallace was surprised when she was greeted by her grandmother, who spoke to RaNelle without moving her lips (*The Burning Within*, p. 96).

ELANE DURHAM

In her book, *I Stand All Amazed*, Elane Durham responds to the question, "You describe being taught and spoken to not only by Jesus Christ but by at least one angel. Was this verbal conversation or otherwise?" Elane's response was

"I could not only hear the answers but I could feel them."

> Actually, it was both. Except for the brief view of myself as a premortal spirit, I don't think I ever uttered a sound verbally. I had only to think and my thoughts were instantly responded to—oftentimes before they were even fully formed in my mind. On the other hand, when I was spoken to it was verbal, but it was also so much more than that. I could not only hear the answers but I could feel them with every particle of my being, so that there was *no chance for misunderstanding* on my part. It was verbal, mental, spiritual; all at the same time. (*I Stand All Amazed*, p. 160; emphasis added)

Going Home

RAYMOND A. MOODY JR.

Dr. Raymond Moody writes about the method of communication many of his subjects use when they meet a being of light during their experience.

"An unimpeded transfer of thoughts"

> Shortly after its appearance, the being [of light] begins to communicate with the person who is passing over. Notably, this communication is of the same direct kind which we encountered earlier in the description of how a person in the spiritual body may "pick up the thoughts" of those around him. For, here again, people claim that they did not hear any physical voice or sounds coming from the being, nor did they respond to the being through audible sounds. Rather, it is reported that direct, unimpeded transfer of thoughts takes place, and in such a clear way that there is no possibility whatsoever either of misunderstanding or of lying to the light. (*Life After Life*, p. 60; emphasis added)

"Exchange does not take place in the native language"

"Furthermore, this unimpeded exchange does not even take place in the native language of the person. Yet, he understands perfectly and is instantaneously aware. He cannot even translate the thoughts and exchanges which took place while he was near death into the human language which he must speak now, after his resuscitation" (*Life After Life*, p. 60).

An eleven-year-old boy who had had a near-death experience told Dr. Moody, "I could tell what they were thinking and they could tell what I was thinking" (*The Light Beyond*, p. 65).

"It was more like knowing what they were thinking."

Dr. Moody surmises regarding communication in the spirit world and quotes from several other of his case histories.

> "Hearing" in the spiritual state can apparently be called so only by analogy, and most say they do not really hear physical voices or sounds. Rather, they seem to pick up the thoughts of persons around them, and . . . this same kind of direct transfer of thoughts can play an important part in the late stages of death experiences.

Keith A. Haslem

> As one lady put it:
> I could see people all around, and I could understand what they were saying. I didn't hear them, audibly, like I'm hearing you. It was more like knowing what they were thinking, but only in my mind, not in their actual vocabulary. I would catch it the second before they opened their mouths to speak. (*Life After Life*, p. 52)

"Things that are not possible now, are then. Your mind is so clear. It's so nice. My mind just took everything down and worked everything out for me the first time, without having to go through it more than once. After a while everything I was experiencing got to where it meant something to me in some way" (*Life After Life*, p. 51).

Severe damage to the physical body does not affect the spiritual body.

> Finally, on the basis of one unique and very interesting report, it would appear that even severe damage to the physical body in no way adversely affects the spiritual one. In this case, a man lost the better part of his leg in the accident that resulted in his clinical death. He knew this, because he saw his damaged body clearly, from a distance, as the doctors worked on it. Yet, while he was out of his body,
> I could feel my body, and it was whole. I know that, I felt whole, and I felt that all of me was there, though it wasn't. (*Life After Life*, pp. 52–53)

Ability to learn rapidly

BETTY J. EADIE

"[I] comprehend[ed] the mysteries of the universe."

> My comprehension was such that I could understand volumes in an instant. It was as if I could look at a book and comprehend it at a glance—as though I could just sit back while the book revealed itself to me in every detail, forward and backward, inside and out, every nuance and possible suggestion. All in an instant. As I comprehended one thing, more questions and answers would come to me, all building on each other, and interacting as if all truth were intrinsically connected. . . . Knowledge permeated me. In a sense it became me, and

I was amazed at my ability to comprehend the mysteries of the universe simply by reflecting on them. (*Embraced by the Light*, pp. 44–45)

A spirit world library accessed by "simply by reflecting on a topic."

I was taken to another large room similar to a library. As I looked around it seemed to be a repository of knowledge, but I couldn't see any books. Then I noticed ideas coming into my mind, knowledge filling me on subjects that I had not thought about for some time—or in some cases not at all. Then I realized that this was a library of the mind. By simply reflecting on a topic, as I had earlier in Christ's presence, all knowledge on that topic came to me. I could learn about anybody in history—or even in the spirit world—in full detail.

No knowledge was kept from me, and it was impossible not to understand correctly every thought, every statement, every particle of knowledge. There was absolutely no misunderstanding here. History was pure. Understanding was complete. I understood not only what people did but why they did it and how it affected other people's perceptions of reality. . . .

But this was more than a mental process. I was able to feel what the people felt when they performed these actions. I understood their pains or joys or excitement because I was able to live them. Some of this knowledge was taken from me, but not all. I cherish the knowledge granted to me of certain events and people in our history which were important for me to understand. (*Embraced by the Light*, pp. 76–77)

RANELLE WALLACE

RaNelle Wallace describes communication with her grandmother.

"[Able to] think on several levels at once and communicate them all simultaneously"

All of this rang utterly true to me. She had communicated it with lightning speed, faster than computers can talk. It was instant and total knowing. I found that Grandmother and I could think on several levels at once and communicate them all simultaneously. You can't know something without knowing everything around it, what causes it, what sustains it. Knowledge dovetails in the spirit world, each piece

Keith A. Haslem

fitting with other pieces. Every fact connected to it is seen instantly, in totality. We have nothing like it on earth. We can't even approach it. Our knowledge and ability to communicate is like a child's who hasn't yet learned a language. We struggle to communicate, but we don't possess the tools. We're like little children. (*The Burning Within*, p. 99)

During her time with her grandmother, RaNelle observed that:

"Floodgates of knowledge opened"

Floodgates of knowledge opened and truth poured into me without end or constraint. Its source was the light and truth all around me, and it was clarified, or explained at my level, by my grandmother. She gave me knowledge about God, life, the creation of the world, and even the reaches of eternity. The truths were comprehensive and complete and rushed upon me in such enormous volume that I thought my head would explode. It was coming too fast. I wanted to be able to absorb it, remember it all, but it was too much. "I can't take this!" I said. "Stop!"

"I can't handle all you're giving me. How can I possibly retain it all?"

"RaNelle, don't worry about it," she said to me. "Let go of the fear. Don't doubt yourself. You will recall things as you need them, and they will be brought back to your memory by the Spirit. Have faith. Believe in the power of God." (*The Burning Within*, p. 106)

RAYMOND A. MOODY JR.

Some of Dr. Moody's subjects spoke about remarkable learning abilities in the spirit world.

A realm where all knowledge coexists

Several people have told me that during their encounters with "death" they got brief glimpses of an entire separate realm of existence in which all knowledge—whether of past, present or future—seemed to co-exist in a sort of timeless state. . . . In trying to talk about this aspect of their experience, all have commented that this experience was ultimately inexpressible. Also, all agree that this feeling of complete knowledge did not persist after their return; that they did not bring back any sort of omniscience. They agree that this vision

Going Home

did not discourage them from trying to learn in this life, but, rather, encouraged them to do so. (*Reflections on Life After Death*, pp. 9–10)

Another of Dr. Moody's subjects described her experience.

"Whatever I wanted to know could be known."

"There was a moment in this thing—well, there isn't any way to describe it—but it was like I knew all things. . . . For a moment, there, it was like communications weren't necessary. I thought whatever I wanted to know could be known" (*Reflections on Life After Death*, pp. 13–14).

THE CHURCH OF JESUS CHRIST OF LATTER-DAY SAINTS PERSPECTIVE

ORSON PRATT
(one of the members of the original Quorum of the Twelve Apostles, 1811–1881)

We will have more than just the five senses.

> When I speak of the future state of man, and the situation of our spirits between death and the resurrection, I long for the experience and knowledge to be gained in that state, as well as this. We shall learn many more things there; we need not suppose our five senses connect us with all the things of heaven, and earth, and eternity, and space. . . . Suppose He should give us a sixth sense, a seventh, and eighth, a ninth, or a fiftieth. All these different senses could convey to us new ideas, as much so as the senses of tasting, smelling, or seeing communicate different ideas from that of hearing. (*Journal of Discourses*, 2:247)

Orson Pratt described three abilities that will be possessed by spiritual beings.

(1) Increased ability to remember

> We read or learn a thing by observation yesterday, and to-day or tomorrow it is gone . . . through the weakness of the animal system, that we cannot call it to mind . . . but the spirit has a full capacity to remember. . . . Wait until these mortal bodies are laid in the tomb:

when we return home to God who gave us life; then is the time we shall have the most vivid knowledge of all the past acts of our lives during our probationary state. (*Journal of Discourses,* 2:239)

(2) Ability to see with all parts of the body

Suppose that the whole spirit were uncovered and exposed to all the rays of light, can it be supposed that light would not affect the spirit if it were thus unshielded. . . . The spirit is inherently capable of experiencing the sensations of light. . . . I think we could then see in different directions at once, instead of looking in one particular direction, we could then look all around us at the same moment. (*Journal of Discourses,* 2:242–44)

(3) Ability to obtain and consider numerous ideas simultaneously

There is a faculty mentioned in the world of God, which we are not in possession of here, but we shall possess it hereafter; that is not only to see a vast number of things in the same moment, looking in all directions by the aid of the spirit, but also to obtain a vast number of ideas at the same instant . . . knowledge will rush in from all quarters; it will come in like the light which flows from the sun, penetrating every part, informing the spirit, and giving understanding concerning ten thousand things at the same time; and the mind will be capable of receiving and retaining all. (*Journal of Discourses,* 2:245–46)

Traveling with a spirit body at the speed of thought

Traveling at the speed of thought may be one of the most incredible abilities of the spiritual body and will be discussed later in the book.

AUTHOR'S PERSPECTIVE

It is no wonder, with the tremendous abilities of the spirit body, that those who have visited that realm generally have no desire to return to their mortal bodies.

Those with an appetite for learning will find the spirit world a wondrous place, as they are able to acquire knowledge rapidly and retain it perfectly.

20

HOW WILL WE INTERACT WITH PLANTS?

SYNOPSIS

As they enjoyed their brief tours in the beautiful spirit world, both Betty J. Eadie and RaNelle Wallace had a remarkable experience as they somehow merged with the spirit essence of a flower. The effect of this experience had a significant impact upon them emotionally, and they gained a deeper appreciation of the oneness of all creations.

BETTY J. EADIE

"I felt the rose's presence around me."

> As I approached the water, I noticed a rose near me that seemed to stand out from the other flowers, and I stopped to examine it. Its beauty was breathtaking. Among all the flowers there, none captured me like this one. It was gently swaying to faint music, and singing praises to the Lord with sweet tones of its own. I realized that I could actually see it growing. As it developed before my eyes, my spirit was moved, and I wanted to experience its life, to step into it and feel its spirit. As this thought came to me, I seemed to be able to see down into it. It was as though my vision had become microscopic and allowed me to penetrate the rose's deepest parts. But it was much more than a visual experience. I felt the rose's presence around me, as if I were actually inside and part of the flower. I experienced it as if I were the flower. I felt the rose swaying to the music of all the other flowers, and I felt it creating its own music, a melody that

Keith A. Haslem

perfectly harmonized with the thousands of other roses joining it. I understood that the music in my flower came from its individual parts, that its petals produced their own tone, and that each intelligence within that petal was adding to its perfect notes, each working harmoniously for the overall effect—which was joy. My joy was absolutely full again! I felt God in the plant, in me, his love pouring into us. We were all one!

I will never forget the rose that I was. That one experience, just a glimmer of the grander joy that is available in the spirit world, in being one with everything else, was so great that I will cherish it forever. (*Embraced by the Light*, pp. 80–81)

RANELLE WALLACE

"Then the flower became part of me."

I noticed something unusual about the flowers near us. My grandmother waved her arm and, without speaking, commanded them to come to her. Although it was a command the flowers took joy in obeying her. They floated through air and came to a stop, suspended within the circle of her arms. The bouquet was alive. Each blossom was able to communicate, react, and actually enlighten others near it.

"Grandma," I said, "they have no stems."

"Why should they have stems?" she said. "Flowers on earth need stems to receive nourishment, to grow to their fullest potential. Everything God has made is spiritual and is designed to grow toward its own spiritual potential. A flower reaches its fullness in the blossom. Here everything exists in its fullest form. These flowers have no need of stems."

"But they just float."

"Should they fall? Everything here is perfect." She took one of the flowers and handed it to me. "Isn't that beautiful?" she said.

The flower hung inside my cupped hands, barely touching me. It was like a camellia except that it was deeper than any camellia I had seen, and it had many fine tendrils at its center, some long and straight, others coiled. The petals cascaded one upon the other in luminous hues of lavender, orange, and pink. The whole blossom was filled with various shades of light, and its beauty was incredible. Then the flower became part of me. Its soul merged with mine.

It experienced everything I was doing, or had done before. It was acutely aware of me, and at the same time it changed me with its delicate spirit, and its own existence and life. It affected my feelings, my thoughts, my identity. It was me. I was it. The joy that came from this union was more pervasive and delicious and fulfilling than any I had known until that moment, and I wanted to cry. The scriptures say that one day all things shall be as one. That statement has great power for me now.

My grandmother commanded the flowers to return, and they floated gently back to their places just above the ground. The one in my hands also returned, but its essence remained with me. (*The Burning Within*, pp. 102–3)

AUTHOR'S PERSPECTIVE

Several of the Witnesses talk about passing through solid objects or people during their NDE, which might not be so surprising when you consider that physicists tell us that the atoms we are all made of are mostly empty space.

A spirit is even less solid that a physical body, so the possibility of one spirit penetrating another living spirit seems quite reasonable.

21

WHAT ACTIVITIES WILL WE ENGAGE IN?

The old sectarian notion of heaven has the inhabitants floating idly on clouds while playing harps. None of the accounts I've read would support such a notion. On the contrary, it appears that life in the spirit world is quite busy.

SYNOPSIS

According to our resources, some of the activities engaged in by inhabitants of the spirit world include:

- performing manual labor
- acquiring knowledge in libraries or "learning centers"
- attending family events
- attending cultural events
- constructing buildings in the spirit world
- traveling the universe
- developing technology to be applied on earth
- composing music
- performing missionary work
- serving as guardian angels to inhabitants of the earth

Going Home

BETTY J. EADIE

Performing manual labor

As we approached the people, I saw that they were weaving on large, ancient looking looms. My first impression was "how archaic" to have manual looms in the spirit world. Standing by the looms were many spiritual beings, male and female, and they greeted me with smiles. . . .

I went closer and picked up a piece of the cloth they were weaving. Its appearance was like a mixture of spun glass and spun sugar. As I moved the cloth back and forth, it shimmered and sparkled, almost as though it were alive. The effect was startling. . . . The workers explained that the material would be made into clothing for those coming into the spirit world from earth. . . .

I was surprised at how much people like to work with their hands there—those who want to. They enjoy creating devices that are helpful to others—both here and there. I saw a large machine, similar to a computer, but much more elaborate and powerful. . . . Again, I understood that all things of importance are created spiritually first and physically second. I had no idea of this before. (*Embraced by the Light*, pp. 74–76)

Acquiring knowledge and other activities

As will be discussed in Chapter 31: "Do Libraries Exist in the Spirit World?" acquiring knowledge is a major emphasis in the spirit world.

Other accounts I've read talk about family gatherings and cultural events such as concerts. One account alludes to the annual celebration of Christ's birth.

Another account implies that some spirits are involved in the construction of the buildings in the spirit world.

Some accounts imply that we will be able, if we desire, to travel the universe and visit other worlds, doing so at the speed of thought.

Keith A. Haslem

GEORGE G. RITCHIE

Developing technology

George describes visiting a huge building, which he termed a "study center."

> [It was] humming with the excitement of great discovery. Everyone we passed in the wide halls and on the curving staircases seemed caught up in some all-engrossing activity; not many words were exchanged among them. And yet I sensed no unfriendliness between these beings, rather an aloofness of total concentration.
>
> Whatever else these people might be, they appeared utterly and supremely self-forgetful—absorbed in some vast purpose beyond themselves. Through open doors I glimpsed enormous rooms filled with complex equipment. In several of the rooms hooded figures bent over intricate charts and diagrams, or sat at the controls of elaborate consoles flickering with lights. I'd prided myself a little on the beginnings of a scientific education; at the university I had majored in chemistry, minored in biology, studied physics and calculus. But if these were scientific activities of some kind, they were so far beyond anything I knew, that I couldn't even guess what field they were in. Somehow I felt that some vast experiment was being pursued, perhaps dozens and dozens of such experiments.
>
> "What are they doing, Jesus?" I asked.
>
> But although Knowing flamed from Him like fire—though in fact I sensed that every activity on this mighty "campus" had its source in God—no explanation lighted my mind. What was communicated, as before, was love: compassion for my ignorance, understanding that encompassed all my non-understanding.
>
> And something more . . . in spite of His obvious delight in the beings around us, I sensed that even this was not the ultimate, that He had far greater things to show me if only I could see. (*Return from Tomorrow*, p. 82)

Composing music

"Bach is only the beginning!"

And so I followed Him into other buildings of this domain of thought. We entered a studio where music of a complexity I couldn't begin to follow was being composed and performed. There were complicated rhythms, tones not on any scale I knew. "Why," I found myself thinking, "Bach is only the beginning!" (*Return from Tomorrow*, pp. 69–70).

RANELLE WALLACE

"Everyone is quite busy."

Upon meeting her grandmother as she entered the spirit world, RaNelle asked:

> "Aren't people supposed to meet me when I die," I asked. "Aren't there supposed to be people singing hallelujah and coming up to hug me and saying 'Welcome'?"
>
> She giggled again, and I thought it was the most delightful giggle I had ever heard. "Well," she said, "everyone is quite busy." (*The Burning Within*, pp. 96–97)

THE CHURCH OF JESUS CHRIST OF LATTER-DAY SAINTS PERSPECTIVE

Performing missionary work

Members of the Church of Jesus Christ of Latter-day Saints believe that Jesus, after His Resurrection, went among the "spirits in prison" (1 Peter 4:19) and organized a missionary effort to take His gospel to those in the spirit world who had not had the opportunity to hear and accept it on earth. Members believe the missionary work they devotedly engage in on earth will continue in the spirit world.

Keith A. Haslem

JOSEPH F. SMITH
(sixth prophet and president of the Church of Jesus Christ of Latter-day Saints)

Serving as guardian angels

Joseph F. Smith reiterated a teaching of the Prophet Joseph Smith, Jr. who taught that angels who minister to people on earth have a connection as family or friends.

"We are told by the Prophet Joseph Smith, that 'there are no angels who minister to this earth but those who do belong or have belonged to it.' Hence, when messengers are sent to minister to the inhabitants of this earth, they are not strangers, but from the ranks of our kindred, friends, and fellow-beings and fellow-servants" (*Gospel Doctrine*, p. 435).

Joseph F. Smith also taught that "we are all on the road of advancement."

"Every man will have his work to do."

> Some people dream, you know, and think, and teach that all the glory they ever expect to have in the world to come is to sit in the light and glory of the Son of God, and sing praises and songs of joy and gratitude all their immortal lives. We do not believe in any such things. We believe that every man will have his work to do in the other world, just as surely as he had it to do here. We believe that we are on the road of advancement, of development in knowledge, in understanding, and in every good thing, and that we will continue to grow, advance, and develop throughout the eternities that are before us. That is what we believe. (*Gospel Doctrine*, p. 432)

AUTHOR'S PERSPECTIVE

Playing a harp for eternity sounds boring, and I doubt God wants us to have an eternity of boredom. Heaven should be fascinating and engaging, with the exhilaration that comes from personal development.

22

HOW WILL WE TRAVEL IN THE SPIRIT WORLD?

SYNOPSIS

Our resources report that moving around in the spirit world can be by walking, gliding, or moving at the speed of thought. To desire to go to any specific location is to arrive there almost instantly.

SARAH LANELLE MENET

Travel "at the speed of a thought"

> While still beside the lake, I made another discovery. As I turned my head slowly to the left to take in the view, I saw in the distance a beautiful hill blanketed with trees. I thought how much I would like to go in that direction and be there. No sooner did I think this thought than I began moving toward the hill. It was almost as though the movement was initiated by the beginning of my thought. It was wonderful and I was there in a second. It was all so smooth and happened so quickly that before I realized it I stood at the top of the hill. (*There Is No Death*, p. 30)

ELISABETH KÜBLER-ROSS

> "It takes up no space, no time, to go from one star to another, from planet earth to another galaxy" (*On Life After Death*, p. 63).

Keith A. Haslem

THE CHURCH OF JESUS CHRIST OF LATTER-DAY SAINTS PERSPECTIVE

BRIGHAM YOUNG
(second prophet and president of the Church of Jesus Christ of Latter-day Saints)

Travel with "lightning speed to any planet"

"As quickly as the spirit is unlocked from this house of clay, it is free to travel with lightning speed to any planet, or fixed star, or to the uttermost part of the earth, or to the depths of the sea, according to the will of Him who dictates" (*Journal of Discourses*, 13:77).

Brigham Young also said:

"Move with ease and like lightning"

> The brightness and glory of the next [world] is inexpressible. It is not encumbered so that when we advance in years we have to be stubbing along and be careful lest we fall down. We see our youth, even, frequently stubbing their toes and falling down. But yonder, how different! They move with ease and like lightning. If we want to visit Jerusalem, or this, that, or the other place—and I presume we will be permitted if we desire, there we are, looking at its streets. . . . If we wish to understand how they are living here on these western islands, or in China, we are there; in fact, we are like the light of the morning. (*Discourses of Brigham Young*, p. 380)

AUTHOR'S PERSPECTIVE

To travel anywhere in the universe at the speed of thought! Unimaginable vacations with no hassles and no expenses! The only thing more exciting might be time travel.

23

CAN WE TRAVEL THROUGH TIME IN THE SPIRIT WORLD?

SYNOPSIS

Many scientists believe time travel is a theoretical possibility. However, it would require travel at the speed of light, for which we currently do not have the technology.

However, if spirits can travel faster than the speed of light—at the speed of thought—that may suggest that time travel is possible in the spirit world.

SARAH LANELLE MENET

Traveling into the past or the future and to different worlds at the speed of a thought.

> I became aware of many abilities of the spirit body. Spirit bodies have the ability to travel into the past and actually see, hear, and experience things that have already happened. They do not, however, have the power to change or influence outcomes. They are merely in a position of observation. I found that there are many dimensions and spirits can easily travel between them. The future is another dimension, and occasionally spirits are permitted to travel there. Spirits are also able to travel to different worlds and planets if they desire, and it all happens at the speed of a thought. (*There Is No Death*, p. 109)

Keith A. Haslem

AUTHOR'S PERSPECTIVE

The concept of time travel is incomprehensible to most people—including me. However, how many scriptural prophets have described seeing future events?

24

IS TECHNOLOGY DEVELOPED IN THE SPIRIT WORLD?

SYNOPSIS

Betty J. Eadie and George G. Ritchie observed that some technological developments are first developed by inhabitants of the spirit world, and then inspiration is given to specific mortals who are in a position to develop and implement the technological advances. Their aim is to improve the quality of our lives.

BETTY J. EADIE

"Unseen inspiration" spurs important inventions.

> Many times the creative thoughts we have in this life are the result of unseen inspiration. Many of our important inventions and even technological developments were first created in the spirit by spirit prodigies. Then individuals on earth received the inspiration to create these inventions here. I understood that there is a vital, dynamic link between the spirit world and mortality, and that we need the spirits on the other side for our progression. I also saw that they are very happy to assist us in any way they can. (*Embraced by the Light*, p. 48)

GEORGE G. RITCHIE

George saw the development of the atomic submarine engine.

Keith A. Haslem

During his tour of the world of spirits, Dr. Ritchie relates seeing an area where it appeared some sort of technology was being developed.

"Huge laboratories"

"Out we moved again into the hushed and expectant park. Then into a building crowded with technological machinery. Into a strange sphere-shaped structure where a catwalk led us over a tank of what appeared to be ordinary water. Into what looked like huge laboratories and into what might have been some kind of space observatory. And as we went my sense of mystification grew" (*My Life After Dying*, p. 71).

Nine years after his near-death experience, Dr. Ritchie had the following experience:

"I had seen all this before."

> One winter evening in 1952—it was around the middle of December because we had just had our annual Christmas party at the Richmond Academy of Medicine which I had recently joined—I was in the living room reading a copy of *Life* magazine. The issue was full of ads for brand name turkeys and hams, with jolly Santas on every other page, and I was flipping through it without much interest when suddenly my fingers tightened.
>
> On the page in front of me was a drawing of a gigantic sphere-shaped structure cut away to reveal men and machines inside it. There was a kind of traveling crane mounted on steel girders, turbines, a huge circular tank, stairs, catwalks, down in one corner of a small control room.
>
> What set my heart pounding in my throat was not the strange futuristic appearance of these objects but the certainty that I had seen all this before. Not recently, either. Somehow, years ago, I had stood staring not at a drawing of this enormous sphere but at the thing itself. I had wandered about that peculiar interior too: I had seen the stairway just there, peering into that vast tank of water.
>
> But . . .I couldn't have! Skimming the text I saw that what I remembered was impossible:
>
> Last week the Atomic Energy Commission partially lifted its veil of secrecy and allowed *Life*'s artists to make a drawing of some details of the prototype of the second US atomic submarine engine and the strange house that holds it. The building, now going up near

Going Home

Schenectady, N.Y., will be the world's largest man-made sphere, a $2-million, two hundred and twenty-five foot steel shell.

The article went on to say that to avoid possible radioactive contamination scientists would build the submarine engine inside the sphere, then submerge it for tests in the giant tank. Baffled, I lowered the magazine to my lap. I had never been to Schenectady. Anyhow, what I recalled was some time ago and this was just now being built. The thing I had seen was finished and operating, though I hadn't had any idea what—

Then I remembered. It was in that tranquil campus-like realm inhabited by beings wrapped in thought as monks are wrapped in robes, that I had stood in 1943 as the earth measures time, staring at a huge sphere-shaped building, walking through its intricate fittings....

What was that realm? In what mysterious way was it related to the life and thought of the world where I sat in 1952, with Marguerite talking on the telephone in the hall and Christmas cards lining the mantelpiece? I did not think about it very long, except to wonder if philosophers are right when they say that certain ideas seem to drop into widely scattered areas of the world from "somewhere" simultaneously. (*Return from Tomorrow*, pp. 119–21)

In his book *My Life After Dying*, Dr. Ritchie talks about visiting a realm where "all fields of knowledge are advanced":

"A realm . . . for souls . . . who want to keep on researching and learning."

> This is the realm where I believe the souls go who have developed the greatest interest in a particular field of life's endeavor, the ones who want to keep on researching and learning more in their particular fields. This gives hope to all people who want to keep learning and have established enough wisdom to realize we have just begun to scratch the surface in any field when we are on the earth's level of development....
>
> It seemed to me that this dimension is divided into centers of higher learning. The only things on Earth that begin to approach these centers are our most advanced universities and large industrial research centers. (*My Life After Dying*, pp. 28–29)

"Motivated by . . . a desire to help make the universe a better place to live"

Keith A. Haslem

Their work was motivated by sincere interest in what they were learning and a desire to help make the universe a better place to live, not money or fame. They were so far advanced in so many ways that it would be like my taking my son, when he was six years of age, to one of the research laboratories at the University of Virginia and expecting him to comprehend what he was seeing. . . .

Why is it that inventors in different parts of the earth come up with the same ideas about the same time—Ford in America, Bentley in England, Peugeot in France? I believe I was shown the place where those who have already gone before us are doing research and want to help us when we begin to seriously search and turn deep within for answers. I think this is true regardless of our fields of interest. (*My Life After Dying*, pp. 29–30)

AUTHOR'S PERSPECTIVE

"Once a geek, always a geek"? (No disrespect intended! Quite the opposite.)

It seems unlikely that highly intelligent people who pass into the spirit world will suddenly lose their interest in exercising their intelligence and creativity. Without the encumbrances they encounter on earth—limited financial resources, governmental regulations, etc.—they can happily pursue their intellectual passions unconstrained.

At the appropriate time, they need only whisper the details of their work to some person on earth who shares the same interest and is in a position to advance the idea, thereby furthering the development of earth's technology.

25

WILL WE EAT FOOD IN THE SPIRIT WORLD?

SYNOPSIS

Although spiritual beings do not need to consume food, as immortal beings, Sarah LaNelle Menet and Akiane Kramarik both learned that some sort of spiritual food is consumed as a form of pleasure.

SARAH LANELLE MENET

Fruit and "minicakes"

> In one of the very large rooms in the building I was looking at . . . I saw a large group of women involved in some very specific tasks. They were quietly talking and laughing as they worked. Most of their communication was done telepathically or in whispers. My interest was seized by this group because of the pleasure they appeared to have found in what they were doing. They were having a wonderful time and I became curious as to what they were doing.
>
> On closer inspection I realized that they were preparing food, and the room they were in was a very large kitchen. Some of the women were slicing what appeared to be a fruit, shaped somewhat like a pear that also glowed, and arranging the slices on platters that had the look of crystal glass. Others were slicing and arranging what looked like little wafers of a cakelike bread. The wafers, or minicakes, were of a spongy texture and the size and shape of a hard boiled egg and when sliced were about a quarter of an inch in thickness. I watched as one of the women occasionally tasted a wafer as she made the arrangement. I wished that I could taste one too, and instantly a

wafer was literally melting in my mouth. The taste of it was exquisite. More than just a taste or flavor, eating the wafer made me feel good and happy all at the same time. The taste was extremely intense as was everything else. As I watched this activity, I was impressed that people ate more for pleasure than for sustenance. (*There Is No Death*, pp. 39–40)

AKIANE KRAMARIK

Akiane Kramarik, at four years old, started having out-of-body experiences. Not long after, she started painting depictions of Christ (see Chapter 35: What Is the Best Portrayal of Jesus? to learn more about Akiane).

Fruit

Akiane wrote that during her out of body experiences—which started at the age of four—she was given fruit to eat:

"It tastes good, better than anything you've ever tasted. The Light gives me fruit" (*Akiane*, p. 10).

BIBLICAL PERSPECTIVE

As a resurrected being, which I doubt also requires food, Jesus did eat some broiled fish and a piece of honeycomb, apparently as a gesture of social goodwill (see Luke 24:42–43).

AUTHOR'S PERSPECTIVE

Although it seems unlikely that spirits or resurrected beings will *need* food for sustenance, I believe spirit-world food will make the spirit world an even nicer place.

26

WOULD THOSE IN THE SPIRIT WORLD LIKE TO RETURN TO EARTH?

SYNOPSIS

Almost universally, individuals who have near-death or out-of-body experiences, after experiencing the wonderful realm of the spirit world, are very reluctant to return to their bodies.

In most cases, these individuals are given the choice of whether to stay or to return. The primary motivation for those who return is usually for the sake of their families who need them, or to complete their "mission" on earth.

BETTY J. EADIE

"This is my home."

Betty was informed by a council of twelve men that she had died prematurely. The leader of the council told her that she had "died prematurely and must return to the earth."

> I felt them saying it was important that I return to the earth, that I had a mission to fulfill, but I resisted it in my heart. This was my home, and I felt that nothing they could ever say would ever convince me to leave it.

Betty then experienced a "life review," after which she was again told by the council:

Keith A. Haslem

> "You have not completed your mission on earth. . . .
>
> You must go back. But, we will not compel you; the choice is yours."
>
> Without hesitation I said, "No, no. I can't go back. I belong here. This is my home." I stood firm, knowing that nothing could ever make me choose to leave.
>
> One of the men spoke, also firmly. "Your work is not complete. It is best that you return."

Eventually, she did consent to return but with a condition.

> "I made them promise that the moment my mission was complete they would take me back home. I was not willing to spend a minute on earth longer than was necessary. My home was with them."

She then received a promise from Jesus:

> "His last words to me still ring in my ears: 'The days of the earth are short. You will not be long there, and you will return here.'" (*Embraced by the Light*, pp. 111–19)

After returning to her body, Betty writes of her abhorrence to have returned:

> [I] found myself in the hospital room again . . . and lying on the bed under the blankets was my body. I stood in the air and looked down at it and was filled with revulsion. It looked cold and heavy and reminded me of an old pair of coveralls that had been dragged through mud and grime. In comparison, I felt like I had just taken a long, soothing shower, and now I had to put that heavy, cold muddy garment on . . . my spirit slipped back into the body. . . . The body's cumbersome weight and coldness were abhorrent. (*Embraced by the Light*, pp. 123–24)

RANELLE WALLACE

RaNelle did not want to return to her body. But then she met a spirit who she understood was intended to be one of her future children, and she became persuaded that she should return to earth for their sake. (Her poignant story is told in Chapter 62: "Were Families Planned Before We Came to Earth?")

SARAH LANELLE MENET

"I don't want to go back."

Sarah was met by her grandmother, who told her:

"'You cannot stay here. You have to go back.' . . . I protested, 'I don't want to go back. I don't want to go back.'" (*There Is No Death*, pp. 49–50)

In her description of the spirit world, Sarah says:

"There were no feelings of loss . . . [even] my dear children . . . were not on my mind."

> As I looked around, drinking it all in, a tremendous feeling of peace came over me. Here I was, separated from everything that I had known before and there were no feelings of loss for the possessions I had left behind. My material treasures, my dear children, or anyone else that might have loved me were not on my mind. All I could think of was how very wonderful it was to be in this place. (*There Is No Death*, pp. 30–31)

RAYMOND A. MOODY JR.

In his book *The Light Beyond*, Dr. Moody writes:

> For many people, the NDE is such a pleasant event that they don't want to return. As a result, they are frequently very angry at their doctors for bringing them back.
>
> Two physician friends of mine first discovered NDEs for themselves when patients they saved became hostile.
>
> One of them was resuscitating another physician who had just had a cardiac arrest. When the stricken man revived, he said angrily: "Carl, don't you ever do that to me again."
>
> . . . Another physician friend of mine discovered the NDE phenomenon when he resuscitated a man who then yelled at him for taking him out of "that beautiful and bright place."
>
> NDEers frequently act this way. But it is a short-lived feeling. If you talk to them a week or so later, they are happy to have returned. Although they miss the blissful state, they are glad to have the chance to go on living.

Keith A. Haslem

Interestingly, many NDEers feel they are given a choice to return or to stay. It may be the Being of Light who offers this choice to them, or a relative who has died.

All the persons I have talked to would stay if they had only themselves to think of. But they usually say they want to go back because they have children left to raise or because their spouses or parents would miss them. (*The Light Beyond*, pp. 15–17)

AUTHOR'S PERSPECTIVE

For those who are grieving the loss of a loved one, this chapter was meant to help you understand that once your loved one is in a paradisaical realm, it is likely that they would not want to come back even if they could.

This understanding may assuage your grief because you can be at peace knowing that they are in a wonderful new realm, and that they likely would not want to return even if they could.

27

WILL WE BE REUNITED WITH FAMILY AND FRIENDS?

SYNOPSIS

It is only natural to hope that we will be reunited with loved ones and friends when we enter the spirit world. Several of the Witnesses affirm that we will.

- Elane Durham met a group of deceased relatives.
- RaNelle Wallace met her grandmother, and Sarah LaNelle Menet met hers.
- Lance Richardson witnessed an elderly woman, who had just died, coming into the spirit world and being reunited with her husband from mortality.
- Brigham Young taught that we will be reunited with friends from our premortal lives who will be even happier to see us than our loved ones in this world; they having been our friends for perhaps eons of time before mortality.

ELANE DURHAM

Elane writes that immediately after arriving in the spirit world:

"People were gathered, waiting for me."

Keith A. Haslem

> A group of six or seven people were gathered, waiting for me. I "felt" with every part of who I am, someone amongst them say, "She'll soon be here."
>
> Another one, looking my way, exclaimed, "There she is!" And again, I "felt" this rather then heard it with my ears.
>
> "Hurry Elane! Everyone's waiting!" called a man who was standing by a rock under the trees, motioning me to them with a swing of his arm. He was my mother's stepfather who had died when I was about sixteen, and I recognized him immediately.
>
> Two ladies broke away from the group, coming toward me. . . . I recognized my dad's mother who had been dead since I was about nine. Behind her was my husband's Aunt Virginia, who had died the previous spring. She had been so crippled up in life, yet here she appeared physically perfect! They both seemed young, too; in their late twenties or early thirties!
>
> I smiled happily, surprised at Virginia's vibrant good health and thrilled to see all of them. (*I Stand All Amazed*, p. 20)

RANELLE WALLACE

RaNelle recounts a special connection with one spirit in particular as she visited with a group of spirits she had known as friends in her premortal existence:

"I've always been with you."

> My friends embraced me again and committed to stay with me. I felt their perfect love and knew they would never leave me. One female friend lingered and embraced me for a long time. She seemed bonded to me in a unique way, but I didn't quite understand what it was. "You know I've always been with you," she said. "I've never left you. And I never will." She hung on every word I said and I was moved as I recognized her passion to be with me, her absolute devotion and love. "I'll always be there," she said again. (*The Burning Within*, p. 109)

A few years after her near-death experience, RaNelle gave birth to a daughter who she felt was this spirit who had been so devoted to her. That story is told in Chapter 62: "Were Families Planned Before We Came to Earth?"

Going Home

SARAH LANELLE MENET

Sarah meets a "beautiful woman."

> I did not recognize her, though she seemed somewhat familiar. I felt I should know her but had no idea who she was.... She looked to be about thirty years old. Another wonderful thing I understood about spirit bodies was that they all looked to be about the same age. They were all absolutely beautiful and perfect....
>
> Upon reaching me, she said with surprise, "LaNelle, what are you doing here?"
>
> This woman, whom I did not know, was a relative of mine. She had been caught by surprise, somehow knowing that it wasn't my time to cross over, so she had hurried to reach me.
>
> She continued, "You cannot stay here. You have to go back."... I protested, "I don't want to go back. I don't want to go back." (*There Is No Death*, pp. 50–52)

Sarah learns the identity of the "beautiful woman."

> A few years after my return to mortality, my sister and I had to place our elderly mother into a care facility and were going through some old photographs that I had never seen before. I saw a picture of a woman and asked my sister who she was. She was my grandmother, Sarah, who died when I was a baby. When I saw the photograph, I immediately recognized her as the beautiful lady in the spirit world who sent me back. (*There Is No Death*, p. 128)

Sarah also learned that "there was something like a kind of signal that alerts family members in the spirit world when a relative on earth is about to die or 'cross over.' This provides the opportunity for them to be there" (*There Is No Death*, p. 50).

Sarah learns that spirit world associations are primarily with family and friends.

> As I mentioned before, even while looking down into the city from a great distance, I could feel the love that was exchanged between the people as they greeted each other and conversed.... I understood that the small groups of people gathered together were families and friends from earth. It came to me that most activities the people took part in were done within these groups, and I found comfort knowing

that I would continue friendships with those I had known while on earth. (*There Is No Death*, p. 38)

LANCE RICHARDSON

In his book *The Message*, Lance Richardson describes a near-death experience he had on Christmas Day, 1998, after a motorcycle accident.

Lance was met by a group of his relatives as he entered the spirit world. His escort was his deceased cousin Randy. During his visit, he witnessed the reunion of an elderly woman with her husband.

Like coming off an airplane

> Randy assured me that everyone who dies has close relatives and friends present to greet them then they pass through the veil that separates our two worlds.
>
> I watched numerous people pass through that veil while I was there. It was most enjoyable. I witnessed an elderly woman whose family anticipated her arrival. There were about twenty individuals, jumping up and down excitedly, as if waiting for a loved one to come off of an airplane. A slender man, who was obviously the husband of the woman, paced back and forth nervously. Two women kept patting him on the back and excitedly hugging him as they anticipated the arrival.
>
> Another man, who acted as a leader to the group, then stepped partly through the veil so that I could not see him. He then stepped back, announced happily, "It is time," and turned back into the veil. He reached his arm forward and drew it back holding the hand of the elderly woman. She seemed startled, and a bit blinded at first. Then upon seeing the group, her expression turned to one of absolute splendor. They parted for her to see the gentleman standing at the back; the one who appeared to be her husband. They rushed into one another's arms. The entire group encircled them and eagerly welcomed her home.
>
> I was deeply moved. I realized very quickly that a spirit can experience great extremes of emotion, as I was feeling at that moment.
>
> "Is this how it happens?" I asked Randy, choked with emotion.
>
> "Isn't it beautiful? I never tire of seeing it," he answered me.
>
> The family began to walk away together. "They are going to where a family celebration has been planned," Randy explained.

"Celebration? I guess I had never thought of the Spirit World having celebrations. What is it like?"

"Oh, it's wonderful! Families get together when loved ones pass into our world, and to celebrate other special events and occasions." (*The Message*, pp. 63–64)

THE CHURCH OF JESUS CHRIST OF LATTER-DAY SAINTS PERSPECTIVE

JOSEPH SMITH, JR.
(first prophet and president of the Church of Jesus Christ of Latter-day Saints)

"An eternity of felicity"

I have a father, brothers, children, and friends who have gone to a world of spirits. They are only absent for a moment. They are in the spirit, and we shall soon meet again. . . . When we depart, we shall hail our mothers, fathers, friends, and all whom we love, who have fallen asleep in Jesus . . . it will be an eternity of felicity. (*Teachings of the Prophet Joseph Smith*, pp. 359–60)

BRIGHAM YOUNG
(second prophet and president of the Church of Jesus Christ of Latter-day Saints)

"We have more friends behind the veil than on this side."

We have more friends behind the veil than on this side and they will hail us more joyfully than you were ever welcomed by your parents or friends in this world; and you will rejoice more when you meet them than you ever rejoiced to see a friend in this life; and then we shall go on from step to step, from rejoicing to rejoicing, . . . our happiness becoming more and more exquisite. (*Discourses of Brigham Young*, pp. 379–80)

Keith A. Haslem

AUTHOR'S PERSPECTIVE

Love *does* last forever.

In the lyrics of "What's Forever For" (sung by Michael Martin Murphey), the song's author, Rafe VanHoy laments that so many couples split up—"throwing love away."

In the chorus, he asks the question, "*And if love never lasts forever, tell me, what's forever for?*"

My response to Mr. VanHoy is: Love *does* last forever, and is probably the best part of *forever*.

28

WILL WE BE REUNITED WITH OUR PETS?

Pets are, for some, not merely animals; they are members of the family. Sarah LaNelle Menet learned that we may be reunited with them in the spirit world.

SYNOPSIS

Sarah LaNelle Menet learned that the spirits of animals have their own realm in which to live after they die. However, those animals who would be happiest living with a person who loved them on earth will be allowed to do so.

She also learned that the purpose for our pets is to help us learn how to love—an important first step for those who have a difficulty loving people.

She also learned that our pets can understand us during mortality and that communication after mortality will be two-way.

SARAH LANELLE MENET

"One of the reasons that animals exist on earth is to help us learn to love."

As I looked at the cottage and admired how pretty and perfect it was, I noticed a dog trotting along a path. The dog appeared to be like an Irish setter with long brown hair. I was somewhat surprised and thought to myself, Are there pets here? The response that filled my mind was that there are animals here of all kinds, some of which have been pets to people on earth. I was given to understand that if a person had pets they loved and cared for in mortality and if the animals also loved them and wanted to be with them, they could then be together forever.

As I looked at the dog, it seemed to sense my presence and looked back at me. I could hear and feel its thoughts of recognition. This surprised me a little. Then immediately I understood that the spirits of animals and people could communicate and understand each other the same way I had communicated with the plants earlier, that is, telepathically. The difference being that animals communicated on a higher level than the trees and grass but still well below the level of my thoughts.

It also came to my mind that on earth the animals could understand people but that our ability to understand them had been taken away. The thoughts of animals are simple, like the thoughts of a child, and they have personalities, feelings, and desires as well. One of the reasons that animals exist on earth is to help us learn to love. There are some individuals who have not developed the ability to love other people but are capable of loving animals. I also understood that the spirits of animals are precious, and those who take their lives without cause or are cruel to them will have serious consequences to pay. (*There Is No Death*, pp. 33–34)

I did not see any insects in the spirit world. It was my understanding that when they cross over they go to an entirely different place prepared just for them—a lower world, sort of a spirit world for insects. Most of the animals are the same. They also go to a place where they can be happy and be with their own kind. The exceptions are those animals that would be happiest living with a person who loves them. We will be able to enjoy the company of our pets that we loved and had stewardship over while we were on the earth. (*There Is No Death*, pp. 107–8; emphasis added)

THE CHURCH OF JESUS CHRIST OF LATTER-DAY SAINTS PERSPECTIVE

All living things have a spirit essence.

Members of the Church of Jesus Christ of Latter-day Saints believe that all living things have a spirit essence that resides within the physical body. From the book of Moses, in the Pearl of Great Price, it reads:

"And every plant of the field before it was in the earth, and every herb of the field before it grew. For I, the Lord God, created all things, of which I have spoken, spiritually, before they were naturally upon the face of the earth" (Moses 3:5).

AUTHOR'S PERSPECTIVE

For some individuals their happiness in heaven would be increased significantly if they were reunited with their pets. If heaven is the place of *ultimate* happiness, then it follows logically that some individuals will be reunited with their pets.

29

WHAT DO BUILDINGS LOOK LIKE IN THE SPIRIT WORLD?

SYNOPSIS

The buildings of spirit world are reported to be far more amazing than any on earth; they are perfect in detail, and are complemented by beautiful vegetation and fountains of water.

BETTY J. EADIE

Every structure "a work of art."

"Buildings are perfect there; every line and angle and detail is created to perfectly complement the entire structure, creating a feeling of wholesomeness or inevitability. Every structure, every creation there is a work of art" (*Embraced by the Light*, p. 108).

GEORGE G. RITCHIE

Something like "a well-planned university"

> Enormous buildings stood in a beautiful sunny park and there was a relationship between the various structures, a pattern to the way they were arranged, that reminded me somewhat of a well-planned university. Except that to compare what I was now seeing with anything

on earth was ridiculous. It was more as if all the schools and colleges in the world were only piecemeal reproductions of this reality.

. . . As we entered one of the buildings and started down a high-ceilinged corridor lined with tall doorways, the air was so hushed that I was actually startled to see people in the passageway. (*Return from Tomorrow*, pp. 68–69)

SARAH LANELLE MENET

"The buildings . . . were magnificent."

The tallest of the buildings stood maybe three or four stories high, though most were only one level. They were of various architectural styles. One of the most common designs reminded me a little of Hearst Castle in California. . . . And yet, even the grandeur of the Hearst Castle pales in comparison to the beauty of any of the structures I saw in the city. The buildings, flowers, shrubbery, and the shimmering fountains of water within this city were beyond anything that can be seen on this planet.

The buildings had the appearance of a pinkish-white alabaster or marble so thin that it looked almost transparent. As I concentrated on one of the buildings, I could see right through its walls. Inside, I saw columns and steps and many rooms with large hallways. These corridors were very wide and full of people going places. Fifty people could easily have stood shoulder to shoulder across the width. The rooms were even larger and filled with hundreds of people. (*There Is No Death*, pp. 36–37)

AUTHOR'S PERSPECTIVE

Could it be that all the architects and construction tradespeople out there are just getting started?

I googled "Hearst Castle" to see what it looked like. To me, it resembles the Salt Lake City temple of the Church of Jesus Christ of Latter-day Saints. The design for this temple was reportedly given through heavenly vision to Brigham Young, who was then the president of the Church of Jesus Christ of Latter-day Saints.

30

WHAT DOES A HEAVENLY CITY LOOK LIKE IN THE SPIRIT WORLD?

SYNOPSIS

Dale Black describes seeing "townships" in the spirit world. Both he and George G. Ritchie also describe seeing a "heavenly city" from a distance, although neither had the opportunity to enter the city.

The heavenly city seemed to be far distant from cities on earth. It was a city that seemed to be made of light. There was a wondrous wall around the city, and a magnificent angel attended a beautiful gateway that appeared to be made from pearls that had been liquefied and then solidified on the wall. The inhabitants of the city enjoyed an atmosphere of love, light, and beautiful music. There was a complete absence of any sense of evil.

George G. Ritchie surmised that the inhabitants of the city were individuals who had been devoted disciples of Jesus Christ during mortality.

GEORGE G. RITCHIE

During his near-death experience, George Ritchie traveled a far distance from the earth and saw, at a great distance, a heavenly city, which he surmised was the heavenly city talked about in the book of Revelation.

Inhabited by those "who had indeed kept Jesus the focus of their lives"

Going Home

Up until this point I had had the impression that we were traveling—though in what manner I could not imagine—upon the earth itself. Even what I had come to think of as a "higher plane" of deep thoughts and learning, was obviously not far distant from the "physical plane" where bodyless beings were still bound to a solid world.

Now however, we seemed to have left the earth behind. I could no longer see it. Instead we appeared to be in an immense void, except that I had always thought of that as a frightening word, and this was not. Some unnameable promise seemed to vibrate through that vast emptiness.

And then I saw, infinitely far off, far too distant to be visible with any kind of sight I knew of . . . a city. A glowing, seemingly endless city, bright enough to be seen over all the unimaginable distance between. The brightness seemed to shine from the very walls and streets of this place, and from beings which I could now discern moving about within it. In fact, the city and everything in it seemed to be made of light, even as the Figure at my side was made of light.

At this point I had not yet read the Book of Revelation. I could only gape in awe at this faraway spectacle, wondering how bright each building, each inhabitant, must be to be seen over so many light-years of distance. Could these radiant beings, I wondered, be those who had indeed kept Jesus the focus of their lives? Was I seeing at last ones who had looked for Him in everything? Looked so well and so closely that they had been changed into His very likeness? . . . Even as I asked the question, two of the bright figures seemed to detach themselves from the city and start toward us, hurling themselves across that infinity with the speed of light.

But as fast as they came toward us, we drew away still faster. The distance increased, the vision faded. Even as I cried out with loss, I knew that my imperfect sight could not now sustain more than an instant's glimpse of this real, this ultimate heaven. He had shown me all He could; now we were speeding far away. (*Return from Tomorrow*, pp. 72–73)

DALE BLACK

A city with "an absence of sin"

My eyes were next drawn to a river that stretched from the gathering area in the middle of the city to the wall. It flowed toward the wall and seemed to end there, at least from my vantage point. The river was perfectly clear with a bluish-white hue. The light didn't shine on the water but mysteriously shone within it somehow.

The wall to the city was not a single wall but rather a series of walls layered next to each other. The wall was made of three outer layers, three inner layers, and one higher wall in the center. The outer layers of the wall were about forty feet tall. Each layer of the wall was taller as it got closer to the center, like a stairstep. At its tallest point, the wall was a couple hundred feet. And surprisingly, it was as thick as it was tall. The wall was massive and stretched out to my left and right as far as I could see in both directions.

The outer wall was greenish in color with a hint of blue and a hint of black mingled within it. It was made entirely of translucent stones. Large multicolored stones were built into the base of the wall in layered rows. A powerful light permeated the wall, and you could see all the colors of the rainbow in it. Strangely, whenever I moved, the colors moved ever so slightly as if sensing my movement and making an adjustment. . . .

I was eye-level with the base of the wall now and no longer hovering above it, but standing in front of an impressive opening. It was an archway that seemed to be approximately forty feet high and thirty to thirty-five feet wide.

A tall, majestic angelic being stood to the right side of the gate, dressed similarly to my escorts with the exception of the golden belt wrapped around his upper waist. A large emblem was located on the belt where a buckle would normally be. He appeared very strong and masculine. His hair was either white or it was the light radiating from him. But his entire being, specifically, was illuminated in bright white light. His face seemed to light up with love and joy at seeing me.

The entrance, or gateway, was opalescent in color, as if it had been made of pearls that had been liquefied, and then solidified onto the wall. The entrance was completely composed of this mesmerizing substance that also coated the entire inside of the opening as far as I could see. The ornamentation around the entrance included phenomenal detail. It was the most astounding sight I had ever seen. As I basked in the beauty that adorned the gateway, I noticed large gold letters emblazoned above the opening. They seemed to quiver with life. The single line of letters formed an arch over the entrance. I didn't recognize the letters but knew the words were as important as any words could be. Other words were written in honey-colored gemstones on the ground in front of the entrance and included several lines. The entrance through the thick wall was breathtaking. The opening seemed filled with light that was the purest of white, yet it seemed to have countless hues that changed with even my slightest movement. I was filled with excited anticipation of entering that beautiful gate.

I was immersed in music, in light, and in love. Vibrant life permeated everything. All these weren't just around me, they were inside me. And it was wonderful, more wonderful than anything I had ever experienced. It felt as if I belonged there. I didn't want to leave. Ever. It was as if this was the place I had been searching all my life to find, and now I'd found it. My search was over! . . .

My attention was diverted to the beautiful entrance. I was certain I was going through the gate. Again I turned back toward my precious family and did not want to leave that perfect love. But because of the highly expectant look on their smiling faces, it seemed as if they knew I would be given a gift and what that gift would do for me. . . .

And then, as I was about to travel through the entrance and receive the gift. . . .

I was swept away. (*Flight to Heaven*, pp. 104–10)

At this point in his narrative, Dale Black found himself back in his body.

AUTHOR'S PERSPECTIVE

Whether these cities were indeed "heaven" or just a heavenly city that the Witnesses were permitted to view without entering, we can't be certain. But either way, these cities sound like a wonderful place to call "home."

31

DO LIBRARIES EXIST IN THE SPIRIT WORLD?

SYNOPSIS

According to our resources, acquiring knowledge is a primary pursuit for many in the spirit world. They report seeing amazing libraries to facilitate that endeavor. But the acquisition of knowledge in these libraries is significantly more efficient than the process of learning on earth. In the spirit world, knowledge is seemingly absorbed at a tremendous rate regarding any subject of interest rather than extracted from books through concentrated effort.

BETTY J. EADIE

"Understand volumes in an instant"

> My comprehension was such that I could understand volumes in an instant. It was as if I could look at a book and comprehend it at a glance—as though I could just sit back while the book revealed itself to me in every detail, forward and backward, inside and out, every nuance and possible suggestion. All in an instant. As I comprehended one thing, more questions and answers would come to me, all building on each other, and interacting as if all truth were intrinsically connected. . . . Knowledge permeated me. In a sense it became me, and I was amazed at my ability to comprehend the mysteries of the universe simply by reflecting on them. (*Embraced by the Light*, pp. 44–45)

"No knowledge was kept from me"

Going Home

I was taken to another large room similar to a library. As I looked around it seemed to be a repository of knowledge, but I couldn't see any books. Then I noticed ideas coming into my mind, knowledge filling me on subjects that I had not thought about for some time—or in some cases not at all. Then I realized that this was a library of the mind. By simply reflecting on a topic, as I had earlier in Christ's presence, all knowledge on that topic came to me. I could learn about anybody in history—or even in the spirit world—in full detail.

No knowledge was kept from me, and it was impossible not to understand correctly every thought, every statement, every particle of knowledge. There was absolutely no misunderstanding here. History was pure. Understanding was complete. I understood not only what people did but why they did it and how it affected other people's perceptions of reality....

But this was more than a mental process. I was able to feel what the people felt when they performed these actions. I understood their pains or joys or excitement because I was able to live them. Some of this knowledge was taken from me, but not all. I cherish the knowledge granted to me of certain events and people in our history which were important for me to understand. (*Embraced by the Light*, pp. 76–77)

SARAH LANELLE MENET

"No chairs anywhere ... people never grew tired"

Looking along another corridor, I saw people going in and out of another very large room. The room appeared to be a library, since it had row after row of huge books along all of the walls. I would guess the books were about five or six inches thick and fourteen inches high. They appeared to be beautifully bound and engraved with something that I do not think was leather, though it was dark brown in color. People stood studying and reading at ornate, intricately carved tables while others walked about normally. It was here I noticed that there were no chairs anywhere. This seemed strange, since I had seen people sitting on the lawn while caught up in conversation outside earlier. As I thought about this, I was impressed with the understanding that chairs were not needed here except for some kinds of work, since people never grew tired and had no need to sit and rest. (*There Is No Death*, p. 40)

GEORGE G. RITCHIE

"The important books of the universe"

Next we walked through a library the size of the whole University of Richmond. I gazed into rooms lined floor to ceiling with documents on parchment, clay, leather, metal, paper. "Here," the thought occurred to me, "are assembled the important books of the universe."

Immediately I knew this was impossible. How could books be written somewhere beyond the earth! But the thought persisted, although my mind rejected it. "The key works of the universe," the phrase kept recurring as we roamed the domed reading rooms crowded with silent scholars. Then abruptly, at the door to one of the smaller rooms, almost an annex: "Here is the central thought of this earth." (*Return from Tomorrow*, pp. 70–71)

DR. RAYMOND MOODY

A young man interviewed by Dr. Moody talked about a school.

"You absorb knowledge."

Now, I was in a school . . . and it was real. It was not imaginary. If I were not absolutely sure, I would say, "Well, there is a possibility that I was in this place." But it was real. It was like a school, and there was no one there, and yet there were a lot of people there. Because if you looked around, you would see nothing . . . but if you paid attention, you would feel, sense, the presence of other beings around. . . . It's as if there were lessons coming at me and they would keep coming at me. . . . I cannot describe it. . . . Because this is a place where the place is knowledge. . . . Knowledge and information are readily available—all knowledge. . . . You absorb knowledge. . . . You all of a sudden know the answers. . . . It's like you focus mentally on one place in the school and—zoom—knowledge flows by you from that place, automatically. It's just like you'd had about a dozen speed reading courses. (*Reflections on Life After Life*, pp. 13–14)

AUTHOR'S PERSPECTIVE

I love to see my grandchildren grow and increase in knowledge. I expect God feels the same with regard to His spirit children.

The speed and efficiency of learning in the spirit world will likely make it quite exhilarating.

32

DO PEOPLE HAVE HOUSES IN THE SPIRIT WORLD?

Jesus told His disciples: "In my Father's house are many mansions. . . . I go to prepare a place for you" (John 14:2).

SYNOPSIS

Dale Black talks about "townships" having "picture perfect homes in small, quaint towns." Sarah LaNelle Menet writes of the latitude we will have in choosing a home.

DALE BLACK

"Townships" in the spirit world

> Between the central part of the city and the city walls were groupings of brightly colored picture-perfect homes in small, quaint towns. I'll call them townships, because I can't think of a better word for them. I focused on only three townships, but certainly there were more. A lot more, no doubt. The dwellings in these townships were not arranged in a uniform or symmetrical manner but appeared perfectly balanced somehow. Each home was customized and unique from the others yet blended harmoniously. Some were three or four stories, some were even higher. There were no two the same. If music could become homes, it would look like these, beautifully built and perfectly balanced. . . .
>
> As I described previously, the grass, the sky, the walls, the houses, everything was more beautiful than I ever dreamed anything could be. (*Flight to Heaven*, pp. 104–5)

Going Home

SARAH LANELLE MENET

"You can live in whatever type of building . . . that would make you happy . . . within limits."

As I stood on the hill asking questions and receiving answers, I paused to look at something that caught my interest off in the distance. It was a lovely little cottage in a meadow far away. It seemed so serene and perfect. Situated in an area surrounded by trees, flowers, and little streams, it appeared like a little cottage out of a fairytale book. It had a round-topped door, a cobblestone path leading up to it, and what appeared to be a soft thatched roof. On taking a closer look I realized that it was not as I first assumed and that the cottage was actually very large.

While gazing upon this idyllic scene I thought, I would love to live in such a house. Immediately the answer came: You can. You can live in whatever type of building or house that would make you happy. At the same time I understood that I could live in a simple cottage like this one or in a columned mansion with family and friends. The decision regarding our living circumstances is primarily up to us, although within the limits of what we have earned. (*There Is No Death*, pp. 32–33)

AUTHOR'S PERSPECTIVE

A really nice home *without* a mortgage or taxes. Paradise indeed!

WHAT IS IT LIKE TO MEET JESUS CHRIST?

SYNOPSIS

Four of the six Witnesses write about meeting or seeing Jesus Christ during their experiences in the spirit world.

By all accounts, to meet Jesus is to feel His love for you—a love that is overwhelming.

GEORGE G. RITCHIE

"An astonishing love. A love beyond my wildest imagining."

I wasn't sure when the light in the room began to change; suddenly I was aware that it was brighter, a lot brighter, than it had been. I whirled to look at the nightlight on the bedside table. Surely a single 15-watt bulb couldn't turn out so much light?

I stared in astonishment as the brightness increased, coming from nowhere, seeming to shine everywhere at once. All the bulbs in the ward couldn't give off that much light. All the bulbs in the world couldn't! It was impossibly bright: it was like a million welders' lamps all blazing at once. And right in the middle of my amazement came a prosaic thought probably born of some biology lecture back at the university: "I'm glad I don't have physical eyes at this moment," I thought. "This light would destroy the retina in a tenth of a second."

No, I corrected myself, not the light.

He.

He would be too bright to look at. For now I saw that it was not light but a Man who had entered the room, or rather, a Man made out of light, though this seemed no more possible to my mind than the incredible intensity of the brightness that made up His form.

The instant I perceived Him, a command formed itself in my mind. "Stand up!" The words came from inside me. Yet they had authority my mere thoughts had never had. I got to my feet, and as I did came the stupendous certainty: "You are in the presence of the Son of God."

Again, the concept seemed to form itself inside me, but not as thought or speculation. It was a kind of knowing, immediate and complete. I knew other facts about Him too. One, that this was the most totally male Being I had ever met. If this was the Son of God, then his name was Jesus. But . . . this was not the Jesus of my Sunday School books. That Jesus was gentle, kind, understanding—and probably a little bit of a weakling. This Person was power itself, older than time and yet more modern than anyone I had ever met.

Above all, with that same mysterious inner certainty, I knew that this Man loved me. Far more even than power, what emanated from this Presence was unconditional love. An astonishing love. A love beyond my wildest imagining. This love knew every unlovable thing about me—the quarrels with my stepmother, my explosive temper, the sex thoughts I could never control, every mean, selfish thought and action since the day I was born—and accepted and loved me just the same. (*Return from Tomorrow*, pp. 48–49)

BETTY J. EADIE

Embraced by Jesus

"I felt an utter explosion of love."

I saw a pinpoint of light in the distance. The black mass around me began to take on more of the shape of a tunnel, and I felt myself traveling through it at an even greater speed, rushing toward the light. I was instinctively attracted to it, although again, I felt that others might not be. As I approached it, I noticed the figure of a man standing in it, with the light radiating all around him. As I got closer the light became brilliant—brilliant beyond any description, far more brilliant than the sun—and I knew that no earthly eyes in their natural state could look upon this light without being destroyed. Only

Keith A. Haslem

spiritual eyes could endure it—and appreciate it. As I drew closer I began to stand upright.

I saw that the light immediately around him was golden, as if his whole body had a golden halo around it, and I could see that the golden halo burst out from around him and spread into a brilliant, magnificent whiteness that extended out for some distance. I felt his light blending into mine, literally and I felt my light being drawn to his. It was as if there were two lamps in a room, both shining, their light merging together. It's just hard to tell where one light ands and the other begins; they just become one light. Although his light was much brighter than my own, I was aware that my light, too, illuminated us. And as our lights merged, I felt as if I had stepped into his countenance, and I felt *an utter explosion of love* (emphasis added).

It was the most unconditional love I have ever felt, and as I saw his arms open to receive me I went to him and received his complete embrace and said over and over, "I'm home. I'm home. I'm finally home." I felt his enormous spirit and knew that I had always been a part of him, that in reality I had never been away from him. And I knew that I was worthy to be with him, to embrace him. I knew that he was aware of all my sins and faults, but that they didn't matter right now. He just wanted to hold me and share his love with me, and I wanted to share mine with him.

There was no questioning who he was. I knew that he was my Savior, and friend, and God. He was Jesus Christ, who had always loved me, even when I thought he hated me. He was life itself, love itself, and his love gave me a fullness of joy, even to overflowing. I knew that I had known him from the beginning, from long before my earth life, because my spirit *remembered* him.

All my life I had feared him, and I now saw—I knew—that he was my choicest friend. Gently, he opened his arms and let me stand back far enough to look into my eyes, and he said, "Your death was premature, it is not yet your time." No words ever spoken have penetrated me more than these. Until then, I had felt no purpose in life; I had simply ambled along looking for love and goodness but never really knowing if my actions were right. Now, within his words, I felt a mission, a purpose; I didn't know what it was, but I knew that my life on earth had not been meaningless.

It was not yet my time

I understood that he was the Son of God, though he himself was also a God, and that he had chosen from before the creation of the world to be our Savior. I understood, or rather, I *remembered*, his role as creator of the earth. His mission was to come into the world to teach love. This knowledge was more like remembering. Things were coming back to me from long before my life on earth, things that had been purposely blocked from me by a "veil" of forgetfulness at my birth. (*Embraced by the Light*, pp. 40–42, 44)

ELANE DURHAM

"Love . . . [that was] absolutely overwhelming"

> I . . . felt an immense amount of love from it, a different kind of love than I had ever felt before, love that was completely overwhelming. (*I Stand All Amazed*, p. 26)
>
> I knew then that I had been with Him before, for I absolutely recognized Him. I knew that I had dwelt, with my same exact identity, in an eternal life or existence prior to my mortal life, and in that existence I had come to know this glorious being thoroughly and even intimately. That is both why and how I knew that the voice I had heard and felt, as well as the being I was now gazing upon, was . . . the Lord Jesus Christ. . . .
>
> The love I felt from Christ was the most powerful feeling I had ever experienced. It was absolutely overwhelming, and I knew if I had been in my physical body it would have left me powerless, and perhaps might even have destroyed me. There was heat associated with it, too, a wonderful burning that swept through me again and again, like waves of comforting fire, cleansing me and purifying me so that I felt at peace being with Christ. (*I Stand All Amazed*, pp. 30–33)

In her book, Elane Durham responded to the question, "How did it make you feel to know you were in the presence of the Son of God?"

"I wanted . . . to bask in [His] love."

> If I were to use one word, it would be reverent. . . . The power of love I felt from Christ was so overwhelming that it illuminated my own insignificance, thus giving me reverence for Him. It made me feel small but not diminished, penitent but not fearful, humble but not chastised, understood but not condemned, so that I wanted with all my heart to draw closer, to be one with Him, to bask in the love He was so willingly sharing with me. (*I Stand All Amazed*, pp. 154–55)

Keith A. Haslem

SARAH LANELLE MENET

"It was as if love was emanating from him, permeating time and space."

> But, like most things in the spirit world, it wasn't His appearance that was so overpowering; it was the feelings of love and complete acceptance transmitted to me as I gazed upon Him. The feelings were glorious beyond description and filled my whole being so that it felt as if it would burst.... I thought to myself that these beams of light must spread throughout the universe and to us on earth as well, so that all people everywhere could feel this tremendous love if they wanted to. It was as if love was emanating from Him, permeating time and space, even in his physical absence. (*There Is No Death*, pp. 47–49)

AUTHOR'S PERSPECTIVE

In their accounts, the Witnesses acknowledge their unworthiness. Yet their consistent recollection is the overwhelming love they feel emanating from Jesus to them personally.

Because every person has made mistakes in life, the experience of the Witnesses offers hope to us all that we may be received in like manner by God. Perhaps His most perfect attribute is His ability to offer all His spiritual offspring unconditional love.

34

WHAT DOES JESUS LOOK LIKE?

SYNOPSIS

Witness accounts indicate that Jesus appears to be about thirty-five years of age, a little over six feet tall, and that He is a very attractive, masculine man. His eyes seem to be His most compelling feature—beautiful blue eyes that are captivating to behold.

Some Witnesses observed that the nail prints from His Crucifixion are still visible in His hands and feet.

GEORGE G. RITCHIE

"He had blue eyes and chestnut-brown hair parted in the middle. He was slightly taller than I, which would place His height at over six feet, two inches. Though He was dressed in a magnificent white robe, his powerful, muscular frame shone through. He was ageless and yet appeared about thirty-five years of age" (*My Life After Dying*, p. 20).

ELANE DURHAM

Beautiful blue eyes . . . powerful eyes

> I saw in the light's core the outline of a man—a glorious being apparently made of light that seemed more golden in color than the radiance that shown all about him. And though I thought of Him as light, He certainly had all the physical aspects of a man. I saw His hands, His arms, His body, His neck, His head—I even noted His facial

characteristics, though I am at a loss to describe them now. Yet withal He was a being of power and glorious light so incredible that I could not really comprehend Him.

But I do remember His eyes! They were so clear and bright—yet there was color to them—a beautiful blue color outlined in deeper blue that made me think of the color of the distant ocean on a clear day. But it wasn't so much the color of His eyes as it was the power in them, that awed me. Those fathomless eyes penetrated my very soul. They knew me beyond anything I was ever capable of knowing about myself—and to my absolute and dumbfounded amazement, still He loved me. In fact, the love I had felt from the moment of seeing the light had grown steadily stronger, and now it somehow reached out and literally began to encircle me and draw me closer. (*I Stand All Amazed*, pp. 30–31)

When asked "Can you describe what [Jesus] looks like?" Elane responded:

Jesus is "attractive and masculine."

"To be candid, I can but I won't, other than to state that He looks like a man, very attractive and masculine. I remember His features vividly, but I consider that sacred and personal, and do not discuss it with anyone. I will say that there are numerous paintings of him on the market, and each of them has something of Christ in them, though in my opinion none of them do Him justice" (*I Stand All Amazed*, p. 154).

SARAH LANELLE MENET

An extremely bright light had entered the city and was gradually moving down one of the streets. This moving light was so brilliant that it outshone the light of the city and was blinding beyond our sun or any other light source I am familiar with. . . . It was then that I realized the source of this moving light was a man at its center. He was walking with a crowd of people all around Him. The light came from Him, from His body and His clothing. . . .

The man was incredibly beautiful, and then in an instant I knew that this was Jesus Christ making a visit to the city. . . . He had no beard, and His hair was a reddish golden blond. (*There Is No Death*, pp. 47–49)

In response to the question, "What does Christ look like?" Sarah wrote:

"He is beautiful beyond description."

> There are really no earthly words to do him justice. His brightness and glory are far beyond the brilliance of the sun. He is the light of the world. His hair appeared to be shoulder length and was a dark golden blond. His eyes were a piercing blue, almost unreal. He was not thin and weak, but powerful, and yet he encompassed the word love completely. Seeing the Savior finally helped me understand what the word love means. He Is Love. (*There Is No Death*, pp. 130–31)

DUANE S. CROWTHER

In his book *Life Everlasting*, Duane S. Crowther references a number of accounts where individuals describe the appearance of Jesus. The following physical features were mentioned:

1. fairly young, appearing to be 35 to 40 years of age,
2. approximately six feet in height,
3. extremely attractive, a handsome man,
4. wearing a small beard,
5. having wonderful blue, love-filled eyes,
6. having beautiful golden-brown hair, rather long,
7. having a smooth, kind, thin, fine-featured handsome face with no time lines,
8. being strong, but of average stature, with broad shoulders,
9. having large, strong hands, but still having nail prints in his hands and wrists,
10. radiating intense light, which sometimes makes him appear translucent, and which may affect observer's perceptions of his hair color. (*Life Everlasting*, p. 68)

AUTHOR'S PERSPECTIVE

It's only logical that Jesus, a perfect being, would also be perfect in appearance—handsome and masculine.

The Witnesses' descriptions of Jesus are interesting, but "a picture is worth a thousand words."

In the next chapter, I will introduce you to a painting done by Akiane Kramarik—titled *Prince of Peace*—which I believe is the best representation of Jesus available.

35

WHAT IS THE BEST PORTRAYAL OF JESUS?

I believe a painting done by Akiane Kramarik, titled *Prince of Peace*, gives us the best likeness of Jesus. (Google "Prince of Peace painting Akiane Kramarik") Akiane's story is remarkable.

SYNOPSIS

At the age of four, Akiane, having had no religious training, whispered one day to her mother, "Today I met God." She continued to have out-of-body experiences and told her mother that she was taught how to draw during these experiences.

Akiane's artistic skills were evident at age four, and at age eight she painted a portrayal of Jesus in only forty hours. It was titled *Prince of Peace*.

Years later, Colton Burpo had a near-death experience at the age of four and described meeting Jesus. When his father showed him Akiane's painting he said, "That one's right," after having dismissed all representations of Jesus for the three years since his experience. Colton's experience is the subject of the book titled *Heaven Is for Real*.

A MORE DETAILED BACKGROUND

AKIANE'S PAINTING FEATURED ON THE DVD *HEAVEN IS FOR REAL*

A few years ago, a movie came out based upon the book *Heaven Is for Real*, which told the real-life story of Colton Burpo, who, at four years

Going Home

old, underwent an emergency appendectomy. Afterwards, he told his family that he had visited heaven, and had met Jesus and long-departed members of his family.

For the next three years, Colton's father Todd showed painting after painting to Colton to try to find the most accurate representation of Jesus. One day, he came across Akiane Kramarik's painting. In his book *Heaven Is for Real*, Todd Burpo writes:

> As I watched a montage of Akiane's artwork play across my computer screen, the narrator said, "Akiane describes God as vividly as she paints him."
>
> At that point, a close-up portrait of the face of Jesus filled the screen. It was the same likeness I'd seen before, but this time with Jesus looking "into the camera," so to speak.
>
> "He's pure," Akiane was saying. "He's very masculine, really strong and big. And his eyes are just beautiful."
>
> *Wow.* Nearly three years had passed since Colton's surgery, and about two and a half years since he first described Jesus to me that night in the basement. I was struck by the similarities between his and Akiane's recollections: all the colors in heaven . . . and especially their descriptions of Jesus' eyes.
>
> "And his eyes," Colton had said. "Oh, Dad, his eyes are *so* pretty!"
>
> What an interesting detail for two four-year-olds to key in on. . . . Still, of the literally dozens of portraits of Jesus we'd seen since 2003, Colton had never seen one he thought was right.
>
> *Well,* I thought, *may as well see what he thinks of Akiane's attempt.*
>
> *I got up from the desk and hollered up the stairs for Colton to come down to the basement.*
>
> "Coming!" came the reply.
>
> *Colton bounded down the stairs and popped into the office.* "Yeah, Dad?"
>
> *"Take a look at this," I said, nodding toward the computer monitor.* "What's wrong with this one?"
>
> *He turned to the screen and for a long moment said nothing.*
>
> "Colton?"
>
> *But he just stood there, studying. I couldn't read his expression.*
>
> "What's wrong with this one, Colton?" *I said again.*
>
> *Utter silence.*
>
> *I nudged him in the arm.* "Colton?"
>
> *My seven-year-old turned to look at me and said,* "Dad, that one's right."
>
> (*Heaven Is for Real*, pp. 143–45)

Keith A. Haslem

AKIANE KRAMARIK BACKGROUND

Akiane Kramarik was born July 9, 1994, to Lithuanian parents, who were atheists when she was young. The following sections are taken from a book written by Akiane and her mother, Foreli Kramarik, titled *Akiane: Her Life, Her Art, Her Poetry*. At the age of four, Akiane"s remarkable story begins.

No exposure to the concept of God

Because Akiane and her brothers had only a few acquaintances and had never formed deep relationships with anyone outside the family, they played mostly with one another. Our family never talked about religion, never prayed together, and never went to any church. I had been raised as an atheist in Lithuania, and Markus had been raised in an environment not conducive to spiritual growth. The children did not watch television, had never been out of our sight, and were homeschooled; therefore we were certain that no one else could have influenced Akiane's sudden and detailed descriptions of an invisible realm. We can't remember the exact month, but one morning when Akiane was four, she began sharing her visions of heaven with us.

"Today I met God"

"Today I met God," Akiane whispered to me one morning.

"What is God?" I was surprised to hear this. To me, God's name always sounded absurd and primitive.

"God is light—warm and good. It knows everything and talks with me. It is my parent."

"Tell me more about your dream."

"It was not a dream. It was real!" . . .

About the same time as the visions began, Akiane suddenly began showing an intense interest in drawing. She began sketching hundreds of figures and portraits on whatever surfaces she found at hand, including walls, windows, furniture, books, and even her own legs and arms. . . .

One day we noticed white spots on her front teeth. We asked what had happened, but Akiane just turned away.

Going Home

> "Akiane ate a tube of toothpaste," Delfini accused. "Her angel's teeth are so white, they sparkle. She thought that if she ate toothpaste, her teeth would also get whiter."
>
> The next morning, after unscrewing almost the entire bookshelf to make an easel, Akiane woke me up at 4:00 a.m. by waving a drawing of a woman over my face. "Look! This is her—this is my angel," Akiane explained. "Her skin is so smooth, not one spot. She doesn't smile in my picture, because paper is not white enough to show how white her teeth are, and I wanted to show how she talks to me with her eyes. You see, where God takes me, He teaches me how to draw."
>
> (*Akiane*, pp. 7–9)

Some of Akiane's sketches are included in her book; they are amazing. I will fast forward through the next four years of Akiane's life to when she did her painting of Jesus.

Akiane paints "Prince of Peace" at the age of eight

One of the most uncanny events surrounding Akiane's art was her discovery of one particular model. Desperately wanting to paint portraits of Jesus, whom she had first seen in her dreams, she spent a lot of time searching for the right face. For over a year she had been looking for the perfect representation of Jesus; she stood by supermarkets, shopping malls, parks, and on city streets, watching thousands of faces pass by, only to shake her head.

One morning she asked us to pray with her throughout the day about her Jesus model. "I can't do this anymore, God. This is it. I can't find anyone by myself," eight-and-a-half-year-old Akiane tearfully prayed. "I need You to send me the right model and give me the right idea. Maybe it's too much to ask, but could You send him right through our front door? Yes, right through our front door."

The very next day, in the middle of the afternoon, the doorbell rang and an acquaintance brought her friend, a carpenter, right through our front door. She introduced him to Akiane, thinking that the young artist would like his features. Standing almost seven feet tall, the carpenter had strong hands and a warm smile.

"*Tai Jis*! This is he!" Akiane blushed.

"*Kas jis*? Who is he?" I asked her quietly in Lithuanian.

Keith A. Haslem

... This is the man who'll model for the Jesus painting. He resembles the image that keeps coming back to me in my visions. Maybe he's the reason God moved us to this town."

We were stunned at the prompt response to our prayers. In our excitement, we all touched the man to make sure he was real and that we were not dreaming. ...

But a week later the carpenter called to apologize, stating that he felt unworthy to represent his Master, and that he had to decline the honor. We were all disappointed but Akiane refused to give up, praying even more feverishly, that day, the next day, and the next.

Another week passed before the carpenter called us back. "God wants me to do it, but I have only three days before I have to cut my hair and beard."

Akiane couldn't have been happier. ...

We were amazed by the quick pace at which she was working. ... It took her only forty hours to finish the portrait. ... At one point, desperately needing a thin brush to paint eyelashes, she even cut a strand of her own hair and made a fine brush. Watching the portrait develop was almost like watching a microscopic embryo develop into a newborn. Physically, artistically, and logically, the process of her painting was incomprehensible, as though the Almighty power was vibrating through her every vein.

While the painting was drying on the white wall of the studio, every viewer was quick to notice that no matter where you stood, Jesus's eyes followed you. Although the portrait resembled the model, Akiane had altered his expression and features to mimic the resurrected Jesus she remembered from her dream. Many times we overheard Akiane share the meaning to others. "The light side of His face represents heaven. And the dark side represents suffering on earth. His light eye in the dark shows that He's with us in all our troubles, and He is the Light when we need Him." (*Akiane*, pp. 26–28)

AKIANE'S INFLUENCE

Akiane's talents have expanded to poetry, which often relate to her paintings. She is regarded as a prodigy in both painting and poetry.

At the age of ten, she appeared on the Oprah Winfrey Show, and when asked by Oprah at the end of the interview, "Where does your inspiration come from?" she replied simply, "From God."

"From God," Oprah repeated, and gave her a hug.

Going Home

Akiane has also appeared on CNN and Katie Couric's show.

Wikipedia reports that "By age 12, [Akiane] had completed sixty large paintings. Some of her works have been purchased by the US Embassy in Singapore. She has completed over 200 artworks and 800 literary works and has published two best-selling books" (Wikipedia, "Akiane," last modified 17 March 2018, en.wikipedia.org/wiki/Akiane).

THE REACTION OF SMALL CHILDREN TO AKIANE'S PAINTING

Anonymous account

I know a man who believes that Akiane's painting is accurate based upon how his three young grandsons reacted when they first saw her painting. The following account is in his own words. (The names have been changed.)

> It was my three young grandsons, ages nine months to fifteen months, who really convinced me that Akiane's *Prince of Peace* was a good depiction of Jesus.
>
> We were watching the movie *Heaven Is for Real* shortly after it came out on DVD. My young grandson Mike, about fifteen months old at the time, was playing happily, oblivious to the movie. At the end of the movie, the portrait of Jesus done by Akiane, affirmed by Colton to be accurate, came on the screen. My son stopped Mike from his play, pointed to the TV, and asked him, "Who is that?" I thought the question was ridiculous because Mike had only a few words in his entire vocabulary. Mike stared intently at the picture for several moments, then said "Esu." He missed the "J" and the "S." I was astounded. I'm sure, at that young age, that his parents had not yet begun to teach him about Jesus.
>
> The next day, I went online and ordered a 5" by 7" replica of Akiane's painting *Prince of Peace*. When it arrived, we placed in on the top of our upright piano in the living room.
>
> Shortly afterward, another of my sons brought his son Johnnie to our home, who was about nine months old at the time. Immediately after coming through the front door, Johnnie saw the painting of Jesus on the piano. He extended his arms and leaned toward the

picture. We handed it to him. He brought the portrait to his lips and kissed it.

Johnnie's parents bought the painting for their home. Some time later when they asked him who it was he said "Jesus . . . Bobo." Who is Bobo? Johnnie's uncle Bob died several years before Johnnie was born.

Another of my sons has a boy named Matt, who was about a year old, just barely walking. We were sitting in the family room and Matt comes toddling in from the living room holding the portrait of Jesus. So unstable was he that he fell and dropped the picture. I gathered it up and put it back on top of the piano, mystified as to how he retrieved it. I don't think anyone in the house handed it to him.

Is it possible that very young children have recollections of their premortal lives, though they are unable to communicate about it? Dr. Mary C. Neal believes they do.

Dr. Mary C. Neal

"Very young children . . . are still quite connected to God's world."

In her book *To Heaven and Back*, Dr. Mary C. Neal expresses her opinion that young children maintain a connection with the spirit world during the early years of their lives:

> I need to categorically state, once again, that I believe very young children clearly remember where they came from and are still quite connected to God's world. I believe they easily recall the images, knowledge, and the love of the world they inhabited before their birth. I believe children may still be able to see angels, and many other people have written about this phenomenon. As young children become more engaged with the world, their memories fade and they begin their personal journey, often filled with detours and dead-ends, of finding their way back to God. (*To Heaven and Back*, pp. 147–48)

AUTHOR'S PERSPECTIVE

Is Akiane's *Prince of Peace* a good representation of Jesus? I believe so. Has any other painting of Jesus been done by a painter who asserts that they met Jesus?

Going Home

Regardless of what Jesus looks like, I don't believe Christians will have any trouble recognizing Him when they see Him again. I believe they will recognize Him from their association with Him in their lives before this earth.

When non-Christians die I believe they will see Christ as a being of light and will probably assume that He is the central figure of their own faith. I don't believe He will force a knowledge to the contrary upon them.

36

DOES JESUS HAVE A SENSE OF HUMOR?

SYNOPSIS

It is easy to imagine a very sober God. But George Ritchie, Betty J. Eadie, and one of Dr. Jeffrey Long's patients all commented on God or Jesus's sense of humor.

GEORGE G. RITCHIE

Soon after meeting Jesus, George asked a question that he immediately regretted.

"A kind of holy laughter—not at me"

> "What about the insurance money coming when I'm seventy?" The words were out, in this strange realm where communication took place by thought instead of speech, before I could call them back. A few months ago I had taken out the standard life insurance policy offered to servicemen; in some subconscious part of me had I believed this piece of paper guaranteed life itself? If I'd suspected before that there was mirth in the Presence beside me, now I was sure of it: the brightness seemed to vibrate and shimmer with a kind of holy laughter—not at me and my silliness, not a mocking laughter, but a mirth that seemed to say that in spite of all error and tragedy, joy was more lasting still. (*Return from Tomorrow*, p. 54)

BETTY J. EADIE

"Nobody could out-do his humor."

"I'll never forget the Lord's sense of humor, which was as delightful and quick as any here—far more so. Nobody could out-do his humor. He is filled with perfect happiness, perfect goodwill" (*Embraced by the Light*, p. 72).

"As more questions bubbled out of me, I became aware of his sense of humor. Almost laughing, he suggested that I slow down, that I could know all I desired. But I wanted to know *everything*, from beginning to end" (*Embraced by the Light*, p. 44).

JEFFREY LONG

Dr. Long quotes one of his patients.

"God has a fantastic sense of humor."

A man we'll call Leonard had a heart attack. He described a 360-degree vision as he watched the frantic efforts to resuscitate him:
"On the other side, communication is done via telepathy (thought transfer). I must tell you that God has a fantastic sense of humor; I never laughed so much in all my life!" (*Evidence of the Afterlife*, p. 131–32)

AUTHOR'S PERSPECTIVE

We all get amused watching foolish people on YouTube. Jesus has the ultimate YouTube channel—viewing everyone's foolish errors. Hopefully, He has a liberal sense of humor.

PART III
WHAT THE WITNESSES LEARNED

Life 181

Death 229

Spirits 284

Family 293

Women 312

Emotions 321

Creation of Life 357

37

WHAT IS THE PURPOSE OF LIFE?

SYNOPSIS

"Why am I here [on earth]?" is a question that most people will ask themselves at some point in their lives. Our resources suggest several reasons.

Elane Durham and Betty J. Eadie learned that God wants us to become like Him and learn to love all people unconditionally.

Many of the Witnesses learned that life is, as expressed by Elisabeth Kübler-Ross, "nothing but a school" (*On Life After Death*, p. 11), and we should actively seek knowledge.

Members of the Church of Jesus Christ of Latter-day Saints believe life is a time to "prepare to meet God" (Alma 34:32) and to "progress toward perfection" ("The Family: A Proclamation to the World").

ELANE DURHAM

Learn "how to become like God . . . through joyfully giving service to others."

"I knew that every single individual who has ever lived had been "in training" from the eternities, learning how to become like God. That, I was given to understand, means learning how to love unconditionally. And learning to love, just as it has been through the eternities, is accomplished through joyfully giving service to others" (*I Stand All Amazed*, p. 38).

Keith A. Haslem

BETTY J. EADIE

"God wants us to become as he is."

Now I knew that there actually was a God. . . . I understood with pure knowledge that God wants us to become as he is, and that he has invested us with god-like qualities, such as the power of imagination and creation, free will, intelligence, and most of all, the power to love. I understood that he actually wants us to draw on the powers of heaven, and that by believing that we are capable of doing so, we can. (*Embraced by the Light*, p. 61)

Focus on our "schooling"

"I was actually relieved to find that the earth is not our natural home, that we did not originate here. I was gratified to see that the earth is only a temporary place for our schooling" (*Embraced by the Light*, p. 49).

RANELLE WALLACE

Focus on the "simple principles"

RaNelle's grandmother encouraged her to focus on "the simple principles."

My grandmother took my hand, and as we walked through the garden she explained some of the basic purposes of our life on earth, the need to live by the golden rule, the need to help others, the necessity of a Savior, the need to read scriptures and have faith, and I said, "Grandma, I already know this; I learned it all in Sunday school. Why are you teaching it to me again?"

She spoke simply, "It is within the simple principles of the gospel that the mysteries of heaven are found." (*The Burning Within*, pp. 104–5)

RAYMOND A. MOODY JR.

Seek knowledge

NDEers also have newfound respect for knowledge. Some say that this was the result of reviewing their lives. The being of light told them that learning doesn't stop when you die; that knowledge is something you can take with you. Others describe an entire realm of the after life that is set aside for the passionate pursuit of knowledge.

One woman described this place as a big university, where people were involved in deep conversations about the world around them. Another man described this realm as a state of consciousness where whatever you want is available to you. If you think of something you want to learn about, it appears to you and is there for you to learn. He said it was almost as though information was available in bundles of thought.

This includes information of any kind. For instance, if I wanted to know what it was like to be the president of the United States, I would need only to wish for the experience and it would be so. Or if I wanted to know what it was like to be an insect, I would merely have to "request" the experience by wishing for it, and the experience would be mine.

This brief—albeit powerful—learning experience has changed the lives of many NDEers. The short time they were exposed to the possibility of total learning made them thirst for knowledge when they returned to their bodies.

Often, they embark on new careers or take up serious courses of study. None that I know of, however, have pursued knowledge for the sake of knowledge. Rather, they all feel that knowledge is important only if it contributes to the wholeness of the person . . . knowledge is good if it helps make something whole. (*The Light Beyond*, pp. 43–44)

ELISABETH KÜBLER-ROSS

Life is "nothing but a school."

"You will come to know that all your life on earth was nothing but a school that you had to go through in order to pass certain tests and learn special lessons. As soon as you have finished this school and mastered your lessons, you are allowed to go home, to graduate!" (*On Life After Death*, p. 11).

BIBLICAL PERSPECTIVE

Jesus gave His disciples many commandments. Perhaps Matthew 5:48 is an all-encompassing directive: "Be ye therefore perfect, even as your Father which is in heaven is perfect."

Keith A. Haslem

THE CHURCH OF JESUS CHRIST OF LATTER-DAY SAINTS PERSPECTIVE

"Progress toward perfection"

Members of the Church of Jesus Christ of Latter-day Saints believe that achieving perfection is possible, although it will not be achieved during mortality. An official statement issued by the First Presidency of the Church on September 23, 1995, titled "The Family: A Proclamation to the World," reads in part: "In the premortal realm, spirit sons and daughters knew and worshipped God as their Eternal Father and accepted His plan by which His children could obtain a physical body and gain earthly experience to progress toward perfection and ultimately realize their divine destiny as heirs of eternal life."

Members of the Church of Jesus Christ of Latter-day Saints believe there are several specific purposes for mortality.

(1) Obtain a body

Perhaps the most important reason for coming to earth is to obtain a body, and to be obedient to the first commandment given to Adam—to "be fruitful, and multiply, and replenish the earth" (Genesis 1:28). God needs mortals to create bodies for His spirit offspring.

Gaining a body provides experience and knowledge that cannot be obtained in any other way; it is essential in the course of eternal progression of the soul.

For many individuals in this world who die young or who are born into circumstances devoid of opportunities for education of any kind, this one event is sufficient reason for this mortal life. (Consider how many people are born into primitive conditions devoid of an opportunity for growth.) Members of the Church of Jesus Christ of Latter-day Saints believe that opportunities for additional growth and development—for all individuals—will come after mortality.

(2) Learn to love God and keep His Commandments

Members of the Church of Jesus Christ of Latter-day Saints believe, as taught in the Bible, that the "first and great commandment" is "Thou shalt love the Lord thy God with all they heart, and with all thy soul, and with all thy mind" (Matthew 22:37–38).

John quoted Jesus saying, "If ye love me keep my commandments" (John 14:15). Members of the Church of Jesus Christ of Latter-day Saints believe that obedience to the laws and ordinances of Christ's gospel manifests that love for God.

(3) Learn to love all men unconditionally

Jesus told His disciples that the second commandment is "Thou shalt love thy neighbour as thyself" (Matthew 22:39).

Members of the Church of Jesus Christ of Latter-day Saints believe that God loves all men unconditionally, and that our ultimate goal, which is to become like Him, should inspire us to do the same.

(4) Gain knowledge

Members of the Church of Jesus Christ of Latter-day Saints believe that "Whatever principle of intelligence we attain unto in this life, it will rise with us in the resurrection" (Doctrine and Covenants 130:18).

Therefore, members of the Church of Jesus Christ of Latter-day Saints stress education to their members and are encouraged to "teach one another words of wisdom; yea, seek ye out of the best books words of wisdom, seek learning even by study and also by faith" (Doctrine and Covenants 109:7).

(5) "Prepare to meet God"

The Book of Mormon teaches that life is a time to repent and prepare to meet God:

> And we see that death comes upon mankind, yea, the death which has been spoken of by Amulek, which is the temporal death; nevertheless there was a space granted unto man in which he might repent; therefore this life became a probationary state; a time to prepare to meet

Keith A. Haslem

God; a time to prepare for that endless state which has been spoken of by us, which is after the resurrection of the dead. (Alma 12:24)

AUTHOR'S PERSPECTIVE

Seek joy

There is a lot to be done in this life, particularly when you take into account the necessity of making money so you can pay your bills. I try to keep in mind my deathbed, and to do those things which will minimize my regrets at that time—and when I have my Life Review. Paul Tsongas, an American politician, once remarked, "Nobody on his deathbed ever said, 'I wish I had spent more on my business.'"

A Book of Mormon scripture teaches, "Adam fell that men might be; and men are that they might have joy" (2 Nephi 2:25).

I believe that joy comes from cultivated relationships with family and friends and from taking advantage of opportunities to help other people. On the other hand, there are plenty of examples of rich, self-absorbed, miserable people. It has been said that "money only makes misery a little more comfortable."

38

DO WE ALL HAVE "MISSIONS" IN LIFE?

SYNOPSIS

Several of our resources came to understand that they had a particular mission in life that they needed to fulfill. It is reasonable to assume that the same applies to everyone.

BETTY J. EADIE

Betty was informed by a council of twelve men that she should return to earth.

"I had a mission to fulfill."

> [The leader of the council told Betty that she had] died prematurely and must return to the earth. I felt them saying it was important that I return to the earth, that I had a mission to fulfill, but I resisted it in my heart. This was my home, and I felt that nothing they could ever say would ever convince me to leave it. . . .
>
> "You have not completed your mission on earth. . . . You must go back. But, we will not compel you; the choice is yours."
>
> One of the men spoke, also firmly. "Your work is not complete. It is best that you return." (*Embraced by the Light*, p. 111, 117)

RAYMOND A. MOODY JR.

Dr. Moody quotes the experience of a man who came to understand that he had a mission to complete in his life before finally passing on:

Keith A. Haslem

"Go back and complete what you began."

I got up and walked into the hall to go get a drink, and it was at that point, as they found out later, that my appendix ruptured. I became very weak, and I fell down. I began to feel a sort of drifting, a movement of my real being in and out of my body, and to hear beautiful music. I floated on down the hall and out the door onto the screened-in porch. There, it almost seemed that clouds, a pink mist really, began to gather around me, and then I floated right straight on through the screen, just as though it weren't there, and up into this pure crystal clear light, an illuminating white light. It was beautiful and so bright, so radiant, but it didn't hurt my eyes. It's not any kind of light you can describe on earth. I didn't actually see a person in this light, and yet it has a special identity, it definitely does. It is a light of perfect understanding and perfect love.

The thought came to my mind, "Lovest thou me?" This was not exactly in the form of a question, but I guess the connotation of what the light said was, "If you do love me, go back and complete what you began in your life." And all during this time, I felt as though I were surrounded by an overwhelming love and compassion. (*Life After Life*, pp. 62–63)

THE CHURCH OF JESUS CHRIST OF LATTER-DAY SAINTS PERSPECTIVE

SPENCER W. KIMBALL
(twelfth prophet and president of the Church of Jesus Christ of Latter-day Saints)

President Kimball taught:

"We were given certain assignments."

"Before we came [to earth, we] were given certain assignments. . . . While we do not now remember the particulars, this does not alter the glorious reality of what we once agreed to" ("The Role of Righteous Women," *Ensign*, November 1979, 102).

AUTHOR'S PERSPECTIVE

Does everyone have a mission in life? I believe so. Those missions may not be grandiose; they may be as simple as being there to help family members or friends through their trials.

Was it part of the missions of these individuals who had near-death experiences to write them down in order to increase the faith of their readers and provide comfort to them? I believe so.

39

WHY ARE SOME BORN WITH DISABILITIES?

A child born with disabilities, whether physical or mental, usually elicits great grief and sorrow from their family members. The family feels as if this condition will prevent the child from having a full and happy life.

SYNOPSIS

However, the experiences of Betty J. Eadie, Sarah LaNelle Menet, and Elane Durham suggest that such individuals accepted these challenges during their premortal existence because it would give them unique opportunities for personal growth.

BETTY J. EADIE

"He had chosen to enter this world mentally handicapped."

> My attention turned to other spirits making preparations to go to earth. One exceptionally brilliant and dynamic spirit was just entering his mother's womb. He had chosen to enter this world mentally handicapped. He was very excited about this opportunity and was aware of the growth he and his parents would achieve. The three of them had bonded with each other and planned this arrangement long before. (*Embraced by the Light*, pp. 94–95)

SARAH LANELLE MENET

"They come to earth . . . to helps others learn how to love and give service."

Going Home

> I learned that those people who are born mentally handicapped, like children with [Down syndrome], knew that they were going to be born with that challenge and chose to come anyway. Children born with those challenges are very special spirits, already full of tremendous love. They are some of the very best and most noble of God's children. They come to earth primarily to receive a body and help others learn how to love and give service. In reality, it is a great blessing to have one of these children born into your home if they are welcomed and cared for with love and gratitude. They do not have to be tried and tested in ways that we do and are already received into Heavenly Father's highest kingdom. (*There Is No Death*, p. 108)

ELANE DURHAM

"[Those with disabilities go through] . . . a soul-building experience they willingly accept."

"I was also given understanding concerning the suffering of children; orphans of wars, victims of abuse and cruelty, sufferers of poor health or maimed bodies, and those who are born or who become either mentally or physically handicapped. In God's plan their suffering becomes a soul-building experience which they willingly accept" (*I Stand All Amazed*, p. 79).

"Earth life [is] only scant seconds in the eternal scheme of things."

Elane was shown three "powerful spirits" which she understood would come to earth in a diminished capacity; one to have something like Down syndrome, along with another woman, and they *"would grow to adulthood, though their mental abilities would never grow beyond those of twelve to fourteen-year-old children"* (*I Stand All Amazed*, p. 81).

Of the third spirit, Elane writes:

> The third woman . . . had the most profound spirit of all. While all of them were exceptionally powerful, this woman's spirit seemed to be such a powerhouse that it somehow spilled beyond the boundaries of her spirit body. She literally glowed with this power.
>
> Unlike the others, however, she was shown to me as a mortal baby, held in the loving, tender arms of a sweet-faced, bright-haired

Keith A. Haslem

woman whom I could see cherished this child dearly. The woman carried her forward for me to see more closely.

In appearance this child was about three to four months old. She had wispy brown hair, chubby cheeks, and sparkling blue eyes rimmed with darker blue, eyes that reminded me a little of Christ's eyes, they reached out to me from under long, dark lashes. Full of laughter she turned her head to look at me, giving me the sweetest smile in the world, and I thought what a pure delight this child would be to her mortal family!

I could see no handicap to her, and was mildly surprised when the woman holding her declared that she would live out her days as a baby. In explanation I was told that this sweet bundle of sheer happiness would be born without a brain. For all of her earthly life, therefore, she would live as an infant. Yet, without ever speaking a word, the woman assured me, she would deeply affect and bless many hundreds of people.

Wondering why such powerful spirits would agree to mortal lives of such hardship and privation, I was given to understand by the angel that each of these three had agreed to come to earth and gain flesh in this manner, and to endure the subsequent hardships of life, because they understood that, by comparison, earth life was only scant seconds in the eternal scheme of things. They also understood that, if they endured well, then upon death they would receive glorious rewards. The little girl who would live with no brain, for instance, would be immediately transformed upon her death into a perfected spirit being, and would ultimately be given eternal and incredible glory. (*I Stand All Amazed*, pp. 80–82)

AUTHOR'S PERSPECTIVE

Most families with a disabled child will affirm that their initial grief evolved into gratitude, as they recognized their child's exceptional spirit and that their child has taught them many things.

Perhaps, most importantly, the family learns compassion, which is—per all the Witnesses' accounts—the most important trait we can develop during mortality.

40

WHAT IS THE PURPOSE OF HAVING TRIALS AND HARDSHIPS IN LIFE?

SYNOPSIS

Several of our resources learned that we experience difficulties in life for a variety of reasons:

- To help us grow
- To make us wiser
- To give us greater understanding
- To make us stronger
- To make us more compassionate and empathetic of others
- To be better prepared to provide service to others

They also gained the understanding that our suffering, in a relative sense, is only a moment in comparison to our immortal lives. Yet, what we learn from suffering can advance us for the eternities.

Dr. M. Scott Peck shares the insight that life is *supposed* to be difficult, and after that concept is accepted, life is no longer difficult. It simply is what it is.

The best long-term attitude is to view trials more as opportunities than afflictions.

Keith A. Haslem

BETTY J. EADIE

Betty was taught during her experience in the spirit world that

"You needed the negative as well as the positive experiences on earth. Before you can feel joy, you must know sorrow" (*Embraced by the Light*, p. 114).

With this revelation, Betty came to a new understanding:

"Every unhappy experience had allowed me to obtain greater understanding. . . . I saw that the guardian angels remained with me through my trials."

> All of my experiences took on a new meaning. I realized that no real mistakes had been made in my life. Each experience was a tool for me to grow by. Every unhappy experience had allowed me to obtain greater understanding about myself, until I learned to avoid those experiences. I also saw myself growing in ability to help others. I even saw that many of my experiences had been orchestrated by guardian angels. Some experiences were sad and some were joyful, but all were calculated to bring me to higher levels of knowledge. I saw that the guardian angels remained with me through my trials, helping me in any way they could. Sometimes I had many guardian angels around me, sometimes just a few, depending on my needs. (*Embraced by the Light*, pp. 114–15)

Betty learned that even bad experiences can produce positive growth.

"All experiences can be positive."

> "Repentance can be as easy as we make it—or as difficult. When we fall down, we need to get up, dust ourselves off, and get moving again. If we fall down again, even a million times, we still need to keep going; we're growing more than we think. In the spirit world they don't see sin as we do here. All experiences can be positive. All are learning experiences" (*Embraced by the Light*, p. 70).

"Although these experiences may be painful, they can help us grow."

> There are far fewer accidents here than we imagine, especially in things that affect us eternally. The hand of God, and the path we chose before we came here, guide many of our decisions and even

many of the seemingly random experiences we have. . . . Even experiences such as divorce, sudden unemployment, or being victim of violence may ultimately give us knowledge and contribute to our spiritual development. Although these experiences may be painful, they can help us grow.

Under the guidance of the Savior I learned that it was important for me to accept all experience as potentially good. (*Embraced by the Light*, pp. 68–69)

ELANE DURHAM

Elane tells of her trials: having a mother who was incapable of showing her love, a father who sexually abused her, and an abusive first husband.

I was given an understanding of adversities in life and why I go through them. They are rarely a punishment as many people seem to believe. In fact, without adversity and the pain that goes with it, I learned that I wouldn't grow spiritually. God knows that, and it is why He allows me to go through such difficulties as I do. He wants me to become spiritually perfected, and the harsh times in my life serve to *polish* me into a more perfected soul.

This earth with the harshness that it affords kind of gives me a jump-start into the higher spiritual realms if I can learn to look at my pain and grief as growing stages. In other words, my attitude is very important. (*I Stand All Amazed*, p. 43; emphasis added)

As she prepared to return to her body, Elane was told:

"Your suffering . . . is just minutes."

"My angel guide then spoke from beside me . . . [and said] my life after my return would not be easy. 'Here there is perfection,' I was reminded. 'Such perfection does not yet exist on earth. The time of your suffering and growing will seem longer while you are there, but it is just minutes in comparison to how long such growth would take in this higher realm'" (*I Stand All Amazed*, pp. 85–86).

Elane learned that we might have gone to other earths.

"Earth was the most dreaded place to go."

The being with me let me know that earth was the most dreaded place to go, but it was also the place to learn the fastest—because of the

Keith A. Haslem

> adversities. Earth was put here for us to learn, and we are here for that purpose....
>
> In a global sense I knew that there were other galaxies and other worlds. There were other places to live, to learn lessons from. Earth was not the only place where lessons could be learned. In fact, I could have stayed where I was and continued to learn, but not as fast as if I returned to earth. *The hardships and adversities of earth accelerate the learning experience, and those lessons help us to reach a more perfected state.* (quoted in *Life Everlasting*, p. 120)

Elane came to understand that adversity in life is necessary if we are to grow spiritually.

As she concludes her book, she contemplates:

"I'm not sure I'd change anything at all."

> At times I think back and ask myself—If I could change anything in my life, what would it be? And having thought about it, I'm not sure I'd change anything at all. Without the pain of my early years, I would have never learned the lessons I needed to learn for the later years.... Without the hardships in life, how would we grow into more perfect people and learn the lessons from which we need to chart our own pathways in life?
>
> No, I think I'd keep everything just as it happened in my life, and I'll spend the rest of it trying to make it better. I've learned that the riches of this world aren't in what I own, but rather in who I am and what I give away. The question I've learned to ask myself, then, is what makes me most happy? I guess I'll know if I've answered it correctly when I go home for good—and I'm looking forward to that day. (*I Stand All Amazed*, pp. 164–65)

SARAH LANELLE MENET

Sarah, who was also terribly abused as a child by her father, addresses the question: why do good people suffer?

"God ... allows unpleasant things to happen to us because of the growth, understanding, and strength we will gain."

> One of the questions I asked while on the hill was, "Why did I have to suffer so much pain during my life, especially at the hands of my father?" The reply was that nothing any of us suffer in this life would

be more than we could stand, and that in every hardship a way is provided to deal with it or to overcome it. Our lives on earth, the things that we experience of good and bad, are designed especially to help us grow and are all part of a great plan for us. . . .

God also allows unpleasant things to happen to us because of the growth, understanding, and strength we will gain. For example, without misery there would be no compassion. Without pain we would not appreciate well-being. God does not interfere with our individual agency to choose good or evil. He does not "cause" bad things to happen to us but allows us to learn our greatest abilities and strengths through adversity. I learned that it is very important for us to understand pain and suffering and that this was one of the reasons we came to earth. I know that as spirits, before coming to earth, we didn't understand physical pain. (*There Is No Death*, pp. 99–100)

"Very little [of what happens in our lives] is by accident."

Almost everything that happens to us in our lives, including every person that we meet, is part of a plan for each one of us. Very little of it is by accident. Our lives and the surrounding circumstances are all part of a huge plan that we are a part of. What we do and how we react when those trials happen is up to us, and so the choices we make have a great deal to do with it as well. But there are forces working hard to arrange circumstances for us and then influence our decisions in responding to them. Both good and evil spirits pull strings in our lives to make events happen. Do you think you could travel down all these paths throughout your life and by coincidence run into just the right person at just the right time, in just the right place, without some help? God arranges things so everything that happens to us can work for our benefit, if we allow it to.

The trials of my life have allowed me to help hundreds of people who are going through similar experiences. I do not ever look at any hardship in my life and think of it as horrible anymore. The Lord does not give us these experience as punishments or even necessarily as trials. We suffer the natural consequences of our actions. However, the Lord orchestrates the outcome for our benefit and learning allowing us an opportunity to overcome adversity. (*There Is No Death*, pp. 115–16)

Keith A. Haslem

ELISABETH KÜBLER-ROSS

"Nothing that comes to you is negative."

> All the hardships that you face in life, all the trials and tribulations, all the nightmares and all the losses, most people view as a curse, as a punishment by God, as something negative. If you would only realize that nothing that comes to you is negative. I mean nothing. All the trials and tribulations, the greatest losses, things that make you say, "If I had known about this I would never have been able to make it through," are gifts to you. It's like somebody has to temper the iron. It is an opportunity that you are given to grow. This is the sole purpose of existence on this beautiful earth. You will not grow if you sit in a beautiful flower garden and somebody brings you gorgeous food on a silver platter. But you will grow if you are sick, if you are in pain, if you experience losses, and if you do not put your head in the sand but take the pain and learn to accept it not as a curse, or a punishment, but as a gift to you with a very, very specific purpose. (*On Life After Death*, p. 22)

MELVIN L. MORSE

One of Dr. Morse's subjects, after having a near-death experience, told him that the experience taught her that *"grief is growth"* (*Closer to the Light*, p. 204).

DUANE S. CROWTHER

Duane quotes a woman who had undergone a near-death experience resulting from an automobile accident.

"It's how you accept [your trials]. That's the real test."

> "One night as I was saying my prayers and thanking my Father in Heaven for all the blessings He had given me and for the miracles that had come into my life, a small voice came to me and said, 'It really doesn't matter what your trials or tests may be here on earth. It's how you accept them. That's the real test'" (*Life Everlasting*, p. 76).

M. SCOTT PECK

In his book *The Road Less Traveled*, Dr. Peck offers remarkable insight as to the purpose of life in the very first line in his book: "Life is difficult." The implication of his statement is that life is *supposed* to be difficult. Having acknowledged this reality, we can then "transcend" it; therefore, "The fact that life is difficult no longer matters."

> Life is difficult.
>
> This is a great truth, one of the greatest truths.* It is a great truth because once we truly see this truth, we transcend it. Once we truly know that life is difficult—once we truly understand and accept it—then life is no longer difficult. Because once it is accepted, the fact that life is difficult no longer matters.
>
> Most do not fully see this truth that life is difficult. Instead they moan more or less incessantly, noisily or subtly, about the enormity of their problems, their burdens, and their difficulties as if life were generally easy, as if life *should* be easy. They voice their belief, noisily or subtly, that their difficulties represent a unique kind of affliction that should not be and that has somehow been especially visited upon them.... I know about this moaning because I have done my share.
>
> Life is a series of problems. Do we want to moan about them or solve them? Do we want to teach our children to solve them?
>
> Discipline ... is the basic set of tools we require to solve life's problems....
>
> It is in this whole process of meeting and solving problems that life has its meaning.... It is only because of problems that we grow mentally and spiritually.... As Benjamin Franklin said, "Those things that hurt, instruct." (*The Road Less Traveled*, pp. 3–5)

* In a footnote, Dr. Peck notes that Buddha taught that the first of the Four Noble Truths was "Life is suffering."

BIBLICAL PERSPECTIVE

God told the Old Testament prophet Isaiah: "Behold, I have refined thee ... in the furnace of affliction" (Isaiah 48:10).

The Apostle Peter taught, "That the trial of your faith, being much more precious than of gold" (1 Peter 1:7).

The Apostle Paul taught: "Now no chastening for the present seemeth to be joyous, but grievous: nevertheless afterward it yieldeth

Keith A. Haslem

the peaceable fruit of righteousness unto them which are exercised thereby" (Hebrews 12:11).

THE CHURCH OF JESUS CHRIST OF LATTER-DAY SAINTS PERSPECTIVE

HENRY B. EYRING
(an apostle for the Church of Jesus Christ of Latter-day Saints, 1995–)

In a message to church membership in the July 2017 edition of the *Ensign*, President Henry B. Eyring, First Counselor in First Presidency of the Church of Jesus Christ of Latter-day Saints, gave a message titled, "The Reward of Enduring Well." He wrote,

Becoming "polished"

> We all have trials to face—at times, very difficult trials. We know that the Lord allows us to go through trials in order for us to be *polished* and perfected so we can be with Him forever. . . .
>
> But a loving God has not set such tests before us simply to see if we can endure difficulty but rather to see if we can endure them well and so become *polished*. . . .
>
> Our trials and our difficulties give us the opportunity to learn and grow, and they may even change our very nature. If we can turn to the Savior in our extremity, our souls can be *polished* as we endure.
>
> Therefore, the first thing to remember is to pray always.
>
> The second thing is to strive continuously to keep the commandments—whatever the opposition, the temptation, or the tumult around us.
>
> The third crucial thing to do is to serve the Lord. . . .
>
> I promise you that the Lord will come to your aid in your trials if you seek and serve Him and that your soul will be *polished* in the process. I challenge you to put your trust in Him in all your adversities. (pp. 4–5; emphasis added)

Going Home

DIETER F. UCHTDORF
(an apostle for the Church of Jesus Christ of Latter-day Saints, 2004–)

President Uchtdorf, as a member of the First Presidency of the Church of Jesus Christ of Latter-day Saints, taught:

God can carry you when your need is greatest.

> God . . . allows adversity to test the just and the unjust. In fact, sometimes it seems that our lives are more difficult because we are trying to live our faith.
>
> No, following the Savior will not remove all of your trials. However, it will remove the barriers between you and the help your Heavenly Father wants to give you. God will be with you. He will direct your steps. He will walk beside you and even carry you when your need is greatest. ("A Yearning for Home," *Ensign*, November 2017)

MY AUNT CAROL

My sweet Aunt Carol lost her husband in 1982 as the result of a fiery truck crash. She suffered third degree burns over most of her upper body and underwent many painful surgeries as the doctors tried to rebuild her beautiful face that had been burned away. She also lost her wonderful husband.

Despite this, Aunt Carol remained a positive person and has spoken in more than five hundred meetings since that tragic day, promoting a message of faith and encouragement to people struggling with their own trials.

In one such meeting, she intimated that she did not begrudge the difficulties of the last thirty-five years: "If someone were to come to me and say they could reverse everything that had happened and put everything back to 'normal' I would say 'no way.' It has been just a super blessing in our lives. . . . [God] loves us enough to let us have these experiences to help us grow."

Happily, for my Aunt Carol, she was able to be reunited with her husband, her daughter, my own dear mother, her parents, and many other family members.

Keith A. Haslem

AUTHOR'S PERSPECTIVE

Based upon my own personal experience and my personal faith, I believe that there is divine purpose in all our sufferings and trials.

Develop faith in God

I believe the foremost value of experiencing trials in life is to help us realize that we are, ultimately, dependent upon God. This dependence is fundamental to the biblical teaching that we need to accept Jesus Christ as our Savior, and have faith in His Atonement.

It has been said, "There are no atheists in foxholes." The trials of life are our own personal "foxholes" where we are given opportunity to look to God in faith that He will help us through whatever difficult situation we may be in.

With faith our whole attitudes can change from bemoaning a trial to embracing the challenge—confident that ultimate success, with God's help, is assured.

Develop character

As we are successful, with God's help, in getting through difficult times—without becoming bitter or cynical—we develop more confidence in God's love for us, His willingness to help us, and our own strength to overcome difficult times.

Develop compassion

Having successfully overcome a difficult situation will make us more compassionate and empathetic to others who may be going through trials. For example, how many recovered abuse victims become victim advocates and become actively involved in helping such victims?

Develop wisdom

Many of the difficulties we find ourselves in are of our own making, the natural consequences of foolish decisions. When the price of such foolishness is finally paid we have acquired a wisdom we didn't have before, and are in a position to counsel others so they can avoid the unhappy consequences of such decisions.

41

DID WE SIGN UP FOR OUR TRIALS IN THE PREMORTAL WORLD?

Previously, we discussed the concept that some people born with disabilities had chosen, while in the premortal world, to be born with those limitations. One might ask whether we all had the opportunity to assent to certain trials during mortality.

SYNOPSIS

Betty J. Eadie, Sarah LaNelle Menet, and Elane Durham learned that during our premortal lives we were shown some of the hardships we would face—to see if we were willing to accept them.

BETTY J. EADIE

"We had actually chosen many of our weaknesses and difficult situations."

> I was told that we had all desired to come here [to the earth], that we had actually chosen many of our weaknesses and difficult situations in our lives so that we could grow. I also understood that sometimes we were given weaknesses which would be for our good. The Lord also gives us gifts and talents according to his will. We should never compare our talents or weaknesses to another's. We each have what we need; we are unique. Equality of spiritual weaknesses or gifts is not important. (*Embraced by the Light*, pp. 89–90)

Keith A. Haslem

"We were very willing, even anxious . . . to accept all of our ailments, illnesses."

To my surprise I saw that most of us had selected the illnesses we would suffer, and for some, the illness that would end our lives. . . . All experience is for our good, and sometimes it takes what we would consider negative experience to help develop our spirits. We were very willing, even anxious, as spirits to accept all of our ailments, illnesses, and accidents here to help better ourselves spiritually. I understood that in the spirit world our earth time is meaningless. The pain we experience on earth is just a moment, just a split second of consciousness in the spirit world, and we are very willing to endure it. Our deaths are also often calculated to help us grow. When a person dies of cancer, for example, he will often experience a long, painful death that may give him opportunities for growth that he cannot get otherwise. (*Embraced by the Light*, pp. 67–68)

"Each of us is receiving more help than we know."

We are where we need to be.
    As all of these things came to me, I understood the perfection of the plan. I saw that we all volunteered for our positions and stations in the world, and that each of us is receiving more help than we know. I saw the unconditional love of God, beyond any earthly love, radiating from him to all his children. (*Embraced by the Light*, p. 53)

SARAH LANELLE MENET

"I had been shown how difficult this journey would be . . . [and chose] to come anyway."

As we made this choice, we were shown some of what our life on earth would be like. We were given small glimpses into our future life. God could somehow look into the future and show some of the things that would happen to us. He was able, to a great degree, to show us some of the joys, some of the suffering, and some of the challenges we would face. Even with that we were still excited for the opportunity to come to earth and experience mortality.
    . . . I understood that I had been shown how difficult this journey would be, and I had chosen to come anyway. As a spirit I understood that the greater the trials were, the greater the growth and learning

would be. Terrible problems looked like exciting challenges that we would surely be able to overcome. Of course the actual experiences here on earth seem much harder than they looked on our "preview screen." Seeing a movie where someone is hurt or in pain is very different from actually feeling the pain ourselves. (*There Is No Death*, p. 105)

ELANE DURHAM

"I had been shown . . . specific trials I would need to endure."

I could see myself as an adult spirit seated together with three other spirit beings, with two angels standing close by. . . .

My angel guide helped me understand that in the scene before me I was at the point of getting ready to enter earth, and that I had already helped choose the lessons I would like to learn from my stay in mortality. To learn these particular lessons, I had been shown specific circumstances I would encounter, and specific trials I would need to endure. These, if I made correct choices and appropriate responses to them, would provide the soul-growth I desired. And that was how everything in that realm was looked at, in terms of soul or spiritual growth. Not just our own, I knew, but everyone else's as well. I saw that we were all sincerely interested in helping everyone else, and in working harmoniously with each other for spiritual growth. This was true even though such a concept seems quite foreign here. (*I Stand All Amazed*, pp. 82–83)

"'Are you sure?'"

As I watched myself . . . one of the other spirit beings asked if I was sure that I could deal with so many trials and difficulties. Apparently he thought I was taking on a pretty heavy load.

"Yes," I told him.

"Are you sure?" he asked again.

"Yes," I responded firmly.

"This is how it must be for her," one of the teaching angels then declared, "if she is to accomplish all that she wants to do on earth." (*I Stand All Amazed*, p. 84)

Elane's angel-guide told her:

"Your suffering . . . is just minutes [in comparison to eternity]."

Keith A. Haslem

"The time of your suffering and growing will seem longer while you are there, but it is just minutes in comparison to how long such growth would take in this higher realm" (*I Stand All Amazed*, pp. 85–86).

Elane did have a difficult life. As a child, her mother seemingly did not know how to show her any love, and her father sexually abused her. On top of that, her first marriage was to an abusive husband.

DUANE S. CROWTHER

In his book *Life Everlasting*, Duane S. Crowther cites the near-death experience of Delynn, a victim of cystic fibrosis.

During Delynn's experience, he asked his escort:

> Why was it necessary for me to suffer so? . . . I kept all the commandments. Why me?
>
> Then I received a most startling answer: He said to me: "You chose your disease and the amount of pain you would be willing to suffer before this life—when you were in a premortal state. It was your choice. . . ."
>
> When he told me that it was my choice, in a premortal environment, to suffer when I came to earth, I was both astonished and incredulous. He must have understood my incredulity, because I was immediately transported to my premortal existence.

DeLynn then saw himself in his premortal state, where he was being instructed prior to coming to earth.

"Learn dignity in suffering. . . . I was now able to look upon my [cystic fibrosis] as my truest mentor."

> [An angel instructor] was instructing us about things we had to know in order to come to earth and get our bodies. Then he said, and I'll never forget this: "You can learn lessons one of two ways. You can move through life slowly, and have certain experiences, or there are ways that you can learn lessons very quickly through pain and disease." He wrote on the board the words: Cystic Fibrosis, and he turned and asked for volunteers. I was a volunteer; I saw me raise my hand and offer to take the challenge. The instructor looked at me and agreed to accept me.
>
> That was the end of the scene, and it changed forever my perspective of the disease that I previously felt was a plague on my life.

No longer did I consider myself a victim. Rather, I was a privileged participant, by choice, in an eternal plan. That plan, if I measured up to the potential of my choice, would allow me to advance in mortal life in the fastest way possible.... The specific choice of cystic fibrosis was to help me learn dignity in suffering.... I no longer felt picked on because of my pain and illness. I understood the choices I had made and the reasons for them. And I understood the tremendous love that God had for me to allow me to make those choices—and to suffer pain.

The realization that this was all by my choice had an enormous rejuvenating effect on me. I was no longer a victim of chance, or worse yet, of some punishment for wrong doing. In the broadest sense, I now saw myself as a master of my own destiny—if I lived up to the possibilities of my choices. Instead of looking at cystic fibrosis as a severe disability, I was now able to look on it as my truest mentor. (*Life Everlasting*, pp. 102–3)

AUTHOR'S PERSPECTIVE

Is God malicious?

If God *can* see the future and show it to those in the premortal world, why would He *not* do so? By doing so, He would obtain the agreement of those He perceives would grow the most by being set on a particular path.

Although life is difficult, the Witnesses learned that God has provided us with heavenly resources, although we may not be aware of it. (See Chapter 44 on guardian angels.)

You *can* handle it

The Bible teaches "There hath no temptation taken you but such as is common to man: but God is faithful, who will not suffer you to be tempted above that ye are able; but will with the temptation also make a way to escape, that ye may be able to bear it" (1 Corinthians 10:13).

My interpretation of that verse would be that God does not ask us to go through anything that He knows we can't handle.

It's been said, "Whatever doesn't kill you makes you stronger." If we know we *can* handle it, and that we aren't going to be "killed," then a trial is simply an opportunity to become stronger.

Keith A. Haslem

So rather than be a "victim" with a pity-poor-me attitude, the better approach would be a competitive refuse-to-lose attitude, knowing that we can bear it and ultimately overcome.

And when that battle is won, you may as well get ready for the next one because that is what life is all about. Other than periodic brief respites, the real rest comes when we go home.

So no one need feel "picked on" because life is difficult for everyone. The only relevant question is how will we respond to our particular trials and what can be gained from the experiences?

AUTHOR'S NOTE

Appendix B: "Inspiring Books" lists the accounts of a number of individuals who endured tremendous trials in their lives and did so with courage and grace.

42

HOW LONG IS OUR MORTAL LIFE IN COMPARISON TO OUR IMMORTAL LIFE?

SYNOPSIS

Sarah LaNelle Menet, Elane Durham, and Elisabeth Kübler-Ross all point out that, on a relative scale, our mortal lives are like minutes compared to our eternal lives.

ELANE DURHAM

As she prepared to return to her body, Elane was told:

"The time of your suffering . . . is just minutes . . . in comparison."

> My angel guide then spoke from beside me . . . [and said] my life after my return would not be easy. "Here there is perfection," I was reminded. "Such perfection does not yet exist on earth. The time of your suffering and growing will seem longer while you are there, but it is just minutes in comparison to how long such growth would take in this higher realm." (*I Stand All Amazed*, pp. 85–86)

SARAH LANELLE MENET

"We are only here on earth for a relatively short span."

Keith A. Haslem

"We spent thousands of years as spirits before coming to earth, and we will spend millions more in the spirit world and beyond after we leave this existence. We are only here on earth for a relatively short span, which seems like a few minutes to everyone in the spirit world" (*There Is No Death*, p. 96).

ELISABETH KÜBLER-ROSS

"On the other side, one minute could be equal to one hundred years of our earth time."

"This time that you are in a physical body, is a very, very short span of your total existence. It's a very important time because you are here for a very special purpose which is yours and yours alone" (*On Life After Death*, p. 18).

"For those on the other side, one minute could be equal to one hundred years of our earth time" (*On Life After Death*, pp. 8–9).

AUTHOR'S PERSPECTIVE

Life is the opportunity to make the best investment ever.

I see this life as an investment—the best investment we could ever make. The investment we make is the effort to overcome the trials that come our way, to seek knowledge, to grow, and to develop unconditional love. That effort is akin to only a few moments, but the dividends—a wonderful realm in which to live—will continue for eternity.

And we have great investment advisors. The Lord has provided plenty of resources (in the form of guardian angels—see Chapter 44) to guide us through the perplexities of our investment program.

So however hard this life—the short run—is, it can be so worth it, in the long run.

43

DO ADDICTIONS GO WITH US TO THE SPIRIT WORLD?

SYNOPSIS

In his account, George G. Ritchie observed spirits of deceased people who were seemingly still addicted to cigarettes or alcohol.

GEORGE G. RITCHIE JR.

"Begged her . . . as though she wanted it more than anything in the world."

> I noticed this phenomenon repeatedly, people unaware of others right beside them. I saw a group of assembly-line workers gathered around a coffee canteen. One of the women asked another for a cigarette, begged her in fact, as though she wanted it more than anything in the world. But the other one, chatting with her friends, ignored her. She took a pack of cigarettes from her overalls, and without ever offering it to the woman who reached for it so eagerly, took one out and lit it. Fast as a striking snake the woman who had been refused snatched at the lighted cigarette in the other's mouth. Again she grabbed at it. And again. . . .
>
> With a little chill of recognition I saw she was unable to grip it.
>
> (*Return from Tomorrow*, p. 56–57)

George Ritchie observed others spirits who had apparently developed other addictions.

"[They had] a dependence on alcohol that went beyond physical. . . . That became mental . . . spiritual."

Keith A. Haslem

> At this point the Light drew me inside a dingy bar and grill near what seemed to be a large naval base. A crowd of people, many of them sailors, lined the bar three deep, while others jammed wooden booths along the wall. Though a few were drinking beer, most of them seemed to be belting whiskeys as fast as the two perspiring bartenders could pour them.
>
> Then I notice a striking thing. A number of men standing at the bar seemed unable to lift their drinks to their lips. Over and over I watched them clutch at their shot glasses, hands passing through the solid tumblers, through the heavy wooden counter top, through the very arms and bodies of the drinkers around them. (*Return from Tomorrow*, p. 59)

Dr. Ritchie concluded that these spirits

> had developed a dependence on alcohol that went beyond the physical. That became mental. Spiritual, even. Then when they lost that body . . . they would be cut off for all eternity from the thing they could never stop craving.
>
> An eternity like that—the thought sent a chill shuddering through me—surely that would be a form of hell. . . . To want most, to burn with the most desire, where you were most powerless—that would be hell indeed. (*Return from Tomorrow*, p. 61)

AUTHOR'S PERSPECTIVE

For those spirits with lingering physical addictions, I wonder if breaking those addictions might not be possible until the reuniting of the spirit with the body. According to the doctrine of the Church of Jesus Christ of Latter-day Saints, that reuniting—the resurrection of all men—won't be completed until a thousand years after the Second Coming of Christ.

44

DO WE ALL HAVE GUARDIAN ANGELS?

Life is difficult, but it's only logical that a loving God would have a system in place to help His children through difficult times.

Most people of faith believe in guardian angels, but may not understand the breadth of their involvement in our lives. Several of the Witnesses make reference to these heavenly helpers.

SYNOPSIS

Betty J. Eadie, Elane Durham, George G. Ritchie, and Elisabeth Kübler-Ross wrote about the role of guardian angels in everyone's lives. In reality, these unseen beings do much more than warn us of danger. They provide assistance in the everyday matters of life—prompting us to do or not do things that will make a difference to our well-being. They might be compared to a best friend who is *always* with you, who loves you, and who is trying to help you in any way possible—and having incredible abilities to do so.

These spirit guides can provide comfort and guidance and can open doors of opportunity and orchestrate positive experiences.

The most common way these heavenly helpers communicate with us is through feelings or thoughts that come into our minds; these thoughts can easily be mistaken for ideas of our own.

BETTY J. EADIE

Betty witnessed that guardian angels attended to all people on earth.

"We are all precious and carefully watched over."

Keith A. Haslem

When the heavens scrolled back, I saw the earth with its billions of people on it. I saw them scrambling for existence, making mistakes, experiencing kindness, finding love, grieving for death, and I saw angels hovering above them. The angels knew the people by name and watched over them closely. They cheered when good was done and were saddened by mistakes. They hovered about to help and give direction and protection. I saw that we could literally call down thousands of angels to our aid if we ask in faith. I saw that we are all equal in their eyes, great or small, talented or handicapped, leaders or followers, saints or sinners. We are all precious and carefully watched over. Their love never fails us.

No one is insignificant in the eternities. Every soul is of infinite worth. (*Embraced by the Light*, p. 121)

"Doors of opportunity were opened to me [by my guardian angels]."

Many of my experiences had been orchestrated by guardian angels . . . all were calculated to bring me to higher levels of knowledge. . . .

. . . The more I learned, the more doors of opportunity were opened to me. . . . Many things I thought I had done by myself were shown to have been extended by divine help. (*Embraced by the Light*, p. 115)

ELANE DURHAM

"Minister to my needs throughout my life"

"This teaching angel then let me know that he and the other one had always been 'with' me, or very aware of me, and that they would continue to minister to my needs throughout my life on earth. I would have their protection whenever I needed it, and at times I would even recognize that they were near" (*I Stand All Amazed*, p. 84).

GEORGE G. RITCHIE

Dr. Ritchie tells of an experience he had in the war where his life was preserved as a result of a spiritual prompting. He was stationed in

France and had received a one-day pass to go to Rheims. That morning he had written a letter to his wife Marguerite.

"Get off this carrier."

> I climbed into the back of one [of the carriers taking the soldiers to Rheims] and took my seat between my two friends. . . . We were waiting for the other carrier to fill when something deep inside me placed a thought in my mind, "Get off of this carrier and go write Marguerite a letter."
>
> "This is absolutely ridiculous. I have just written her a letter. I have fought too hard to get this pass into Rheims and besides, what will my friends, whom I had talked into going with me, think?" Again the voice deep inside me: "I said, get off and go write Marguerite a letter."
>
> But I wanted to see the Cathedral of Rheims and I ignored the second warning. The third repeat order was so loud in my mind I was afraid my friends could hear it. Looking utterly confused and surprising them when I arose, I tried to make some plausible explanation as I was leaving the truck . . . the top sergeant was even more surprised when I handed him my pass.
>
> The young soldier picked by the sergeant to fill my place took my seat between my two buddies. The carrier had not gone eight miles from the hospital when it hit a land mine that the Germans had planted in the road. It blew the carrier over, instantly killing the soldier who took my place and causing severe injuries to my buddies. (*My Life After Dying*, pp. 44–45)

ELISABETH KÜBLER-ROSS

Based upon her many years of studying and interacting with individuals who were dying or had had near-death experiences, Dr. Elisabeth Kübler-Ross believes that we all have guardian angels, who will also help us "in the transition . . . to life after death." She comments,

"Every human being . . . is guided by a spirit entity."

> What the church tells little children about guardian angels is based on fact. There is proof that every human being, from his birth until his

death, is guided by a spirit entity. Everyone has such a spirit guide, whether you believe it or not. . . .

It is important to know that every single human being, from the moment of birth until the moment when we make the transition and end this physical existence, is in the presence of these guides or guardian angels who will wait for us and help us in the transition from life to life after death. Also, we will always be met by those who preceded us in death who we have loved. (*On Life After Death*, p. 9, 51)

SARAH HINZE

In her book *Coming from the Light*, Sarah Hinze relates the account of Sarah Skidmore, a three-year-old girl who was kidnapped in Arizona on October 7, 1986. After she was returned to her family, Sarah told her parents that she was helped by a "shining girl" in the desert after she was released by her abductor.

On a normal Tuesday in October, Sarah was taken from her family's car. Sarah's distraught parents—Mark and Rhonda—reported the kidnapping to the police and an intense media coverage began with the hopes that the kidnapper would let Sarah go.

As Mark and Rhonda prayed for the safe return of their daughter, Mark said the following words, which he felt were not his own: "Sarah is alive and well. She is protected from evil and the deeds of evil men. There are angels attending her and protecting her from harm. . . . Sarah will return to you and grow up in your household and be your little girl again" (*Coming from the Light*, p. 114).

Three days later, Sarah was discovered in the desert by a hunter, who took her to a local hospital, where she was reunited with her parents.

They learned that the kidnapper had abused her for "probably less than an hour" then let her out of the truck. She had found shelter under some trees near the road and remained there. Her mother recounts:

> When it got dark she went to sleep. Awakening when it was still dark, Sarah was alone and scared. She then saw a small child in the desert. The child had short, blond hair and slightly resembled her little sister Heather. The little girl was wearing a white robe that looked like a T-shirt. She was surrounded or encircled by a brilliant light. Sarah thought the leaves of the trees would catch fire because it was so bright. When later asked how she could see this personage, Sarah

said, "In my eyes. She wasn't really in the desert, but she wasn't in my mind either. I didn't pretend. I could see her in my eyes." The shining girl of comfort just stood there and smiled but did not speak to her aloud. Sarah stayed by the trees for two days, as she was constantly attended to by her comforting little friend.

While in the hospital, Sarah told her parents:

"I saw Heather playing in the desert."

"I saw Heather playing in the desert," referring to her desert companion. We did not understand at the time what Sarah meant. We knew she could not have seen Heather because Heather was with us from the time Sarah was taken. . . . The first words she spoke were about this comforting friend who looked like her little sister.

It would be over three years before the identity of Sarah's shining guardian angel in the desert was discovered.

"Jessica . . . was my shining friend in the desert!"

When we gradually returned to a semi-normal family life, about a year after Sarah's ordeal, a baby sister, Jessica, was born. As Jessica grew, she had blond hair. When Jessica was nearly three years old, Sarah stopped suddenly one day and looked at her little sister intently. Then she became excited as a look of amazement came over her face. "Mommy," she said, "it was Jessica in the desert. Her hair is the same as it was then. She is the same size now. . . . She was my helper. Jessica was my shining friend in the desert!" (*Coming from the Light*, pp. 111–19)

BIBLICAL PERSPECTIVE

During Old Testament times, the King of Syria "warred against Israel" (2 Kings 6:8), and at one point, they had Israel surrounded.

"They that be with us are more than they that be with them."

An host compassed the city both with horses and with chariots. And [the prophet's servant] said unto him, Alas, my master! how shall we do?

And he answered, Fear not: for they that be with us are more than they that be with them.

And Elisha prayed, and said, Lord, I pray thee, open his eyes, that he may see. And the Lord opened the eyes of the young man; and he saw: and, behold, the mountain was full of horses and chariots of fire round about Elisha. (2 Kings 6:15–17)

In the New Testament, Jesus warns against abusing children.

"Their angels"

"Take heed that ye despise not one of these little ones; for I say unto you, That in heaven their angels do always behold the face of my Father which is in heaven" (Matthew 18:10).

Does God love children more than adults? I think not. If little children have angels assigned to them then it's logical that adults also have "their angels."

THE COKEVILLE MIRACLE

On May 16, 1986, David Young and his wife entered an elementary school in Cokeville, Wyoming, with a homemade bomb. They held 156 children and teachers hostage. Eventually the bomb went off. All of the hostages survived. Richard Haskell, a bomb expert, made the following comment: "To say it was a miracle would be the understatement of the century" (*Trial by Terror*, Wixom, p. 144).

Many of the surviving children told their parents about communicating with angels who told them what to do to be safe. Several of the children identified their angels using pictures of long-deceased family members.

A movie called *The Cokeville Miracle* was released in 2015 depicting this event.

THE CHURCH OF JESUS CHRIST OF LATTER-DAY SAINTS PERSPECTIVE

JEFFREY R. HOLLAND
(an apostle for the Church of Jesus Christ of Latter-day Saints, 1994–)

Elder Holland addressed the membership of the Church of Jesus Christ of Latter-day Saints in the October 2008 general conference. In his talk titled, "The Ministry of Angels," he taught:

"[Angels] are always near. . . . God never leaves us alone, never leaves us unaided."

> From the beginning down through the dispensations, God has used angels as His emissaries in conveying love and concern for his children. Time in this setting does not allow even a cursory examination of the scriptures or our own latter-day history, which are so filled with accounts of angels ministering to those on earth, but it is rich doctrine and rich history indeed.
>
> Usually such beings are not seen. Sometimes they are. But seen or unseen they are always near. Sometimes their assignments are very grand and have significance for the whole world. Sometimes the messages are more private. Occasionally the angelic purpose is to warn. But most often it is to comfort, to provide some form of merciful attention, guidance in difficult times. . . .
>
> My beloved brothers and sisters, I testify of angels, both the heavenly and the mortal kind [referring to kind people who are anxious to serve one another]. In doing so I am testifying that God never leaves us alone, never leaves us unaided in the challenges we face. . . . And always there are those angels who come and go all around us, seen and unseen, known and unknown, mortal and immortal. (Holland, "Like a Broken Vessel")

Keith A. Haslem

DALLIN H. OAKS
(an apostle for the Church of Jesus Christ of Latter-day Saints, 1984–)

Elder Dallin H. Oaks addressed the membership of the Church of Jesus Christ of Latter-day Saints in the October 1998 general conference. His talk was titled "The Aaronic Priesthood and the Sacrament." In it, he taught: "Angelic messages can be delivered by a voice or merely by thoughts or feelings communicated to the mind. . . . Most angelic communications are felt or heard rather than seen" (Oaks, "The Aaronic Priesthood and the Sacrament").

JOSEPH F. SMITH
(sixth prophet and president of the Church of Jesus Christ of Latter-day Saints)

Our guardian angels are our kindred or friends.

Joseph F. Smith said, "We are told by the Prophet Joseph Smith, that 'there are no angels who minister to this earth but those who do belong or have belonged to it.' Hence, when messengers are sent to minister to the inhabitants of this earth, they are not strangers, but from the ranks of our kindred, friends, and fellow-beings and fellow-servants" (*Gospel Doctrine*, p. 435).

Speaking of those who are spreading the gospel of Jesus Christ, scriptures of the Church of Jesus Christ of Latter-day Saints record a promise of the Lord.

"Mine angels round about you, to bear you up."

"And whoso receiveth you, there I will be also, for I will go before your face. I will be on your right hand and on your left, and my Spirit shall be in your hearts, and mine angels round about you, to bear you up" (Doctrine and Covenants 84:88).

Can the wicked and rebellious count on the assistance of guardian angels?

Might a guardian angel be repelled by conduct offensive to God? Would a father force his benevolence upon a son who wants nothing to do with him and is willfully rebellious?

In the Book of Mormon, the Lord chastised the brother of Jared, who had not been praying faithfully:

"My Spirit will not always strive with man."

"And the Lord said unto him: I will forgive thee and thy brethren of their sins; but thou shalt not sin any more, for ye shall remember that my Spirit will not always strive with man; wherefore, if ye will sin until ye are fully ripe ye shall be cut off from the presence of the Lord" (Ether 2:15).

AUTHOR'S PERSPECTIVE

Perhaps a more descriptive label than guardian angel would be ministering angel. I believe that everyone is entitled to one or more such spirits—not only to help protect them but to guide them in every aspect of their lives, including giving inspiration regarding daily decisions and offering comfort when needed.

After all, we can still learn from adversity without "going it alone."

45

HOW SHOULD WE PRAY?

SYNOPSIS

The importance of prayer is universally recognized, but perhaps is not correctly applied.

Betty J. Eadie learned that God doesn't refuse to answer our prayers until we have asked Him a minimum number of times. Indeed, to endlessly ask for the same blessing is more a "demonstration of doubt" than an exhibition of faith.

Spencer W. Kimball suggested that God answers our prayers by inspiring people around us to help us.

Gordon B. Hinckley expressed his faith when he said: "Things have a way of working out."

BETTY J. EADIE

Prayer is not "an exercise of hours."

> I was told that there is no greater prayer than that of a mother for her children.
>
> I understood that once our prayers of desire have been released, we need to let go of them and trust in the power of God to answer them. He knows our needs at all times and is simply waiting for an invitation to help us.
>
> This all seemed so simple—too simple at first. I had always thought prayer was an exercise of hours. I thought that we had to nag the Lord and to continue nagging him until something happened. (*Embraced by the Light*, p. 104)

Going Home

Betty came to understand that nagging, begging, and bargaining with the Lord were actually *"demonstrations of doubt"* (*Embraced by the Light*, p. 106).

"I saw that it was never necessary for me to repeat my requests unremittingly, as though he couldn't understand. Faith and patience are needed" (*Embraced by the Light*, pp. 106–7; emphasis added).

Gratitude for our blessings is important: "The more we thank God for the blessings we receive, the more we open the way for further blessings" (*Embraced by the Light*, p. 107).

God doesn't intervene in our lives unless we request it.

"We were given agency to act for ourselves here. Our own actions determine the course of our lives, and we can alter or redirect our lives at any time. I understood that this was crucial: God made the promise that he wouldn't intervene in our lives unless we asked him" (*Embraced by the Light*, p. 49).

THE CHURCH OF JESUS CHRIST OF LATTER-DAY SAINTS PERSPECTIVE

People of faith pray to God for help at various times in their lives. Recognizing when a prayer has been answered can sometimes be obscure.

SPENCER W. KIMBALL
(twelfth prophet and president of the Church of Jesus Christ of Latter-day Saints)

President Kimball offers his perspective as to how God answers prayers

"Through another person"

"God does notice us, and he watches over us. But it is usually through another person that he meets our needs" (*Teachings of Presidents of the Church*, p. 82).

Keith A. Haslem

GORDON B. HINCKLEY
(fifteenth prophet and president of the Church of Jesus Christ of Latter-day Saints)

President Hinckley reflected his faith in the following statement:

> It isn't as bad as you sometimes think it is. It all works out. Don't worry. I say that to myself every morning. It will all work out.... Put your trust in God, and move forward with faith and confidence in the future. The Lord will not forsake us ... if we put our trust in Him, if we will pray to Him, if we will live worthy of His blessings, He will hear our prayers. (Jordan Utah South regional conference, priesthood session, March 1, 1997)

AUTHOR'S PERSPECTIVE
God may choose to not answer our prayers.

It would be nice if God would just speak to us and always answer our prayers, even if the answer is "No!" But for the vast majority of us, that doesn't happen. Why?

My guess is that He figures that He's already given us adequate resources to make most of the decisions we are confronted with. He's given us sufficient intellect and reasoning abilities to logically compare options. We may also have wise family and friends with whom we can counsel. Also, He may frankly not care whether we choose Option A or Option B, because He knows that either option will turn out fine for us in the long run. He knows this because He knows the future.

He knows that—with the help of angelic beings—He can "steer" us on a day-to-day basis regarding events that may seem be coincidental and fortuitous to us, but that are in fact arranged for our welfare.

So rather than always hounding Him for help, perhaps we should just trust that He, with his vast network of angelic resources, will steer our best efforts so that everything will turn out fine in *His* due time.

As Gordon B. Hinckley said, "Things have a way of working out." If you google that statement, you will find many sources echo that sentiment. I believe there is a lot of coordination on the other side engaged in responding to our prayers and needs. I believe these individuals are beings who love us, already know our needs, and work on our behalf without even waiting for us to ask.

46

WHY ARE THERE SO MANY CHURCHES?

The number of unique Christian denominations, depending on the source, ranges from 30,000 to 40,000. If, as the Bible says, "God is not the author of confusion" (1 Corinthians 14:33), then why are there so many different churches?

SYNOPSIS

Betty J. Eadie learned that different churches accommodate different individuals' varying stages of spiritual development.

Elane Durham writes that we choose the church we want to attend based upon the level of spiritual comfort we feel with it.

BETTY J. EADIE

"Each of us, I was told, is at a different level of spiritual development."

I wanted to know why there were so many churches in the world. Why didn't God give us only one church, one pure religion? The answer came to me with the purest of understanding. Each of us, I was told, is at a different level of spiritual development and understanding. Each person is therefore prepared for a different level of spiritual knowledge. All religions upon the earth are necessary because there are people who need what they teach. People in one religion may not have a complete understanding of the Lord's gospel and never will have while in that religion. But that religion is used as a stepping stone to further knowledge. Each church fulfills spiritual needs that perhaps others cannot fill. No one church can fulfill everybody's needs at every level. As an individual raises his level of understanding about God and his own eternal progress, he might feel discontented with the teachings of his present church and seek a different philosophy or religion to fill that void. When this occurs he has reached another level of understanding and will long for further truth and knowledge, and for another opportunity to grow. And at every step of the way, these new opportunities to learn will be given.

Having received this knowledge, I knew that we have no right to criticize any church or religion in any way. They are all precious and important in his sight. Very special people with important missions have been placed in all countries, in all religions, in every station of life, that they might touch others. There is a fullness of the gospel, but most people will not attain it here. (*Embraced by the Light*, pp. 45–46)

ELANE DURHAM

Prior to her NDE, Elane had spent a lot of time investigating various churches, trying to find the "right" church. During her experience, she gained the following understanding:

"We will each choose our church according to the degree of spiritual comfort we feel with it."

It was in connection with my understanding of how to become one of the select ones of God, that my questions concerning the Holy Bible and the "right" church were answered. . . .

. . . I was informed that my term the "right" church was not a proper designation. Rather it was the "perfect" church, which was a part of heaven and had been created there. It was designated perfect because it was composed of a perfect organizational structure and taught as saving doctrines and ordinances the perfect and complete truth as known by God the Father and His Beloved Son.

In its perfected state Christ's church had been brought to earth and given to mortals. However, it didn't take long for us to begin to change the Church and cause it to lose truth . . . the "perfect" church became so weakened that it fragmented into numerous less perfect churches. This had not only happened once, I was told, but on many different occasions and in many different lands.

Going Home

I was told by the angel that all these churches have a portion of the truth. . . . But only the Church as it was created in heaven has all of it.

. . . The angel explained to me that . . . we who go to various churches that contain portions of God's truth travel the spiritual pathway leading to our ultimate heavenly home. Some of us go rapidly, others slowly; some go a great distance, others not so far; and both our speed and our distance are determined by the amount of God's truth taught by the church we choose to join. The more of God's truth in the church we unite ourselves with, and the more we personally adhere to that truth, the faster and farther we will go. And only Christ's perfect church . . . could take us all the way to the highest heavenly realm in the shortest amount of time.

According to the angel, who was confirming what Christ had explained to me earlier, we will each choose our church according to the degree of spiritual comfort we feel with it, and will grow from there through spiritual enlightenment as fast as we desire, and are willing, to receive it.

Though I was not informed by the angel which church it was, he did tell me that Christ's heavenly church is on the earth again today, organized just like it was organized in days of old. He also told me that if I truly desired to find it, I would.

. . . I was told in connection with this . . . that within fifteen or twenty years I would find a new "people," and if I chose, I could join and become part of them. The angel said I would know these people when I found them because I would recognize among them, the same spirit of peace and joy that I had felt with him in that higher spiritual realm.

Then he cautioned me not to become disillusioned by some of the individuals among the new people, whom I would discover had little or no concern for spiritual growth. I was not to be distracted by their petty negativity or their judgmentalism, nor was I to be troubled by it. I had learned from Christ that God loves all of us unconditionally, and . . . I was given to understand that the elimination of negativity and judgmentalism among those people needed to begin with me, and that was all I needed to worry about. (*I Stand All Amazed*, pp. 68–69)

Keith A. Haslem

AUTHOR'S PERSPECTIVE

I believe that any church that teaches its members that they should love God and their fellow man is doing a good work. I believe that those churches are satisfying, to some degree, the current spiritual needs of their members.

Ultimately—and it may not be during our mortal lives—I believe that every person who has lived, or who will ever live, will have the opportunity to accept what the Apostle Paul referred to as, "One Lord, one faith, one baptism" (Ephesians 4:5).

47

DO WE ALL HAVE AN APPOINTED TIME TO DIE?

SYNOPSIS

Sarah LaNelle Menet, Betty J. Eadie, and Mary C. Neal all believe that everyone has an appointed time to leave mortality. When that time comes it doesn't matter by what means the death comes—the effects of old age, a sickness, an accident, or even violent means. The important thing is whether or not the dying person has fulfilled their mission and is prepared to meet God.

However, not every death is according to God's plan. Some individuals abuse their bodies or take foolish risks that result in their death, prior to their appointed time. However, perhaps premature death is not catastrophic. It simply means that the individual loses the opportunity for the development that they would have had.

SARAH LANELLE MENET

"No righteous person in this world dies before his or her time."

> I tried to grasp the thought that it wasn't my time to die, and more understanding began to flood into my mind. Apparently all of us have an allotted length of time to spend on the earth. No righteous person in this world dies before his or her time. So when a beautiful little child dies, or a beloved grandma or grandpa, or a sixteen-year-old nephew or sweet neighbor, we should not be overly grieved. If they were good people their death is correct according to their plan, even though it may be a time of sadness to those left behind. Sometimes a

Keith A. Haslem

person's time can be cut short by use of drugs or other poor choices regarding how they care for their body. They lose the benefit of that time on earth, But, as I perceived it, the timing is more important than the way or manner a person dies. (*There Is No Death*, p. 51)

BETTY J. EADIE

"Their deaths had been appointed before their births, as were all of ours."

"I saw many spirits who would only come to the earth for a short time, living only hours, or days after their birth. They were as excited as the others, knowing that they had a purpose to fulfill. I understood that their deaths had been appointed before their births—as were all of ours" (*Embraced by the Light*, pp. 95–96).

MARY C. NEAL

Dr. Neal tells the story of her own son, who was certain even at the age of five that he would not live past the age of eighteen.

"I'm never going to be eighteen. That's the plan. You know that."

> Willie and I had always been very close and I always felt a sense of deep spiritual connection with his soul. When he was young, perhaps four or five, he and I were chatting before bed. I do not recall what prompted the comment, but I said, "When you are eighteen. . ."
>
> Willie looked startled and said, "But I'm not going to be eighteen."
>
> I asked him "What did you say?" with a somewhat joking tone. He looked back at me with serious intensity, curiosity, and disbelief, as he said, "You know. I'm never going to be eighteen. That's the plan. You know that." He said it as though I must be kidding with him. Surely, I must know the plan for his life.
>
> This exchange was like a knife to my heart. I never forgot it and did not dismiss it. I cherished each subsequent day I had with this son, wondering which one would be his last.
>
> In the years following [her near-death experience], I intermittently thought about my conversation with the angel regarding Willie and contemplated the reasons for my return to Earth. Given Willie's

Going Home

> long-ago stated certainty that he would not reach the age of eighteen, I assumed that the expectations regarding Willie had less to do with his protection and more to do with my expected role in helping my husband and family after Willie's death. Not wanting to burden others with these thoughts, I held them inside and did not tell anyone. It seemed to become a waiting game, but as Willie's eighteenth birthday neared, I became filled with anticipatory grief.
>
> I finally told my husband about my conversation with our son that had occurred so many years earlier. I'm not sure that he was glad to share my burden of worry, but it certainly made me feel just a little bit better to tell him about it. (*To Heaven and Back*, pp. 149–50)

Just prior to Willie's eighteenth birthday, Mary had an experience that gave her hope that Willie's expectation of dying young would not come to pass.

He went on to graduate from high school and completed an internship in Senator John Kerry's office in Washington, D.C. After his brother Eliot graduated, the two brothers moved to northern Maine to pursue ski training with the Maine Winter Sports Club. Mary recounts:

> The day before their departure, Willie asked me about writing a will. He wanted to know who writes a will, why a person would write a will, and whether he should write one. He also wanted to know if I had a life insurance policy for him and, upon discovering that I had never thought of it, wanted to know how I could get one. He really pestered me about it. Although I felt strange having this conversation with a healthy nineteen-year-old, I assured him that I would look into the matter.
>
> Emotionally, I am even-keeled and I have never been particularly emotional when any of my kids began something new or left for an adventure. . . . The morning my two boys left for Maine was different. . . .
>
> As the boys and I stood next to the Subaru saying "good bye" I kept telling them how much I loved them, told them to be careful driving, to call me from the road, and other such things mothers generally say in those moments. When we embraced, I started crying and almost couldn't let them go. I remember holding Willie just a little bit longer than I normally would have, looking directly into his eyes and telling him how much I loved him and what an extraordinary young man he had become. I told them both how proud Bill and I were of them and what a great adventure they would have together. They

Keith A. Haslem

drove off and, despite speaking with them many times each day while they were on the road, I still felt entirely out of sorts.

Perhaps I was uneasily awaiting a future that I had already seen. (*To Heaven and Back*, pp. 167–68)

One of the activities the brothers engaged in during their training was roller skiing. Mary explains:

Roller skis are the dry-land version of cross country ski equipment. They look a little bit like very short skis, with ski bindings mounted on the top and polyethylene wheels at either end. An athlete can then use them to "ski" on pavement, with or without the use of ski poles. They are used by Nordic skiers to increase endurance, work on technique, and develop ski-specific strength when there is no snow.

June 21, 2009 was the summer solstice, the longest day of the year, and it was a beautiful time in New England. As they skied past a cemetery, Willie told Hilary [a training partner] the story of how he had told me that he would not reach his eighteenth birthday. . . . They went on to talk about death and what it meant to each of them. He then became quite specific in describing his feelings about death and told Hilary what he wanted done in the event of his death. He was clear, for example, about his desire to be cremated. He expressed his opinion that using land for burial was not consistent with his love for the planet and his passion for being a responsible steward of the land.

As they skied toward their half-way point, they crested a hill overlooking a beautiful river. The sun was setting and the golden rays played on the water, the trees, creating a magical quality to the scene as they stopped to take it all in. Willie's final comment as they resumed skiing was, "If we died, wouldn't this be an incredible last vision." Less than three minutes later, Willie was dead.

Erik, a Fort Fairfield youth who had celebrated his eighteenth birthday just weeks earlier, had decided to "just drive around" that evening. When his car approached the section of road upon which Hilary and Willie were skiing, they both heard the car engine and moved as far to the right side of the road as was possible. They continued skiing along the road's edge and waited for the car to drive by. . . . As they waited for the car to pass, they could not have known that Erik was distracted by his cell phone. For the almost-quarter-mile of clear vision of Hilary and Willie he would have had if he were paying attention while he was driving, he saw nothing.

Erik missed hitting Hilary, who was skiing behind Willie, by a few inches. Startled, she looked up and watched in horror as Erik's

Going Home

speeding car struck Willey from behind. My beautiful son was killed instantly. (*To Heaven and Back*, pp. 173–75)

Sometime later, Dr. Neal visited the spot where her son was killed.

"We visited the site of Willie's death and I was struck by many emotions as we slowly examined and absorbed the details of the area.... I had the sense that he had tried to make it as nice a spot for us as was possible—accessible, identifiable, and beautiful. His crumpled body had landed in an area blanketed by blossoming wild *Alpine Roses*, overlooking a valley with a meandering stream and rolling hills" (*To Heaven and Back*, p. 178); emphasis added).

Upon arriving home, the Neal's found that neighbors had "lined [their] front porch with a loving collection of flowering plants."

> My job was to decide where the flowers should be planted. Our home sits on six acres of previous ranchland. Other than the wild grasses, the only vegetation consists of the trees, shrubs, and patches of domestic grass that we planted when we built and landscaped our house....
>
> In the days after our return from Maine, walking our property was the one activity that brought a small semblance of calm to my turbulent and broken spirit. As I walked, I tried to make sense of my life, contemplated what to say at my son's memorial service, and made detailed mental accountings of our property, trying to decide on a site for Willie's flowering garden. One morning, as I was walking past a small grouping of willow trees, I came upon a great surprise. The area around and within every willow was overflowing with the vivid, bold, deep pink-colored blossoms of wild Alpine Roses. These flowers were of the exact color, shape, and appearance as had been the ones blooming in the field in which Willie died. Prior to Willie's accident site, I had never seen one of these blossoms and most definitely had never seen one on our property.
>
> Willie knew the story of the pink blossoms on the Bradford pear tree that had appeared immediately after the death of my stepfather. [See Chapter 55]. He knew how significant and emotional that event had been for my mother and me, and he would have seen the painting of the tree hanging in my bathroom many, many times. I know that Willie sent us a message that day through the roses; one of appreciation, love, gratitude and a sense of apology for leaving. I believe he

knew this would be one of the few ways of communicating we would not question.

Completing the story of the Bradford pear tree, after beautifully blooming for five years, it was suddenly and unexpectedly struck by lightning and destroyed, serving as a message telling my mother that it was "time to move forward" in her life. It makes me wonder if the beautiful Alpine roses that we now lovingly nurture on our property will one day disappear. (*To Heaven and Back*, pp. 178–81)

THE CHURCH OF JESUS CHRIST OF LATTER-DAY SAINTS PERSPECTIVE

SPENCER W. KIMBALL
(twelfth prophet and president of the Church of Jesus Christ of Latter-day Saints)

"There is a time to die."

I am confident that there is a time to die, but I believe also that many people die "before their time" because they are careless, abuse their bodies, take unnecessary chances, or expose themselves to hazards, accidents, and sickness. In Ecclesiastes 7:17 we find this statement, "Be not over much wicked, neither be though foolish: why shouldest thou die before thy time?" . . . God controls our lives, guides, and blesses us, but gives us our agency. We may live our lives in accordance with his plan for us or we may foolishly shorten or terminate them. (Sorenson, *The Journey Beyond Life*, pp. 25–26)

HENRY HART MILMAN

"Death cannot come untimely to him who is fit to die."

"It matters not at what hour the righteous fall asleep. Death cannot come untimely to him who is fit to die. The less of this cold world, the more of heaven; the briefer life, the earlier immortality" (Evans, *Richard L. Evan's Quotebook*, p. 116).

BIBLE PERSPECTIVE

In the book of Acts, the Apostle Paul wrote to the superstitious Athenians:

"God . . . hath determined the times before appointed, and the bounds of their habitation."

> For as I passed by, and beheld your devotions, I found an altar with this inscription, to the unknown God. Whom therefore ye ignorantly worship, him declare I unto you.
> God . . . dwelleth not in temples made with hands. . . .
> And hath made of one blood all nations of men for to dwell on all the face of the earth, and hath determined the times before appointed, and the bounds of their habitation. (Acts 17:23–24, 26)

"A time to die."

> To every thing there is a season, and a time to every purpose under heaven:
> A time to be born, and a time to die. (Ecclesiastes 3:1–2)

AUTHOR'S PERSPECTIVE

Does God do anything randomly?

How much of our mortality was planned before we ever come to earth? The Holy Bible implies that the when and where of our existence on earth was determined before we arrived. That's only logical. Would an omniscient God do anything randomly?

48

WHY DO SOME DIE SO YOUNG?

The loss of a baby or a young child may be one of the most devastating events parents can experience. "Why did God take my child?" is a question that is frequently asked during the anguish of this experience.

SYNOPSIS

Betty J. Eadie, Elane Durham, Sarah LaNelle Menet and resources from the Church of Jesus Christ of Latter-day Saints offer insight that some spirits live a short mortal life because they advanced so far in the premortal world that they don't need a prolonged mortal experience. They can progress faster after moving on to the post-mortal world.

BETTY J. EADIE

"Did not need the development"

> I saw many spirits who would only come to the earth for a short time, living only hours, or days after their birth. They were as excited as the others, knowing that they had a purpose to fulfill. I understood that their deaths had been appointed before their births—as were all of ours. These spirits did not need the development that would result from longer lives in mortality, and their deaths would provide challenges that would help their parents grow. The grief that comes here is intense but short. After we are united again, all pain is washed away, and only the joy of our growth and togetherness is felt. (*Embraced by the Light*, pp. 95–96)

ELANE DURHAM

"Except for the need of flesh, individuals who die as infants didn't have to be born."

> For some reason I was focusing on a whole new thought or idea concerning the deaths of babies and young children, which was one of the questions I had asked Christ. I did not understand how their suffering and premature passing from earth could be God's will?
>
> Instantly my teacher gave me further guidance. Except for the need of flesh, individuals who die as infants didn't have to be born, he said. This was because of the spiritual stature they had reached in their premortal lives. But in order to gain flesh they had agreed to come, and to suffer, and to depart this life quickly and go on toward immortality. (*I Stand All Amazed*, p. 78)

SARAH LANELLE MENET

"No righteous person dies before his or her time."

> I tried to grasp the thought that it wasn't my time to die, and more understanding began to flood into my mind. Apparently all of us have an allotted length of time to spend on the earth. No righteous person in this world dies before his or her time. So when a beautiful little child dies, or a beloved grandma or grandpa, or a sixteen-year-old nephew or sweet neighbor, we should not be overly grieved. If they were good people their death is correct according to their plan, even though it may be a time of sadness to those left behind. (*There Is No Death*, p. 51)

THE CHURCH OF JESUS CHRIST OF LATTER-DAY SAINTS PERSPECTIVE

JOSEPH SMITH JR.
(first prophet and president of the Church of Jesus Christ of Latter-day Saints)

Joseph Smith Jr., who lost six of his own children, taught:

Keith A. Haslem

"They were too pure, too lovely, to live on this earth."

The Lord takes many away even in infancy, that they may escape the envy of man, and the sorrows and evils of this present world; they were too pure, too lovely, to live on this earth; therefore, if rightly considered, instead of mourning we have reason to rejoice as they are delivered from evil, and we shall soon have them again. . . . The only difference between the old and the young dying is, one lives longer in heaven and eternal light and glory than the other, and is freed a little sooner from this miserable, wicked world. (*History of the Church*, 4:553–54)

HEBER J. GRANT
(seventh prophet and president of the Church of Jesus Christ of Latter-day Saints)

A story was told by Heber J. Grant regarding the experience of losing his seven-year-old son.

Two years after he lost his first wife—which he felt was in accordance with the Lord's will—Heber J. Grant faced losing his seven-year-old son. Of that experience he wrote:

"No person that . . . has a knowledge of the Gospel . . . can really mourn for his loved ones."

I had been blessed with only two sons. One of them died at five years of age and the other at seven.

My last son died of a hip disease. I had built great hopes that he would live to spread the Gospel at home and abroad and be an honor to me. About an hour before he died I had a dream that his mother, who was dead, came for him, and that she brought with her a messenger, and she told this messenger to take the boy while I was asleep. In the dream I thought I awoke, and I seized my son and fought for him and finally succeeded in getting him away from the messenger who had come to take him, and in so doing I dreamed that I stumbled and fell upon him.

I dreamed that I fell upon his sore hip, and the terrible cries and anguish of the child drove me nearly wild. I could not stand it, and I jumped up and ran out of the house so as not to hear his distress. I dreamed that after running out of the house I met Brother

Going Home

Joseph E. Taylor [an early leader in the Church of Jesus Christ of Latter-day Saints] and told him of these things.

He said: "Well, Heber, do you know what I would do if my wife came for one of her children—I would not struggle for that child. I would not oppose her taking that child away. If a mother who had been faithful and had passed beyond the veil, she would know of the suffering and anguish her child may have to suffer. She should know whether that child might have to go through life as a cripple or whether it would be better or wiser for that child to be relieved from the torture of life. And when you think, Brother Grant, that the mother of that boy went down into the shadow of death to give him life, she is the one who ought to have the right to take him or leave him."

I said, "I believe you are right, Brother Taylor, and if she comes again, she shall have the boy without any protest on my part."

After coming to that conclusion, I was awakened by my brother, B. F. Grant, who was staying that night with us, helping to watch over the sick child. He came into the room and told me that the child was dying. I went in the front room and sat down. There was a vacant chair between me and my wife who is now living, and I felt the presence of that boy's deceased mother sitting in that chair. I did not tell anyone what I felt, but I turned to my wife and said, "Do you feel anything strange?" "Yes, I feel assured that Heber's mother is sitting between us, waiting to take him away."

Now, I am naturally, I believe, a sympathetic man, I was raised as an only child with all the affection that a mother could lavish upon a boy. I believe that I am naturally affectionate and sympathetic and that I shed tears for my friends—tears of joy for their success and tears of sorrow for their misfortunes. But I sat by the deathbed of my little boy and saw him die, without shedding a tear. My living wife, my brother, and I upon that occasion experienced a sweet, peaceful, and heavenly influence in my home, as great as I have ever experienced in my life. (Burton, *For They Shall Be Comforted*, pp. 66–68)

Infants and young children who die will go to heaven, and do not require baptism.

Members of the Church of Jesus Christ of Latter-day Saints believe that "power is not given unto Satan to tempt little children" (Doctrine and Covenants 29:47). Therefore, young children are not capable of committing sin. Consequently, if a young child dies, the Atonement of Christ ensures that the child will inherit the celestial kingdom—terminology in the Church of Jesus Christ of Latter-day Saints for the highest degree of heaven.

Members of the Church of Jesus Christ of Latter-day Saints do not baptize their children until the "age of accountability," which has been revealed to be eight years of age (Doctrine and Covenants 68:25). At this point, they become "accountable and capable of committing sin."

THE PROPHET MORMON

The prophet Mormon taught this principle emphatically to his son Moroni:

> Listen to the words of Christ, your Redeemer, your Lord and your God. Behold, I came into the world not to call the righteous but sinners to repentance; the whole need no physician, but they that are sick; wherefore, little children are whole, for they are not capable of committing sin; wherefore the curse of Adam is taken from them in me, that it hath no power over them; and the law of circumcision is done away in me.
>
> And after this manner did the Holy Ghost manifest the word of God unto me; wherefore, my beloved son, I know that it is solemn mockery before God, that ye should baptize little children.
>
> Behold I say unto you that this thing shall ye teach—repentance and baptism unto those who are accountable and capable of committing sin; yea, teach parents that they must repent and be baptized, and humble themselves as their little children, and they shall all be saved with their little children. (Moroni 8:8–10)

AUTHOR'S PERSPECTIVE

In any school, some students are exceptional and advance more quickly than their peers. In the case of those who die young, perhaps they advanced to a point during their eons of time prior to their mortality that these mortal experiences were no longer necessary for them; their continued development is better enabled by moving on to the spirit world.

And might the loss of a child also serve to motivate those left behind to so live as to eventually be reunited with that child in an exalted state?

49

WHEN IS DEATH A BLESSING FROM GOD?

SYNOPSIS

RaNelle Wallace gained the insight that sometimes a premature death may be a blessing from God in the case where the individual is set on a course that will only degrade the progress they've already made.

RANELLE WALLACE

During her NDE, RaNelle asked her grandmother about a friend who had recently died who had been a drug dealer.

Taken "home [by God] . . . rather than jeopardize spiritual progression

> "Wait, what about Jim?"
> Jim was a friend who had been killed in an automobile accident several months earlier . . . and then I saw him in the distance, walking toward us. Instantly I wanted to run and embrace him, but my grandmother put out her arm and said, "No, you cannot."
> "Why not?" I asked.
> "Because of the way he lived his life," she said.
> He had come closer now and had stopped ten or twelve feet away. He was dressed in jeans and a blue shirt that was unbuttoned to mid-chest. This was how he normally wore his shirts on earth, but I thought, my goodness, that's risqué. "Do they let you dress like that in heaven?"

Keith A. Haslem

He smiled, and I could feel his happiness. Although he didn't possess the same kind of light or power that my grandmother did, he seemed content. He gave me a message to give to his mother, asking that I tell her to stop grieving over his death, to let her know that he was happy and progressing.

He explained that he had made certain decisions in life that had hindered his growth on earth. He had made the decisions knowing they were wrong, and now he was willing to accept their consequences. When he was thrown from the van that he and his wife and a friend had been in, his head hit a rock, and he had been killed instantly. When he got to the other side, he was given a choice to stay in the spirit or return to earth. He could see that his growth on earth had come to a stop and that if he returned he might even lose that light which he had gained. So he chose to stay. He asked me to explain this to his mother, and I said I would, not knowing how I would accomplish it since I had no thought of going back myself. Then he said that he had a lot of work waiting for him and he turned and left. I could tell that he was very busy, engaged in matters that were vital to him, that would help him, though I didn't know what they were.

I looked at my grandmother and asked why she had prevented me from embracing him. She explained that this was part of damnation.

I was taken aback.

"The powers we are given" she explained, "are self-given. We grow by the force of our desires to learn, to love, to accept things by faith that we cannot prove. Our ability to accept truth, to live by it, governs our progress in the spirit, and it determines the degree of light we possess. Nobody forces light and truth upon us, and nobody takes it away unless we let them. We are self-governed and self-judged. We have total agency. Jim decided to limit his growth on earth by rejecting things he knew to be true. He hurt himself and others by using and selling drugs. Some of the people were hurt severely. He had various reasons for turning to drugs but the fact remains that he knew these things were wrong. He chose darkness over light often enough that he would not choose light again. And, now, to the degree that he became spiritually dark, he is consigned to a similar degree of darkness—or lack of light—here in the spirit. Yet he still has agency. He can grow. He can still find all the joy he is willing to accept, all that he is capable of receiving. But he knows that he does not have the same powers to progress and achieve joy that others with more light have. This is a part of damnation, because his progress is limited. But he is choosing to grow. And he is happy."

"The Lord never gives more challenges in life than can be handled," she continued. "*Rather than jeopardize someone's spiritual progression or cause more suffering than can be endured, he will bring that spirit home, where he or she can continue progressing.*" (*The Burning Within*, pp. 97–99; emphasis added)

AUTHOR'S PERSPECTIVE

Consider a crude analogy:

Little children are fascinated by campfires and invariably get too close. A wise and loving parent will "deprive" the child of his agency to pursue a fascination that will be painful and damaging.

Free agency is a wonderful gift and even bad choices can have positive outcomes. But God knows when someone's errant course will never be corrected, and He can take them home to protect them from themselves.

50
HOW DO WE "LET GO" OF A DYING LOVED ONE?

SYNOPSIS

Dr. Elisabeth Kübler-Ross laments that dying children, who know their own death is at hand and who have had glimpses of the "other side" and are ready to go, are put on a guilt trip by their parents who aren't ready to live without them. Effectively, they are restraining these children from doing what they are ready and want to do.

Dr. Kübler-Ross also believes that we can still be heard by a dying loved one, though they may not be conscious, so it is not too late to conclude unfinished business, such as saying, "I love you" or "I'm sorry."

Based upon his many case histories, Dr. Melvin Morse believes dying individuals often have predeath visions—seeing spirit relatives awaiting their graduation. He laments that medical professionals often conclude that the dying person is delusional and administer drugs that prevent the person from dying "in control and with dignity."

ELISABETH KÜBLER-ROSS

Based upon her extensive interaction with dying patients, Dr. Kübler-Ross believes that the dying often have out-of-body experiences that prepare them for their final transition. The dying, who become ready to make that transition, may delay it in deference to their loved ones who desperately want to postpone their departure.

Going Home

Don't put your loved one on a guilt trip when it's their time to go.

"No one can die alone."

Dr. Kübler-Ross outlines a hypothetical case:

> Little Suzy, who is dying of leukemia in a hospital, may be attended by her mother for weeks and weeks. It becomes very clear to the dying child that it is increasingly difficult for her to leave mommy who sometimes implicitly or explicitly conveys: "Honey, don't die on me, I can't live without you." So, what we are doing to those patients, is to make them, in a sense, guilty for dying on us. Suzy, who has become more and more tuned in with total life, has the awareness of her existence after death and the full awareness of a continuation of life. Suzy, during the night and during normal state of consciousness has been out of her body and is aware of her ability to travel and to literally fly anywhere she wants to be. She simply asks mommy to leave the hospital. Often children say: "Mommy you look so tired, why don't you go home, take a shower, take a rest. I am really okay now." The mother leaves, and half-an-hour later the nurse may call from the hospital and say: "I'm sorry, Mrs. Smith, your daughter just passed away."
>
> Unfortunately, those parents are often left with a tremendous amount of guilt and shame and reprimand themselves for not having stuck it out so they would have been with their child at the moment of death. They do not understand or comprehend that no one can die alone. Suzy, unburdened of their needs, is able to let go of the cocoon and free herself quite quickly. She will then, at the speed of her thoughts, be with mommy or daddy or whoever she needs to be with. (*On Life After Death*, p. 52)

"It is not too late to say 'Sorry' or 'I love you'."

Dr. Kübler-Ross also expresses the opinion that those who are in a coma or who are unconscious and close to death can still hear those who may wish to communicate with them.

> You, too, have to know when approaching the bed of your dying mother or father, who may be in a deep coma, that this woman or man can hear everything you say. At those moments it is not too late to say "Sorry," or "I love you," or whatever else you want to say. For

these words, it is never too late to say them, even to the dead ones, because they can still hear you. Even then you can finish "unfinished business" which you might have carried with you for ten or twenty years. In this way you can unburden yourself of your guilt so that you yourself may live more fully. (*On Life After Death*, p. 6)

MELVIN L. MORSE

In his book *Closer to the Light*, Dr. Morse devotes a chapter to the subject of "Predeath Visions." He talks about how frequently children who are close to death have interactions with deceased relatives shortly before their deaths. They may even make brief excursions into the spirit world to see how wonderful it is going to be for them. Dr. Morse endorses:

"Allowing patients to die in control and with dignity."

> I advocate listening to the dying patient. Rather than making the wrong assumption about the meaning of these predeath visions, we should analyze what we are attempting to achieve when we routinely place dying patients on drugs "to make them more comfortable." We should learn new routines and forge different attitudes that incorporate this new information about death and dying. By changing these attitudes, we can learn new methods of allowing patients to die in control and with dignity. (*Closer to the Light*, p. 68)

Dr. Morse laments that sometimes, when these children speak of these predeath visions, the attending medical personnel often administer drugs to eliminate such hallucinations. This makes the child less able to communicate to their parents that they are ready to make the transition. Dr. Morse calls this "a shocking commentary on how far we have fallen from the time-honored deathbed scene in which the dying person was in control" (*Closer to the Light*, p. 206).

"It's my time to die."

Dying children often know that their lives are at an end. Dr. Morse recites the following case told to him by a physician in Utah.

> A five-year-old boy was in a coma, dying from a malignant brain tumor. He had been in a coma for three weeks and was surrounded almost the entire time by his family . . . [who] prayed constantly for his recovery.

At the end of the third week, the pastor of the family's church came into the hospital room and told them a remarkable story. He'd had a dream, he said, in which the boy told him, "It's my time to die. You must tell my parents to quit praying. I am supposed to go now."

The pastor was nervous about delivering this message to the family. Still, he said, it was a message too vivid to ignore. "It's as though he was right there in the room, talking to me face to face."

The family members accepted the minister's dream as a message from their son. They prayed, they touched his comatose body, and they told him that he would be missed, but he had permission to die.

Suddenly the boy regained consciousness. He thanked his family for letting him go and told them he would be dying soon. He died the next day.

Perhaps the most important aspect of this story is its cathartic nature. This family was allowed to assuage its grief because they knew that their son was ready to die. (*Closer to the Light*, p. 71–72)

Dr. Morse cites several such cases where the dying child knew that it was their time to move on.

AUTHOR'S PERSPECTIVE

I wonder if the bedside vigil is a deterrent to the individual who is ready to make the transition.

When my own mother was close to death, and we knew her time was near, we all whispered in her ear, even though she was not conscious, that it was okay for her to go. Nevertheless, the whole family sat vigil by her bedside awaiting the moment.

I expressed my opinion that we were holding her back, so I left. Several others left shortly thereafter. With just one of my sisters still in the room, she finally passed on within the hour. This reinforced my belief that it is easier for those who are ready to make the transition without the presence of so many loved ones "hanging on."

As stated by Dr. Kübler-Ross, "No one dies alone"; they are received by loved ones and escorted into the spirit world. So it is not like we are abandoning them, but rather that we are *releasing* them to do what they want to do.

51

HOW LONG SHOULD WE MOURN THE DEPARTED?

SYNOPSIS

Several accounts suggest that those who pass to the spirit world would prefer that their loved ones not go through prolonged mourning.

During his near-death experience, Lance Richardson met a deceased friend who expressed to him that he wished his wife would stop grieving his death.

RaNelle Wallace met a friend who asked her to tell his mother that he was now happy and progressing—although he had been a troubled person on earth.

In Marlene Sullivan's book *Gaze into Heaven*, she tells the story of May Nevill—deceased—who gave a similar message to be relayed to her loved ones. Duane S. Crowther tells two other related stories from Heber Q. Hale and Ella Jensen—both of who had messages for loved ones back on earth.

The spirit of a friend of mine appeared to his mother in a dream and asked her to stop grieving for him, telling her that he was happy.

LANCE RICHARDSON

In his book *The Message*, Lance describes his near-death experience, and the moment when he met a friend who had died a year before.

"My wife's pain is hurting me . . . it was right that I died."

As we traveled on our way . . . we came upon two separate friends of mine had died almost exactly one year before. They had been notified

I was there and had come to say hello. It was wonderful to see each of them. Both looked so good. One had died of cancer, while the other had been caught in an avalanche while snowmobiling. It had been difficult for their families and friends to lose them, and so it was particularly good to see them again.

We embraced, and I felt their love radiating to me. My friend who had died of cancer then had to leave.

I asked my friend, whom we will call Rick, how he was doing.

"I absolutely love it here!" Rick began. "But my wife's pain is hurting me." I knew she had been having a very difficult time coping with his loss. They are the parents of five children, which made it all the more difficult for her to handle all of this alone. "Lance, you need to go talk to her and let her know that it was right that I died. I know that now." He then shared how it had been difficult for him to accept when he first found out that he was dead.

"But after they escorted me into this world and showed me the plan for me and my family, I then knew it was right."

We talked of his family, especially of his children, and how he is able to help them in ways he could not have from our world. The work with his family was a very important reason for why he had died when he did. (*The Message*, pp. 102–3)

RANELLE WALLACE

Even troubled individuals who have died can find happiness in the world of spirits.

RaNelle inquired about a friend who had been recently killed in an accident. He had been involved in selling drugs and had made other poor choices in his life. When she inquired about him, he appeared.

"He gave a message to give to his mother . . . to stop grieving . . . he was happy and progressing."

"He smiled, and I could feel his happiness. Although he didn't possess the same kind of light or power that my grandmother did, he seemed content. He gave me the message to give to his mother, asking that I tell her to stop grieving over his death, to let her know that he was happy and progressing." (*The Burning Within*, p. 97)

Keith A. Haslem

MAY NEVILL

"Wished the family not to mourn for him"

May Nevill came back briefly from the spirit world to deliver a message to her mother from her brother, Merrill, who had died the day before: "Merrill wished the family not to mourn for him. He said that if the family fretted and mourned for him he couldn't accomplish the work which his grandfather had for him to do." (Sullivan, *Gaze Into Heaven*, p. 183)

HEBER Q. HALE

Heber Q. Hale had a vision of the spirit world, where he met a family who had suffered violent deaths.

"Tell the children . . . that they should not mourn our departure."

> I met Brother John Adamson, his wife, his son James and daughter Isabelle, all of whom were killed by a band of assassins in Carrey, Idaho, in the evening of October 29, 1915. They seemed to divine that I was on my way back to mortality and immediately said, Brother Adamson speaking: "Tell the children that we are very happy, and that they should not mourn our departure, nor worry their minds over the manner by which we were taken. There is a purpose in it and we have a work here to do which requires our collective efforts and which we could not do individually!" I was at once made to know that the work referred to was that of genealogy on which they were working in Scotland and England. (Crowther, *Life Everlasting*, p. 189)

ELLA JENSEN

During Ella's near-death experience she saw a young child who had recently died. When she returned, she told the little boy's parents that

The departed child would be happier if his parents did not "grieve so much."

"It was not right for [the parents] to grieve so much for him and that he would be happier if we would not do so" (Crowther, *Life Everlasting*, pp. 174–75).

Going Home

MY FRIENDS' EXPERIENCE

I have some friends who lost their son as a young adult and were struggling with the grief. Then one day, the mother described how her son appeared to her in a dream and told them to stop grieving, that he was happy where he was.

DAVID M. ROMANO'S POETIC PERSPECTIVE

David M. Romano offers a lovely poetic perspective of one deceased.

"When Tomorrow Starts Without Me"

When tomorrow starts without me,
And I'm not there to see,
If the sun should rise and find your eyes
All filled with tears for me;

I wish so much you wouldn't cry
The way you did today
While thinking of the many things,
We didn't get to say.

I know how much you love me,
As much as I love you,
And each time you think of me,
I know I'll miss you too:

But when tomorrow starts without me,
Please try to understand,
That an angel came and called my name,
And took me by the hand,

And said my place was ready,
In heaven far above
And that I'd have to leave behind
All those I dearly love.

But as I turned to walk away,
A tear fell from my eye
For all my life, I'd always thought,
I didn't want to die.

Keith A. Haslem

I had so much to live for,
So much left yet to do,
It seemed almost impossible,
That I was leaving you.

I thought of all the yesterdays,
The good ones and the bad,
I thought of all the love we shared,
And all the fun we had.

If I could relive yesterday
Just even for a while,
I'd say good-bye and kiss you
And maybe see you smile

But then I fully realized
That this could never be,
For emptiness and memories,
Would take the place of me.

And when I thought of worldly things
I might miss come tomorrow,
I thought of you, and when I did
My heart was filled with sorrow.

But when I walked through heaven's gates
I felt so much at home
When God looked down and smiled at me,
From His great golden throne,

He said, "This is eternity,
and all I've promised you.
Today your life on earth is past
But here it starts anew.

I promise no tomorrow,
But today will always last,
And since each day's the same way,
There's no longing for the past.

You have been so faithful,
So trusting and so true.
Though there were times you did some things
You knew you shouldn't do.

But now you've been forgiven
And now at last you're free.
So won't you come and take my hand
And share my life with me?"

So when tomorrow starts without me,
Don't think we're far apart,
For every time you think of me,
I'm right here, in your heart.

RUSSELL M. NELSON
(seventeenth prophet and president of the Church of Jesus Christ of Latter-day Saints)

In the April 1992 general conference, Russell M. Nelson gave a talk titled "Doors of Death," and he spoke of mourning the loss of a loved one.

"The only way to take the sorrow out of death is to take the love out of life."

> Irrespective of age, we mourn for those loved and lost. Mourning is one of the deepest expressions of pure love. . . .
>
> Moreover, we can't fully appreciate joyful reunions later without tearful separations now. The only way to take the sorrow out of death is to take the love out of life. ("Doors of Death," *Ensign*, May 1992)

AUTHOR'S PERSPECTIVE

Mourning is normal, and even healthy, after a separation from someone we love. However, we don't need to stay in that state for a long period of time. If the graduates are happy in their new realm, it makes sense they would not want us to be unhappy in ours.

ARE TRAUMATIC DEATHS PAINFUL?

SYNOPSIS

Several of our resources offer the hope that traumatic deaths may not be painful.

Through science, we have already learned that endorphins are released to dull the pain as prey in the animal kingdom are killed. Sarah LaNelle Menet and Betty J. Eadie learned that God affords His children the same protection in the case of traumatic deaths.

SARAH LANELLE MENET

"The spirit leaves the body before much of the pain occurs."

> I asked a question about people who are murdered and experience so much terrible pain when they die. I wondered what happened to those who suffer before they die? The answer was comforting. Often, especially in the case of children, the spirit leaves the body before much of the pain occurs so that they do not feel it. Somehow, with his infinite love, God has made provisions so that *the body will still appear alive, but the person or spirit does not inhabit it* any longer and is cut off from experiencing much of the torment and pain. Those people who participate in the shedding of innocent blood will forever suffer a torment far worse than their victims ever did. (*There Is No Death*, p. 108; emphasis added)

Going Home

BETTY J. EADIE

"If our deaths are traumatic, the spirit quickly leaves the body . . . before much pain."

> When we "die," my guides said, we experience nothing more than a transition to another state. Our spirits slip from the body and move to a spiritual realm. If our deaths are traumatic, the spirit quickly leaves the body, sometimes even before death occurs. If a person is in an accident or fire, for example, their spirit may be taken from their body before they experience much pain. *The body may actually appear still alive for some moments, but the spirit will have already left and be in a state of peace.* (*Embraced by the Light*, p. 83; emphasis added)

SCIENTIFIC PERSPECTIVE

Endorphins released at the time of death dull the pain.

A number of scientific studies have suggested that the brains of both animals and humans have the ability to release chemicals in the brain that relieve physical pain and emotional distress during the moments prior to death.

JAMES BRADLEY

An account from *Flyboys*, written by James Bradley, illustrates this concept for the case of humans.

World War II bomber pilot Charlie Brown was shot down by the Japanese as he bombed Tokyo. Downed pilots were almost always executed, and Charlie expected nothing else when he was captured. The usual form of execution was beheading, so when he was blindfolded and instructed to kneel by a freshly dug grave, he expected death to be imminent. For whatever reason, he was not executed. Of the incident, James Brady writes:

"No fear or panic. . . . A calm went through me."

> What did it feel like at that moment? Pilot Charlie Brown had thought he was about to have his head chopped off after he was shot down over Tokyo on February 16. He was blindfolded and made to kneel

Keith A. Haslem

and extend his neck. "I thought, Here it comes," Charlie said. "But there was no fear or panic when I thought my head was going to be chopped off. Actually, it was the reverse: A calm went through me. Maybe it was blood rushing out of my head like I was about to faint . . . there was just calmness. All I remember thinking was, I hope my parents don't find out how I died." (*Flyboys*, p. 223–24)

James Bradley quotes Dr. Sherwin Nuland on endorphins.

Dr. Sherwin Nuland, in his book *How We Die*, suggests that Charlie's feeling of calm had a medical basis. Nuland writes that the body releases self-generated opiates called endorphins when confronted with terror. "Endorphin elevation appears to be an innate physiological mechanism to protect mammals and perhaps other animals against the emotion and physical danger of terror and it probably appeared during the savage period of our prehistory when sudden life-threatening events occurred with frequency." Commenting on the case study of one murdered young girl, Dr. Nuland writes, "I am convinced that nature stepped in, as it so often does, and provided exactly the right spoonful of medicine to give a measure of tranquility to a dying child." (*Flyboys*, pp. 223–24)

AUTHOR'S PERSPECTIVE

It's only reasonable that a loving God would devise a way to protect His creations, and particularly His *children*, from painful or traumatic deaths.

53

ARE OUT-OF-BODY EXPERIENCES POSSIBLE?

In his book *Evidence of the Afterlife*, Jeffrey Long defines "out-of-body" as "the separation of the consciousness from the physical body" (p. 69).

SYNOPSIS

The experience of Captain Dale Black in the spirit world occurred while his physical body was in a comatose condition. Therefore, if his account is authentic, it is possible to have an out-of-body experience where the spirit leaves the body for a period of time while the physical body is still functioning.

Dr. Elisabeth Kübler-Ross believes that out-of-body experiences are possible during sleep.

Based upon his extensive research, Dr. Raymond Moody also believes that out-of-body experiences are possible.

IANDS (International Association of Near-Death Studies) has compiled hundreds of such accounts. Perhaps the most common scenario for an out-of-body experience to occur is during a medical emergency, where the individual, outside of their body, watches as medical personnel work on their physical body.

ELISABETH KÜBLER-ROSS

"All of us have these out-of-body experiences during certain stages of sleep."

When slowly preparing for death, as is often the case with children who have cancer, prior to death many of these children begin to be aware that they have the ability to leave their physical body and

Keith A. Haslem

have what we call an out-of-body experience. All of us have these out-of-body experiences during certain stages of sleep. Very few of us are consciously aware of it. Dying children especially, who are much more tuned in, become more spiritual than healthy children of the same age. They become aware of these short trips out of their physical bodies which help them in the transition, which help them familiarize themselves with the place they are going to.

It is during these out-of-body trips which dying patients, young and old, experience that they become aware of the presence of beings who surround them, who guide them and who help them. Young children often refer to them as their playmates. The churches call them guardian angels. Most researchers would call them guides. It is not important what label we give them, but it is important to know that every single human being, from the moment of birth until the moment when we make the transition and end this physical existence, is in the presence of these guides or guardian angels who will wait for us and help us in the transition from life to life after death. Also, we will always be met by those who preceded us in death who we have loved. (*On Life After Death*, p. 49–50)

She continues:

"We have all been endowed with a facet of divinity. We received... the ability to shed our physical body—not only at the time of death but in times of crisis, in times of exhaustion, in times of very extraordinary circumstances, and during a certain type of sleep. It is important to know this can happen before death" (*On Life After Death*, p. 52).

Many people have an out-of-body experience during surgery, and in fact are watching the surgeons at work (*On Life After Death*, p. 5).

Dr. Kübler-Ross wrote the foreword of Dr. Kenneth Ring's book *Heading Toward Omega*. In it, she spoke briefly of two of her own out-of-body experiences.

"I was lifted out into a realm of such love and care."

I will never forget when I had my own personal experience after a busy and exhausting workshop. I was lifted out into a realm of such love and care, floating and uplifted as by invisible, tender arms and experienced a rejuvenation and a recharging of my energies as if half a dozen mechanics had lovingly fixed up an old car and made it new. When I returned to my physical body I felt refreshed and strong again and had a conviction that we are truly looked after beyond all our comprehension.

Going Home

It was many years later, during a much more intense experience of this nature, that I was allowed to experience and become part of that light that so many people try to explain in words. Anyone who has been blessed enough to see this light will never again be afraid to die. The unconditional love, the understanding and compassion in the presence of this light are beyond any human description. (Ring, *Heading Toward Omega*, pp. 11–12)

RAYMOND A. MOODY JR.

Dr. Moody also believes that people can have out-of-body experiences.

Experiences "took place spontaneously."

"Many people have told me of out-of-body experiences which took place spontaneously. The persons involved were not "dead" or even ill or in jeopardy. Further, in most cases these experiences were not being sought out in any way. They came as complete surprises" (*Reflections on Life After Death*, p. 97).

Dr. Moody hypothesizes:

"[The] hypothetical mechanism for releasing the soul [might not always] work perfectly."

Now, we don't assume that our bodily mechanisms work perfectly every time. The organs of our body sometimes malfunction. . . . Analogously, we have no reason to assume that this hypothetical mechanism for releasing the soul from the body always would work perfectly. Might it not be that different kinds of situations—stresses, etc.—could sometimes work to set off this mechanism prematurely? If all this were true, then it could explain the similarity between near-death experiences and other kinds, such as out-of-body experiences. It could also explain the fact that the phenomena reported by those who find themselves in life-threatening situations without even being injured can be identical with the experiences of those who are revived from an apparent clinical "death." (*Reflections on Life After Death*, pp. 98–99)

AUTHOR'S PERSPECTIVE

Based upon my own experience, I believe it is possible for anyone to have an out-of-body experience as they sleep (see Chapter 61).

54

DO THE SPIRITS OF THE DEAD STAY WITH US FOR AWHILE?

SYNOPSIS

Do the spirits of the departed go immediately to the world of spirits or do they stay in close proximity to their earthly home for a short period of time? Betty J. Eadie writes that either is possible.

BETTY J. EADIE

"We are given the choice to remain . . . or to move on."

> At the time of death, we are given the choice to remain on this earth until our bodies are buried or to move on, as I did, to the level to which our spirit had grown. I understood that there are many levels of development, and we will always go that level where we are most comfortable. Most spirits choose to remain on earth and comfort their loved ones; families are subject to much more grief than the departed one. Sometimes the spirits will remain longer if the loved ones are in despair. They remain to help the loved ones' spirits heal. (*Embraced by the Light*, pp. 83–84)

ANONYMOUS ACCOUNT

A young man, at his funeral, encourages his grandfather.

Going Home

A number of years ago, a young man I know died tragically. The whole family was grief-stricken. The young man's grandfather was asked to speak at his funeral, and with his emotions so raw he wondered whether he could get through his talk.

As he began, he saw the spirit of his grandson, who offered him verbal encouragement, giving him added strength to finish his remarks.

AUTHOR'S PERSPECTIVE

I believe the spirits of the dead all attend their own funerals. Might it be relevant for them to know where their bodies are buried, as they look forward to the eventual resurrection of their bodies?

55

CAN THE DEAD GIVE US SIGNS THAT THEY ARE ALL RIGHT?

SYNOPSIS

Are the dead somehow able to give us signs in order to communicate their love for us? Dr. Mary C. Neal relates two accounts in her book, *To Heaven and Back,* that support this possibility.

Based upon personal experience, I also believe it is possible.

MARY C. NEAL

While still in the process of recovering physically from her accident and her near-death experience, Dr. Mary C. Neal's stepfather, George, who she was very close to, contracted pneumonia. Although the attending physician indicated that her stepfather was responding well to the antibiotics and thought they should not be overly concerned, Mary was impressed that she needed to visit him in the hospital. So, she made the trip from Jackson Hole, Wyoming, to his hospital in North Carolina. She recounts the story of his death.

"This tree, which had been barren just twenty-four hours earlier, was now filled beyond capacity with large, beautiful, perfect pink blossoms."

When we finally arrived at the side of my stepfather's hospital bed, we found him to be in good spirits. . . . We all celebrated my mother's

Going Home

birthday in George's hospital room the next day. George laughed, felt great, and was even able to eat a bit of his favorite food: cookies.

My mom and I were quite relieved at his condition and were in high spirits the next morning. We sat at her breakfast table sipping coffee and contemplating George's health and the possibility of his release from the hospital. As we chatted, we looked out the picture window and gazed upon a large, entirely barren Bradford pear tree. My mother then told me the story of that tree.

She and George loved the large, pink blossoms of the many Bradford pear trees in their neighborhood, so they had planted this tree many years prior with the hope of enjoying its annual display of color. While this particular tree had continued to grow taller and taller, it had never produced a single blossom. She said that George was so dismayed by the tree's inability to blossom that he planned to cut it down in the spring and plant a new one. He loved color and wanted to see blossoms from their breakfast table.

We were still feeling hopeful as we drove to the hospital, but encountered a radically different situation upon our arrival. George had taken a turn for the worse and his organs were failing. God was calling to him, and we knew his remaining time on Earth was short. My mom, Larry, and I decided to let him pass into the next world with dignity and love. We removed the feeding tube and chose not to place him on a ventilator. We each expressed our deep love for George and each gave him permission to leave. We held each other and held George as his spirit peacefully left this world.

The following morning, as we sat down for coffee at my mom's breakfast table, we looked out the window and gasped. Their once forlorn Bradford pear tree was bursting with color. This tree, which had been barren just twenty-four hours earlier, was now filled beyond capacity with large, beautiful, perfect pink blossoms.

These colorful blossoms stayed on that tree until well after frost had felled the blossoms of neighboring trees. When the tree finally began to drops its leaves, it did so on the side facing away from the window before dropping a single blossom on the side that faced my mother's breakfast window. What a gift from my stepfather. What a miracle. My mother subsequently commissioned a painting of that tree, with its bounty of blossoms, which she gave to me in celebration of George and our shared experience. I have hung this painting in my bathroom dressing area and it gives me a deep sense of peace and contentment every time I look at it. (*To Heaven and Back*, pp. 131–33)

Keith A. Haslem

AUTHOR'S EXPERIENCE

My mother's "weeping headstone."

Just seconds before she passed away, although in an unconscious state, a tear rolled down my sweet mother's face.

Some time later, some of our family gathered around her headstone at the cemetery. The headstone was square, inscribed with the relevant data, and was inlaid in a stone that surrounded the inscribed portion. Then we noticed two small streams of water trickle down from between the inlaid portion of the headstone and the stone that surrounded it at both bottom corners (see the circled corners in the image below). We were all probably thinking the same thing but thought it too ridiculous to say anything, until finally my brother-in-law remarked in amazement, "It looks like the stone is crying!"

I returned to the headstone the next day with a straight pin, to see if there was space enough between the inlaid stone and the surrounding stone that water could somehow have seeped through from beneath. The fit was so tight that I couldn't get a straight pin even started. I do not think it possible that water could seep through that seam even if it were pressurized from beneath the stone.

I attribute mom's tears at the moment of her death and the "weeping headstone" to be signs from my mother that she was there with us, that she wanted us to know that she loved us, and that she was sad to be apart from us.

AUTHOR'S PERSPECTIVE

I have no doubt that thousands of people could recount similar experiences. Skeptics might easily dismiss such events as simply curious coincidences. However, individuals of faith find such experiences comforting and faith confirming, believing that their loved ones found a subtle way to communicate their love despite their lack of a physical body.

56

CAN THE SPIRITS OF THE DEAD VISIT US?

SYNOPSIS

Thousands of accounts exist of people seeing the spirits of deceased loved ones. Several of our resources corroborate that possibility.

SARAH LANELLE MENET

In response to the question, "Do we as spirits ever get to come back to earth after we die?" Sarah answered:

"For special occasions [such as funerals or marriages]"

> Yes, we do. For example, everyone is allowed to come back for his or her own funeral. People can come back for special occasions, like seeing their *son or daughter getting married* or some other important event. It would be possible to be assigned as a guardian angel for a relative and therefore spend a lot of time with them on earth. But good people who cross over are busy doing important work in the spirit world and do not have time to waste without purpose. (*There Is No Death*, p. 120; emphasis added)

"Most often in our dreams"

> "I understand that when our loved ones who have crossed over visit us, it is most often in our dreams during our 'alpha awareness state' when we are more easily susceptible to spiritual communication. They whisper and tell us things, encourage us, and give us ideas during this time" (*There Is No Death*, pp. 120–21).

Going Home

JAMES BRADY

Saying "Goodbye"

In his book *Flyboys*, James Brady tells the story of twenty-year-old Dick Woellhof, a bomber pilot shot down by the Japanese on July 4, 1944, during a bombing run over Chichi Jima. Woellhof was captured by the Japanese and executed. James Brady recounts:

"I was awake. I saw him."

> On August 16, Laura Woellhof received a telegram from the navy notifying her that Dick had been shot down on July 4. The navy wrote that Dick was "missing in action" and that Laura should wait for further word before jumping to conclusions.
>
> It would be a year and a half before the navy would learn that Dick was dead. But Laura told her granddaughter Laura Lucero that by then she already knew that her son's spirit had left the earth.
>
> "Dick flew over the house," his mother told Lucero. "It was like a dream, but not a dream. I was awake. I saw him. Dick waved the American flag and said, 'Good-bye, mom'." (*Flyboys*, p. 191)

James Brady recounts another story that corroborates this idea.

Broken picture . . . shattered dreams

> After he was shot down and executed, pilot Jimmy Dye's girlfriend, Gloria Nields, also received an indication of his demise; hers was more obscure but still effective.

"I knew something had happened."

> "I had a big eight-by-ten framed picture of Jimmy," she told me decades later. "It was shot of him in his sailor uniform with a big smile. Every night I would kiss his picture and sleep with it. One night it fell on the floor and broke. I woke up and it scared me. I knew something had happened. Later I learned that was when Jimmy died" (*Flyboys*, p. 247).

ANONYMOUS ACCOUNTS

Attending a marriage

I have a friend who was attending his sister-in-law's marriage in one of the temples of the Church of Jesus Christ of Latter-day Saints. At one

Keith A. Haslem

point, he happened to turn around and look behind him. On the back row of the room was his mother-in-law, the bride's mother, who had died several years earlier. He nudged his brother-in-law, who was sitting next to him, who also turned and witnessed her presence.

Just stopping by

I have another friend whose elderly wife passed away. A few years afterward, he awoke from a nap to see the spirit of his wife looking at him with a concerned look on her face. When she realized he could see her, she vanished. This man told me she was dressed in a green dress and looked like she had when she was in her thirties.

AUTHOR'S PERSPECTIVE

The deceased may be quite busy in the spirit world, but I'm sure they still like to "stay in touch" with what is going on in our lives. We can't generally see or communicate with them, and I suspect our spiritual growth would be impaired if we frequently had access to immortal beings.

57

DO SOME SPIRITS GO TO NEITHER HEAVEN NOR HELL?

The concept of heaven and hell are commonly acknowledged. However, based upon the accounts of some of the Witnesses it appears that some spirits go to areas that resemble neither heaven nor hell.

SYNOPSIS

Betty J. Eadie referred to earthbound spirits who were seemingly unable to relinquish their interest in worldly things.

Elane Durham also referred to earthbound spirits who were miserable, confused, and uncertain of what they should do.

George G. Ritchie observed spirits "who seemingly were unable to leave their mortal lives behind."

Dr. Raymond Moody describes "a realm of bewildered spirits" seemingly "unable to surrender their attachments to the physical world" (*Reflections on Life After Death*, p. 18) Some spirits wandered aimlessly, unsure of where to go and what to do.

BETTY J. EADIE

"Prisoners of this earth . . . earth-bound"

They [her spirit world escorts] told me that it is important for us to acquire knowledge of the spirit while we are in the flesh. The more

Keith A. Haslem

knowledge we acquire here, the further and faster we progress here, the further and faster we will progress there. Because of lack of knowledge or belief, some spirits are virtual prisoners of this earth. Some who die as atheists, or those who have bonded to the world though greed, bodily appetites, or other earthly commitments find it difficult to move on, and they become earth-bound. They often lack the faith and power to reach for, or in some cases even to recognize, the energy and light that pulls us toward God. These spirits stay on the earth until they learn to accept the greater power around them and to let go of the world. (*Embraced by the Light*, p. 84)

ELANE DURHAM

"Earthbound spirits . . . a terrible amount of confusion and anger"

A large group of people—probably a hundred or more—and all of them had their heads down. They weren't far from me, not more than thirty or forty feet. I knew that they were spirit beings like myself, though there was such darkness about them that they felt to me wicked or unclean. I knew that they had once lived in mortality just as I had, and I remember thinking of them as *earthbound*, not because they *had* to be earthbound so much as because they chose to be. From them I felt a terrible amount of confusion and anger, which I didn't understand, along with a sense of being lost in their own misery—uncertain of which way to go. I wanted to make them understand that all they had to do was look up—up there was the light, and they could go to it with me. But when I tried to tell them, they ignored me completely. It was as if I didn't even exist.

Even more amazing to me was that neither did the light exist to them. Either they could not, or would not, see it. (*I Stand All Amazed*, p. 26; emphasis added)

GEORGE G. RITCHIE JR.

Dr. Ritchie observed spirits who were unable to leave their mortal lives behind and move on to experience all the possibilities of the spirit world.

Going Home

"For where your treasure is, there will your heart be also! . . . They could no longer contact the earth, [but] still had their hearts there."

In fact the streets were impossibly crowded. Just below us two men bore down on the same section of sidewalk and an instant later had simply passed through each other. It was the same inside the humming factories and office buildings—where I could see as easily as I could see the streets—too many people at the machines and desks. In one room a grey-haired man was sitting in an armchair dictating a letter onto a rotating cylinder. Standing behind him, not an inch away, another man, maybe ten years older, kept snatching repeatedly at the speaking tube as though he would tear it away from the seated man's hand.

"No!" he was saying, "if you order a hundred gross they'll charge more. Take a thousand gross at a time. Pierce would have given you a better deal. Why did you send Bill on that Treadwell job?" On and on he went, correcting, giving orders, while the man in the chair appeared neither to see nor hear him. . . .

. . . I remembered myself yelling at a man who never turned to look at me. And then I recalled the people here in this town trying in vain to attract attention, walking along a sidewalk without occupying space. Clearly these individuals were in the same substance-less predicament I myself was in.

Like me, in fact, they were dead.

But—it was so very different from the way I had always imagined death. I watched one woman of maybe fifty following a man of about the same age down the street. She seemed very much alive, agitated and tearful, except that the man to whom she was addressing her emphatic words was oblivious to her existence.

"You're not getting enough sleep. Marjorie makes too many demands on you. You know you've never been strong. Why aren't you wearing a scarf? You should never have married a woman who thinks only of herself." There was more, much more, and from some of it I gathered that she was his mother, in spite of the fact that they appeared so nearly the same age. How long had she been following him this way? Was this what death was like—to be permanently invisible to the living, yet permanently wrapped up in their affairs?

"Lay not up for yourself treasures on earth! For where your treasure is, there will your heart be also!" I'd never been any good at memorizing Scripture, but those words of Jesus from the Sermon on the Mount sprang into my mind now like an electric shock. Perhaps these insubstantial people—the businessman, the woman begging cigarettes, this mother—although they could no longer contact the earth, still had their hearts there. Did I? With a kind of terror I thought of that Eagle Scout badge. Being a Phi Gam. Getting into med school. Was my heart, the focus of my being, fixed on things like these? (*Return from Tomorrow*, pp. 56–58)

RAYMOND A. MOODY JR.

"A realm of bewildered spirits"

From his interviews with NDErs, Dr. Raymond Moody describes what he terms "a realm of bewildered spirits."

"Bound to some particular object, person, or habit"

Several people have reported to me that at some point they glimpsed other beings who seemed to be "wrapped" in an apparently most unfortunate state of existence. . . . First, they state that these beings seemed to be, in effect, unable to surrender their attachments to the physical world. One man recounted that the spirits he saw apparently "couldn't progress on the other side because their God is still living here." That is, they seemed bound to some particular object, person, or habit. (*Reflections on Life After Death*, p. 18)

Dr. Moody quotes a woman who was reported to be dead for fifteen minutes.

"What am I doing? What's it all about?"

These bewildered people? I don't know exactly where I saw them. . . . What you would think of as their head was bent downward: they had sad, depressed looks; they seemed to shuffle, as someone would on a chain gang. . . . They seemed to be forever shuffling and moving around, not knowing where they were going, who to follow, or what to look for. . . . They seemed to be thinking, "Well, it's all over with. What am I doing? What's it all about?" . . . They seemed to be forever moving, rather than just sitting, but in no special direction. They would start straight, then veer to the left and take a few steps and veer back to the right. And absolutely nothing to do. Searching, but for

> what they were searching I don't know. . . . It looks like they have lost any knowledge of who they are, what they are—no identity whatsoever. (*Reflections on Life After Death*, pp. 18–20)

Some of Dr. Moody's subjects reported seeing spirits trying to communicate with family members who were still on earth. He quotes a man who had a near-death experience.

"Don't do as I did, so this won't happen to you."

> You could see them trying to make contact, but no one would realize that they were around; people would just ignore them. . . . They were trying to communicate, yet there was no way they could break through. People seemed to be completely unaware of them. . . . One seemed to be a woman who was trying so hard to reach through to children and to an older woman in the house . . . it seems more or less that she was trying to get through to them, trying to tell them, seemingly, to do things differently from what they were doing now . . . to make a change in their life style. Now this sounds kind of put on, but she was trying to get them to do the right things, to change so as not to be left like she was. "Don't do as I did, so this won't happen to you. Do things for others so that you won't be left like this." . . . It seemed that in this house there was no love, if you want to put it that way. . . . It seemed that she was trying to atone for something she had done. . . . It's an experience I'll never forget. (*Reflections on Life After Death*, pp. 21–22)

AUTHOR'S PERSPECTIVE

It's logical to envision that faithful individuals will go to a paradisaical region of the spirit world. It's also logical to envision that individuals who spent their lives rebelling against God will go to a hellish region. But, in reality, most of the population seems to fit into neither category. Where do those people go who were fundamentally good people but were ambivalent about God, or lackadaisical about keeping His commandments? What about those who, because of the time and region of their birth, were never able to be introduced to the true nature of God?

My faith, as taught in the Church of Jesus Christ of Latter-day Saints, is that these people will inhabit a third realm, at least temporarily, until they finally comply with the laws and ordinances of the gospel

Keith A. Haslem

of Jesus Christ. In the Church of Jesus Christ of Latter-day Saints, the term for this realm is "spirit prison." That term may be a misnomer, as conditions there will not be prisonlike; in fact, they may be paradisaical by our present standards. The Apostle Peter alluded to this spirit prison in 1 Peter 3:18–19.

> For Christ also hath once suffered for sins, the just for the unjust, that he might bring us to God, being put to death in the flesh, but quickened by the Spirit:
>
> By which also he went and preached unto the spirits in prison.

I wonder of the descriptions of "earthbound spirits" could include those in this "spirit prison."

58

WHAT HAPPENS TO THOSE WHO COMMIT SUICIDE?

For some, life can seem so unbearable that they choose to end their own lives. Several of the Witnesses were given the understanding that this is an inappropriate act and that the results may not be what the individual hoped for.

SYNOPSIS

During his experience, Dr. Ritchie learned that those who commit suicide have to witness and feel the pain, grief, and anguish their act has brought upon their loved ones.

Dr. Joyce H. Brown also saw the torment of two suicides during her near-death experience.

Betty J. Eadie wrote that those who commit suicide will feel pain and sorrow for their lost opportunities.

Dr. Raymond Moody's research brought him to the conclusion that those who attempt suicide find no relief from whatever they are trying to escape.

Elane Durham and Sarah LaNelle Menet allude to the concept that not all suicides will be judged the same.

Bruce R. McConkie believes that some victims of suicide may not be accountable for their act.

GEORGE G. RITCHIE JR.

"They are suicides, chained to every consequence of their act."

Keith A. Haslem

In one house a younger man followed an older one from room to room. "I'm sorry, Pa!" he kept saying. "I didn't know what it would do to Mama! I didn't understand!"

But though I could hear him clearly, it was obvious that the man he was speaking to could not. The old man was carrying a tray into a room where an elderly woman sat in bed. "I'm sorry, Pa," the young man said again. "I'm sorry, Mama." Endlessly, over and over, to ears that could not hear.

Several times we paused before similar scenes. A boy trailing a teenaged girl through the corridors of a school. "I'm sorry, Nancy!" A middle-aged woman begging a grey-haired man to forgive her.

"What are they so sorry for, Jesus?" I pleaded, "Why do they keep talking to people who can't hear them?"

Then from the Light beside me came the thought: They are suicides, chained to every consequence of their act.

The idea stunned me, yet I knew it came from Him, not me, for I saw no more scenes like these, as though the truth He was teaching had been learned. (*Return from Tomorrow*, pp. 58–59)

JOYCE H. BROWN

In her book *God's Heavenly Answers*, Dr. Brown describes her experience in the world of spirits, including seeing the funerals of two individuals who had committed suicide. Perhaps she was given these views because she had been considering suicide from the time she was eight years old.

The first funeral was of a young woman who left behind two little girls, about four and six years of age.

> The youngest child sat on her grandmother's lap, clinging to her and weeping desperately. The six-year-old stood at the side of her grandmother, her face buried in her hands. Her little shoulders shook with her sobs. The children could not stop crying, but their grandmother, in such pain she hardly seemed to realize they were there, was unable to offer comfort.
>
> I understood her thoughts.... How could she ever love them enough to ease the pain of losing a mother who had left them by choice?
>
> ... Suddenly I saw the spirit of the young woman kneeling at her mother's feet... her face was contorted in sorrow and pain. Her mortal body lay a few feet away in the coffin, yet her essence, her

Going Home

spirit, her soul was here, sobbing at her mother's knees. I heard her thoughts, her words. She was sorry, oh, so sorry, for what she had done to them. She ached for them and the pain they were experiencing because of her actions. . . . Her desperate attempts to make herself heard or understood failed utterly. She tried to take the oldest girl into her arms to comfort her . . . but they didn't even know she was there.

I listened as she begged for their forgiveness. She was desperate to make them understand, but they could not hear her words. All she could do was watch in torment as they suffered from her actions. (*God's Heavenly Answers*, pp. 77–78)

The second funeral Joyce saw was for a teenage boy who had been troubled and taken his own life.

[In his casket, his] facial features were peaceful, as if he merely slept. His spirit face was contorted with torment and despair. Desperately wanting to make contact, he was reaching out his insubstantial, wispy arms to his father who was gazing down at the body in the casket. His father's shoulders were stooped from almost unbearable sorrow, his face drawn, his eyes swollen from crying. . . .

The boy's mother stood at the foot of the casket weeping quietly. Her pain and confusion were profound. The father was speaking softly to two young men; I sensed that they were best friends of the dead boy [and they were contemplating suicide themselves].

The father was telling them . . . "He's at peace now." . . .

"No, Dad!" the boy's spirit cried out, "Stop, don't tell them that.". . .

He was *not* at peace.

"My Father is so wrong, so wrong," he kept saying. . . .

He shrieked, "No peace, I have no peace!" He was futilely trying to communicate with his father, and trying to warn his friends not to make the same mistake. If they did, he knew his misery would be even worse.

Feelings of misery seemed to exude from him. He had taken his own life, falsely believing that in death he would find happiness, peace, and contentment. He thought he could escape from all earthly anxiety—instead he found feelings of intense sorrow and anguish that were greater than any he had experienced while he was alive. . . .

Suicide is like a disease (emphasis added) that kills some and often cripples everyone else involved. (*God's Heavenly Answers*, pp. 80–83)

Keith A. Haslem

Since her experience in the other world, Dr. Brown founded Stress and Grief Relief, Inc., a nonprofit organization seeking to help troubled individuals. Their website is www.helpstopsuicide.org, which lists a suicide hotline number (1-800-734-3439).

BETTY J. EADIE

"We must never consider suicide."

"This act will only cause us to lose opportunities for further development while here on earth. And afterwards, in reflecting back on these lost opportunities we would feel much pain and sorrow" (*Embraced by the Light*, p. 70).

ELANE DURHAM

Elane Durham learned that there are two types of suicide and one is regarded more gently than the other.

"There are two basic kinds of suicide. . . . The first . . . is lovingly understood."

> Suicide was another aspect of understanding that I gained while in the love of Christ. As I understood it, there are two basic kinds of suicide. That which is done in confusion by a person whose mental capacities aren't all together, is one type. And that which is done in spite—to get even with whomever an individual feels they're receiving pain or misunderstanding from is the second type.
>
> The first kind of suicide is lovingly understood and the taker of life is guided gently so that he understands what he has done by preempting his own life. He will still need to learn the lessons his mortality would have provided him if he wishes to reach a higher glory . . . , but now those lessons will be learned in the spirit state—which takes much, much longer. He will also find himself in a lower realm of the spirit world, and if he chooses will have to work his way up the spiritual levels.
>
> For the person who takes his life to spite God or another person, there is a price to pay which takes a great deal more time than the other, and which somehow involves the giving of that individual in service to others. Unfortunately, the specifics of how this was to be

accomplished were taken from my memory. (*I Stand All Amazed*, pp. 46–47)

SARAH LANELLE MENET

Sarah's near-death experience came as a result of her own attempt to commit suicide.

"Different kinds of suicides . . . are judged differently."

> I also understood that we have the choice or option to shorten our allotted time. I had tried to do so by committing suicide, but it was a very great sin and a terrible action to take. I thought about my death and immediately realized that for many suicides there is a great penalty or price that has to be paid. My understanding was that there are different kinds of suicides, and so they are judged differently. Some individuals are not in control of their minds when they make such a decision, and judgment for them would be very different as opposed to those who kill themselves so they will not get caught for some terrible crime they have committed.
>
> Jesus knows and understands all of the circumstances present that cause a person to take such a drastic measure, even though committing suicide for any reason is very wrong. He takes all of that into consideration as no one else can when making assignments in the spirit world. Assignments may not really be the correct word because it seems to indicate decisions made on our behalf by someone else. Quite the opposite is true as our assignments are determined by the choices we have made and how we have lived here on earth. (*There Is No Death*, pp. 51–52)

RAYMOND A. MOODY JR.

In the course of his work, Dr. Raymond Moody was asked "Have you ever interviewed anyone who has had a near-death experience in association with a suicide attempt? If so, was the experience any different?"

Dr. Moody's response was, in part:

"If you leave here a tormented soul, you will be a tormented soul over there, too."

Keith A. Haslem

I do know of a few cases in which a suicide attempt was the cause of the apparent "death." These experiences were uniformly characterized as being unpleasant.

As one woman said, "If you leave here a tormented soul, you will be a tormented soul over there, too." In short, they report that the conflicts they had attempted suicide to escape were still present when they died, but with added complications. In their disembodied state they were unable to do anything about their problems. (*Life After Life*, p. 143)

"Throwing God's gift back in his face"

A man who was despondent over the death of his wife shot himself, "died" as a result, and was resuscitated. He states:

"I didn't go where [my wife] was. I went to an awful place.... I immediately saw the mistake I had made.... I thought, 'I wish I hadn't done it.'"

Others who experienced this unpleasant "limbo" state have remarked that they had the feeling they would be there for a long time. This was their penalty for "breaking the rules" by trying to release themselves prematurely from what was, in effect, an "assignment"—to fulfill a certain purpose in life.

Such remarks coincide with what has been reported to me by several people who "died" of other causes but who said that, while they were in this state, it had been intimated to them that suicide was a very unfortunate act which attended with a severe penalty. One man who had a near-death experience after an accident said:

"[While I was over there] I got the feeling that two things it was completely forbidden for me to do would be to kill myself or to kill another person....

"If I were to commit suicide, I would be throwing God's gift back in his face. (*Life After Life*, pp. 143–44; insertions in the original text)

"Penalty ... witness the suffering [suicide] would cause"

In *Reflections on Life After Life*, Dr. Raymond Moody writes that one of his subjects "who survived an apparent clinical death of some duration said that while he was 'over there' he had the impression that there was a "penalty" to pay for some acts of suicide, and that part of this would be to witness the suffering on the part of others that this act would cause" (*Reflections on Life After Life*, pp. 44–45).

With regard to a number of individuals he talked to who had near-death experiences after attempting suicide, Dr. Moody writes:

"Their suicidal attempts solving nothing."

> All of these people agree on one point: they felt their suicidal attempts solved nothing. They found that they were involved in exactly the same problems from which they had been trying to extricate themselves by suicide. Whatever difficulty they had been trying to get away from was still there on the other side, unresolved.... All mentioned that after their experiences, they would never consider trying suicide again. Their common attitude is that they had made a mistake, and that they were very glad they had not succeeded in their attempts. For instance, when I asked one man whether, in the light of what he had experienced, he would ever choose to try to kill himself, he answered:
>
> "No, I would not do that again. I will die naturally next time, because one thing I realized at that time is that our life here is just such a small period of time and there is so much which needs to be done while you're here. And when you die it's eternity." (*Reflections on Life After Death*, pp. 45–46)

Dr. Moody concludes his discussion on suicide by writing:

"God will take care of these things in accordance with his love and wisdom."

> When asked about such matters, a psychiatrist friend of mine, who had an "other-world" experience during an apparent clinical death from an infection, gave an interesting answer. He expressed the belief that God, in his nature, is much more forgiving, understanding, and just than we as humans are able to comprehend, and that God will take care of these things in accordance with his love and wisdom. What a suicidal person needs from us as fellow humans is not judgment but love and understanding. (*Reflections on Life After Death*, p. 49)

Keith A. Haslem

THE CHURCH OF JESUS CHRIST OF LATTER-DAY SAINTS PERSPECTIVE

Some people who commit suicide may not be accountable for that act.

BRUCE R. MCCONKIE
(an apostle for the Church of Jesus Christ of Latter-day Saints, 1972–1985)

Bruce R. McConkie defined suicide as "the voluntary or intentional taking of one's own life, particularly where the person involved is accountable and has a sound mind" (*Mormon Doctrine*, p. 771).

By this definition, someone who takes their own life while under the influence of drugs or while in a state of severe depression may not be of "sound mind," and therefore, their act may not be accurately termed "suicide,"—an action which is commonly acknowledged as being contrary to the will of God.

Bruce R. McConkie also said:

> Persons subject to great stresses may lose control of themselves and become mentally clouded to the point that they are no longer accountable for their acts. Such are not to be condemned for taking their own lives. It should be remembered that judgment is the Lord's; He knows the thoughts, intents, and abilities of men; and He in His infinite wisdom will make all things right in due course. (*Mormon Doctrine*, p. 771)

AUTHOR'S PERSPECTIVE

If you are considering suicide . . .

You may think that even going to hell would be better that your current life, but what if you don't go anywhere? What if you stay in your present circumstances and have to stand as a helpless witness to the grief and suffering your suicide has inflicted upon those you love and those who love you? Would that not be worse than hell?

Some suicides may not be accountable.

I believe many suicides are committed by individuals suffering severe depression or who are otherwise not of a "sound mind," and therefore may not be accountable for their act. It may become a minor consideration when all the deeds of their lives are "weighed in the balance" (Daniel 5:27).

Working through our grief

If part of these individuals' unpleasant consequences is to witness the anguish of those left behind, then as survivors we can reduce their suffering by working through our grief, forgiving them, and getting on with enjoying our lives.

59

WHEN DOES THE SPIRIT ENTER THE BODY?

SYNOPSIS

Many people assume that the spirit enters the body the moment the mother first feels movement in her womb. Betty J. Eadie's and RaNelle Wallace's experiences suggest that may not always be the case.

The spirit of a fetus may have the agency to decide when to enter it's body. Even though the mother feels life in her womb, it may be that the spirit doesn't enter the body until the moment of delivery.

BETTY J. EADIE

"At any stage of her pregnancy"

I learned that spirits can choose to enter their mother's body at any stage of her pregnancy. Once there, they immediately begin experiencing mortality (*Embraced by the Light*, p. 95).

RANELLE WALLACE

Moments before her son's birth, RaNelle saw her son—who had the appearance of a mature male—standing beside her. He was concerned at the pain she was enduring during his delivery. (See Chapter 62.)

THE CHURCH OF JESUS CHRIST OF LATTER-DAY SAINTS PERSPECTIVE

Nephi, one of the prophets of the Book of Mormon, lived on the American continent at the time Jesus Christ was born in Bethlehem. One night, Nephi was praying fervently to God on behalf of his fellow disciples who were about to be killed because of their faith in the prophecies of Jesus's birth. He records that his prayer was answered by Jesus Christ Himself, who would be born the next day.

"On this night . . . come I into the world."

> And it came to pass that he [Nephi] cried mightily unto the Lord all that day; and behold, the voice of the Lord came unto him, saying:
> Lift up your head and be of good cheer; for behold, the time is at hand, and on this night shall the sign be given, and on the morrow come I into the world, to show unto the world that I will fulfil all that which I have caused to be spoken by the mouth of my holy prophets. (3 Nephi 1:12–13)

If Jesus spoke to Nephi in answer to his prayer, it is logical that Jesus's spirit was not at that moment within the baby which would be born of Mary later that night. The deductive conclusion is that a fetus can be alive and developing without the spirit being present.

AUTHOR'S PERSPECTIVE

And what would be the purpose of confining a mature spirit to a womb for nine months?

60

CAN THE SPIRITS OF COMATOSE PEOPLE LEAVE THEIR BODIES?

SYNOPSIS

Based upon the experiences of several of the Witnesses, it appears possible that the spirits of comatose individuals *can* leave their bodies and go to the world of spirits.

Captain Black's book, *Flight to Heaven,* details his experience in the world of spirits while his body was in a coma for three days after his crash in a small plane. His experiences have been referenced a number of times in this book.

Dr. Mary C. Neal believes death is a function of when the spirit leaves the body, not when the body's physical functions cease.

SARAH LANELLE MENET

"Even though the spirit is not in it, the body can still appear to be alive."

Upon returning to her body in the hospital, Sarah made the following observation:

"Like awakening from a bad dream I gradually realized I was re-entering my physical body. Through this process I learned that even though the spirit is not in it, the body can still appear to be alive and functioning. There is a space or period of time that the spirit can be separated from the body, but the spirit must return within that time or it cannot enter again" (*There Is No Death*, p. 75).

MARY C. NEAL

Dr. Neal, an orthopedic surgeon, is of the opinion that it is possible for a person's soul to depart for the spirit world while the body remains behind in a comatose state. Some time after her near-death experience, Dr. Neal wrote of visiting her father in a hospital.

"The departure of the soul defines and determines the moment of death."

> When I entered the room where my father was lying in the hospital bed, I saw that he was sedated and the ventilator was rhythmically pushing air in and out of his lungs. Although he was "alive," I had the overwhelming sense, really more of a deep knowledge, that his soul had already departed from his body. He was already dead. Although it is a commonly-held belief that a person's soul departs at the moment of their physical death, I have come to believe that the departure of the soul defines and determines the moment of death, rather than the body's physical death determining the moment of the soul's departure. With the use of modern medicine and technology, the organism that is our human body may continue to physically function and appear to be "alive," but unless God sees a purpose to return the soul to its body, the person is essentially dead. Not only had I witnessed this during my surgical training, but there are far too many accounts of near-death experiences in which there is a description of the soul departing the shell of its not-yet physically dead body to ignore this reality. (*To Heaven and Back*, pp. 125–26)

CAPTAIN DALE BLACK

Nevertheless, many cases exist, similar to Captain Black's, where a long-time comatose person regains full function. The simple explanation is; "With God all things are possible" (Matthew 19:26).

MELVIN L. MORSE

The possibility exists that the spirit of a comatose person does remain in their body. In that scenario, Dr. Morse suggests that we should

Keith A. Haslem

"Talk positively and frequently . . . to comatose or dying patients."

"It is also important to talk positively and frequently to comatose or dying patients since we now know that they may be much more aware of things around them than we realize. Indeed, they may even be hovering above us as we administer to them!" (*Closer to the Light*, p. 102).

AUTHOR'S PERSPECTIVE

The decision to take a comatose loved one off of life support must be one of the most difficult decisions one can be confronted with. However, it may well be that the loved one's spirit has already crossed over to the spirit world. Based upon the many accounts I've read, once they are in paradise they have *no desire* to return.

Perhaps the survivors should seek to know whether or not their loved one has fulfilled their mission on earth and is fit to die. If the person has fulfilled their mission and is ready to go, perhaps the survivors should release their hold and allow their loved one to go or stay where they likely want to be—*if* that is in accordance with God's will.

CAN SPIRITS APPEAR TO US DURING OUR DREAMS?

Many people tell of dreams in which their deceased loved ones appeared to them. They might think it was "just a dream," but some of our resources state that dreams are an avenue that the dead use to communicate with us.

SYNOPSIS

Sarah LaNelle Menet learned that the spirits of the dead can appear to us during our dreams.

Michele R. Sorenson and David R. Willmore point out that there are many biblical accounts that show that individuals can receive heavenly instructions through their dreams.

Parley P. Pratt taught that our loved ones can communicate with us in dreams.

My own mother appeared to me in a dream.

SARAH LANELLE MENET

"Deceased loved ones may visit us in dreams."

> To counter the influence of those evil spirits, there are also a lot of good spirits around us. . . . Usually these good spirits around us are loved ones, family members who have either passed away or who have not yet come to earth. . . . One of the ways these good spirits communicate with us is through dreams. Deceased loved ones may visit us in dreams and bring feelings of comfort and encouragement. Occasionally when we wake up we can remember specific messages

Keith A. Haslem

or images, but usually it is just impressions and feelings. (*There Is No Death*, pp. 101–2)

Sarah goes on to discuss the cause of nightmares.

"Nightmares are . . . caused . . . by evil spirits."

"Unfortunately, evil spirits can also use dreams as a means of communication. Most nightmares are actually caused or influenced by evil spirits. . . . For this reason it is extremely important to pray at night and ask God to keep us safe from evil" (*There Is No Death*, p. 102).

MICHELE R. SORENSON and DAVID R. WILLMORE

The authors of the book *The Journey Beyond Life* discuss the biblical accounts that reference spiritual communications during sleep.

"Over thirty scriptural references . . . where communications . . . occurred through dreams."

There are over thirty significant scriptural references in the Standard Works where communications from beyond the veil occurred through dreams. One of the more familiar examples is found in the gospel of Matthew, where Joseph is warned in a dream to take Mary and Jesus and flee into Egypt to escape the wrath of King Herod, and then to return once again following his death. (*The Journey Beyond Life*, p. 49)

THE CHURCH OF JESUS CHRIST OF LATTER-DAY SAINTS PERSPECTIVE

PARLEY P. PRATT
(a member of the first Quorum of the Twelve Apostles)

Parley P. Pratt, an apostle during the early years of the Church of Jesus Christ of Latter-day Saints, tells that beings from the spirit world sometimes communicate with mortals during their dreams.

Going Home

"We frequently hold communication with our departed [family members].... Their guardian angels then hover about them with the fondest affection."

When the outward organs of thought and perception are released from their activity, the nerves unstrung, and the whole of mortal humanity lies hushed in quiet slumbers, in order to renew its strength and vigor, it is then that the spiritual organs are at liberty, in a certain degree, to assume their wonted [familiar, normal] functions, to recall some faint outlines, some confused and half-defined recollections, of that heavenly world, and those endearing scenes of their former estate, from which they have descended in order to obtain and mature a tabernacle of flesh. Their kindred spirits, their guardian angels, then hover about them with the fondest affection, the most anxious solicitude. Spirit communes with spirit, thought meets thought, soul blends with soul in all the raptures of mutual, pure, and eternal love.

In this situation, the spiritual organs are susceptible of converse with Deity, or of communion with angels, and the spirits of just men made perfect.

In this situation, we frequently hold communication with our departed father, mother, brother, sister, son or daughter, or with the former husband or wife of our bosom, whose affection for us, being rooted and grounded in the eternal elements . . . , can never be lessened or diminished by death, distance of space, or length of years. . . .

With what tenderness of love, with what solicitude of affection will they watch over our slumbers, hand about our pillow, and seek to communicate with our spirits, to warn us of dangers or temptation, to comfort and soothe our sorrow, or to ward off the ills which might befall us, or perchance to give us some kind token of remembrance or undying love! (*Key to the Science of Theology*, p. 71)

ANONYMOUS ACCOUNT

I know a young lady who lost her elderly grandmother. At about the same time, she realized that the young man she had hoped to marry was not the one that she should marry, and was grieving that realization.

Later, she had a dream where she conversed with her grandmother briefly. She apologized that she hadn't grieved her grandmother's death like she should have. Her grandmother comforted her, and told her she knew how she felt, having had a similar experience with a young man in her own youth.

AUTHOR'S EXPERIENCE

Mom appears to me in a dream.

My mother passed away in 2010. I believed, if permitted by those in authority in the world of spirits, that it was possible for my mother to visit me. So, I made that request in my personal prayers.

Not long afterward, I had, what I thought at the time, was a dream. I was looking out upon a large number of people coming and going. I recognized my mother some distance off. Being cognizant at that moment that she was a spirit and that it might not be appropriate for me to talk to her, I stood there wondering whether or not I should try to seek her out. Suddenly she was in front of me. Still not sure whether it was appropriate for her to talk to me I could only think to ask, "Mom, is it ok for you to be here?" She said nothing but smiled sweetly at me. And then she was gone.

Most dreams are forgotten within hours or days. This dream has remained vivid in my memory for years now. As I've contemplated it's meaning I have come to the following conclusions:

(1) Mom was not "here," rather I was there, in the spirit world, having a brief out-of-body experience.

(2) I had this experience because I requested it. With faith that it could be granted, and it was—as an example of "the tender mercies of the Lord" that we periodically see manifest in our lives.

(3) While I had hoped that Mom would visit me while in a conscious state so it would be an unmistakable event, her appearance in a dream has afforded me the opportunity to exercise a greater level of faith.

AUTHOR'S PERSPECTIVE

I have read many accounts and talked to many people who have had similar experiences, seeing and sometimes conversing with deceased family members during their sleep. We are so busy with the demands of everyday living that perhaps the easiest time a departed spirit can "get through" to us is during our dream state.

62

WERE FAMILIES PLANNED BEFORE WE CAME TO EARTH?

SYNOPSIS

With the understanding that we all lived in a premortal world the question could arise: "Were our mortal families organized while in this pre-existent state?"

The experiences of four of the six Witnesses suggest that the answer may be "Yes."

RaNelle Wallace met a young man and young woman during her experience that were intended as her future children.

Betty J. Eadie also met her future daughter and Sarah LaNelle Menet saw her future son from a distance.

RANELLE WALLACE

RaNelle meets her future children.

While in spirit world, RaNelle met a number of friends, one of whom seemed to bond with her in a unique way.

> My friends embraced me again and committed to stay with me. I felt their perfect love and knew they would never leave me. One female friend lingered and embraced me for a long time. She seemed bonded to me in a unique way, but I didn't quite understand what it was. "You know I've always been with you," she said. "I've never left you. And I never will." She hung on every word I said, and I was moved as I

Keith A. Haslem

> recognized her passion to be with me, her absolute devotion and love. "I'll always be there," she said again. (*The Burning Within*, p. 109)

When told she needed to return to her body, RaNelle was resistant. But after meeting the spirit who was intended to be her future son, she relented:

> Grandma waved her arm and the ground opened before us. I looked and saw a person lying on a hospital bed surrounded by doctors and nurses. The person's face was bandaged.
>
> "You will never be the same, RaNelle," Grandma said. "Your face will be altered and your body filled with pain. When you go back, you will have years of rehabilitation."
>
> "When I go back?" I looked at her. "You expect me to go back?" Sudden understanding came, and I looked at the person on the bed. The arms were spread wide, and both arms and hands had been sliced in several places to allow fluids to drain into plastic bags.
>
> "Is that me?" I was horrified.
>
> "Yes, RaNelle, it is you. You will be badly scarred."
>
> I became frantic. "Grandma, I'm not going back."
>
> "Your children need you, RaNelle."
>
> "No, they don't. They're better off with someone else. I can't give them what they need."
>
> "It's not just your children, RaNelle. You have things to do—things aren't finished yet."
>
> "No, I'm not returning to that body! I'm not going back."
>
> In response, my grandmother swept out her arm and commanded, "Look!"
>
> A rift opened in the space before us, and I saw a young man walking toward us. At first he didn't seem to understand why he was there. Then he saw me and looked stunned.
>
> "Why are you here?" he said almost in disbelief. As I remained silent, his disbelief changed to grief, and he began crying. I felt his grief, his sadness, and I too began crying.
>
> "What's the matter?" I asked. "Why are you crying?" I put my arms around him, trying to comfort him.
>
> "Why are you here?" he repeated.
>
> Then I understood that my refusal to go back to earth was causing him sadness. I belonged on earth for him, I understood, and I immediately felt guilt for my selfishness.

Going Home

His name was Nathaniel, and he hadn't been born on earth yet. He said that if I didn't go back, his own mission would be hindered. Then he showed me his mission, and I saw that I was to open doors for him, to help him, to encourage him.

"I will complete as much of my mission as I can," he said, "but I will never fulfill it without you. I need you."

I thought my heart would break. I was a part of his puzzle, and I was hurting him and everyone he would help by refusing to go back to earth. I felt a great love for this young man, and I wanted to help him in every way I could.

"Oh, Nathaniel," I said, "I swear to you that I will help you. I will go back, and I promise that I will do everything I can to do my part. I will open those doors for you. I will protect and encourage you. I will give you everything I have. Nathaniel, you will complete your mission. I love you."

His grief was replaced with gratitude. His face lit up, and I saw the great spirit he was. He was crying now with gratitude and joy.

"Thank you," he said. "Oh, I love you."

My grandmother took my hand and drew me away. Nathaniel watched me leave, still smiling, and I distinctly heard him say, "I love you, Mom." (*The Burning Within*, pp. 114–16)

A few years after her near-death experience, RaNelle became pregnant. When a baby girl was delivered she was "astonished." She had been expecting a boy—Nathaniel.

> We named her Danielle, and she and I immediately had more than a mother-daughter bond; from the beginning, it was a bond of friends. I began to recognize the kind of bond I had shared within a circle of friends. One of them had clung to me, vowing that she would never leave me. . . . I see the look in her eyes that reminds me of a former world. We have been friends for a long, long time. (*The Burning Within*, pp. 199–200)

Almost seven years after her near-death experience, RaNelle struggled through a difficult childbirth. She recounts:

> It was about four o'clock on Sunday afternoon, August 22, 1992. The soundtrack from "Somewhere in Time" was playing on a stereo near my bed, the beautiful, haunting melody of a story of love beyond this life. As this music soothed me between contractions, an impression came that I was being watched from my right side. I turned and saw

Keith A. Haslem

a man standing there, a tall man with dark hair and blue eyes. He was dressed in a white suit. Was I seeing things? I closed my eyes and looked again, and the young man was still there, next to me. His eyes were wide and mournful. I had seen those eyes before, those sorrowful eyes. But now he was lamenting the pain I was going through, the suffering I was experiencing for him. He opened his mouth and said, "Thank you, Mom," and a wave of love came into me that blew my spirit into a spin. I looked at him through tears and said, "Thank you." Then he was gone.

The baby finally settled down and the contractions became consistent. The nurses and Annie returned. Terry [RaNelle's husband] also came in and stood against a wall at the far end of the room. I gave a final push and heard a little cry. Annie said, "You've got a beautiful baby boy, RaNelle. I hope you've got a name for him."

Terry came forward and looked at the baby, and Annie let him clip the cord. "It's Nathaniel, isn't it?" he said.

I nodded, still crying. (*The Burning Within*, pp. 204–205)

BETTY J. EADIE

"We had bonded together in the spirit world . . . [and] covenanted . . . to come to earth as [a] family."

I was told that we had bonded together in the spirit world with certain spirit brothers and sisters—those we felt especially close to. My escorts explained that we covenanted with these spirits to come to earth as family or friends. This spiritual bonding was a result of the love we developed for each other over an eternity of being together (*Embraced by the Light*, p. 92).

Betty saw the spirit of man trying to get his future father and mother together:

"Playing cupid"

I saw again the spirits who had not yet come to earth, and I saw some of them hovering over people in mortality. I saw one male spirit trying to get a mortal man and woman together on earth—his future parents. He was playing cupid and was having a very difficult time. The man and woman seemed to want to go in opposite directions and were unwittingly very uncooperative. This male spirit was coaching them, speaking to them, trying to persuade them to get together.

Going Home

> Other spirits became concerned as they saw his difficulty, and they took up the cause, several of them trying to "corral" these two young people. (*Embraced by the Light*, p. 92)

During her NDE, Betty meets her future daughter.

> Before this scene of the pre-earth life spirits was closed up, my attention was drawn to another spirit. She was one of the most charming and delightful beings I had ever seen. She was buoyant with energy and radiated a contagious cheer to all around her. Watching her with wonder, I recognized the feeling of a close bond between us and the love that I knew she felt for me. My memory of this moment has been mostly blocked, but I knew that I would never forget her, and there was no doubt that wherever she went she was going to be somebody's special angel. (*Embraced by the Light*, p. 97)

After returning to her body, while still in the hospital, Betty describes the visitation of the spirit of a child to her:

> A beautiful little girl came into the room. She was only two or three years old and was the only child that I had seen in the spirit. A golden halo of light emanated from her, glowing in the room wherever she walked. She seemed quite attracted to Joe [Betty's husband]. . . . I asked him if he could see her. He couldn't. She had the grace of a ballerina, walking almost on the tips of her toes and performing little gestures, as though she were dancing. I was struck immediately by her spontaneity and happiness. She went to Joe and stood on the toe of his shoe. She balanced on one foot and kicked her other leg up behind her like a ballerina might, and leaned forward to reach into his pants pocket. I was mesmerized by this movement. I asked her what she was doing. She turned and laughed, smiling in an impish way, and I knew that she had heard me. But she didn't reply. I sensed her inner joy, the pure, exuberant happiness that filled her inside. She then faded from my view and never reappeared, but I knew I would never forget her. (*Embraced by the Light*, p. 129–30)

Eleven years after her near-death experience, Betty tells the story of agreeing to serve as a foster mother of a Native American baby who was given up by her alcoholic parents. It was supposed to be for just a few months, but the whole family quickly fell in love with the baby. And then came a heartrending turn of events:

Keith A. Haslem

She was ten and a half months old when the case worker called to tell me that they had found relatives for her in another state. The adoptive parents would be by in a few days to pick her up. I was stunned. Joe and I had signed an agreement saying that we would not attempt adoption, but now I was desperate. We had known all along she couldn't be ours, but now I was in the worst agony a mother can know. I was about to lose my child. . . .

When the new parents drove up, I carried her to the car. . . . The baby realized that she was being taken from me and began to scream. My heart broke. As the car drove off, I stood immobile. The vision of my precious little girl crying with hands outstretched, reaching for me, burned into my soul. I broke down and ran into the house, the image searing me. It was to torment me for months to come. . . .

After three months I began praying to the Lord to return her to me. . . .

[One] night I was awakened by a messenger who stood by my bed. I understood that he had come from the spirit world. He said that the situation with my baby was not right, that she would be returned to me. He said I would receive a phone call in which the caller would say, "I have good news, and I have bad news." I did not sleep the rest of the night.

For the next two weeks I would not leave the house. Every time the phone rang I jumped for it. . . .

The phone rang early one morning, and I heard a voice plainly say, "Betty, this is Ellen. I have some good news, and I have some bad news." The voice continued, explaining that my baby was in a hospital. "She wouldn't adjust to the new family" Ellen said, "and she kept crying. You were her mommy for ten months, and she's been looking for you."

Ellen went on to explain that as the baby cried, tempers rose, and one night in a drunken rage the parents beat her and threw her down a flight of stairs. The baby had then been taken to a hospital and abandoned, where she lay critically ill for two weeks. She was not responding to treatment and the doctors recognized that in her emotional state she might never recover. Finally Ellen said, "Betty, our last hope is you. We know we're asking a lot, but could you please take her back for a while, at least until she gets better?"

Betty and her family traveled to an airport to pick the baby up from a case worker:

Going Home

Then to one side I spotted them, but the baby didn't resemble the image in my memories at all. Still, I knew it was her. "That's my baby!" I heard myself screaming as I ran to them and snatched her out of his arms.

The baby was bald except for tufts of hair here and there. Her eyes were swollen, and one eyebrow was cut and bruised. She recognized me immediately and clutched me tightly, with both her arms and little legs wrapped tightly around me. "What have they done? What have they done?" I cried. . . .

For the next few months she wouldn't let me leave her sight. . . .

Joe and I hired an attorney to begin immediate adoption proceedings. . . .

The court reviewed the matter and considered all the evidence. The decision was soon in coming: she was ours. . . .

By the time little Betty [their adopted daughter] was two and a half, she had fully recovered both physically and emotionally. She became once again the most darling and playful child in the house, surprising us constantly with her quick sense of humor. One afternoon she ran over to Joe. As an impish smile came to her face, she stood up on the toe of his shoe, threw her other foot up behind her, and balancing like a ballerina reached up to dig into the pocket of his slacks. A chill ran through me as memories flooded back. Little Betty laughed, and I heard the voice of a little girl years before, a little girl who had kept us company in a hospital room when heaven and earth seemed one. Then I saw and understood more. A vision of a young woman came back to me, a memory of a beautiful and energetic spirit who had once been waiting to come to earth. I remembered her as the young spirit with whom I shared a bond in a previous time, the one in the spirit world whose loveliness and energy captivated me. I wanted to cry as everything about this precious angel came together. I had been allowed to see her as a child in the spirit. Now I knew why I had been shown her as an adult spirit ready to come to earth. I knew also that while she could not be born to me because of my hysterectomy, she had found another way to become part of my life. And now I knew why I had been compelled to take her as a baby. We were closest of friends forever, eternities of experiences behind us, and eternities ahead. (*Embraced by the Light*, pp. 135–46)

Keith A. Haslem

SARAH LANELLE MENET

"We formed groups . . . with those spirits we wanted to have as part of our earthly family."

> We spent thousands of years as spirits before coming to earth, and we will spend millions more in the spirit world and beyond after we leave this existence. . . .
>
> When it came time for us to come here . . . we formed groups and were organized with those spirits we wanted to have as part of our earthly family. Usually we chose to be with those spirits to whom we were closest, the spirit friends we loved the most from whom we could learn the most. (*There Is No Death*, pp. 96, 104–5)

"I was impressed with the feeling that he was to be my child."

While viewing Christ visiting a "city of light" in the spirit world, Sarah saw her future son:

> As I looked down upon this scene, only one person in the city looked back at me. He was a handsome young man with dark hair and dark eyes, and he caught my attention just for a moment. I was impressed with the feeling that he was to be my child. I thought that could not come to fruition because I should not have any more children due to my diabetes, and I was now in a place where this would be impossible. This thought lasted for just a moment, and then he turned back toward the Savior. The full understanding of this experience came later in my life. (*There Is No Death*, p. 49)

Several years after her near-death experience Sarah adopted a baby:

> I met a young girl who was pregnant. I trained her as a waitress at Twains and befriended her. She wanted to have an abortion, but I talked her out of it by agreeing to pay all the expenses of the birth and adopting the baby. For some reason I really wanted the baby. It took every dime I could scrape together for the adoption, including selling most of my furniture, but I felt it was worth it.
>
> While the adoption was in process, a man whom I had never seen before came into the restaurant. He was friendly, and we started talking. It came out that I was working hard to earn enough money to pay for legal fees for the adoption. He said he would like to help. I politely turned him down a couple of times because I didn't know him and was afraid of doing something with "strings attached." The

conversation turned to other things, and he left. The next day he showed up again and handed me an envelope. He said, "Just a little contribution to help." In it was two thousand dollars with a note saying it was for the baby. I never saw him again. I thanked the Lord with all my might for this miracle. It was after [the baby's] birth that I realized that this precious little baby was the spirit who had looked up at me from the city I visited in Paradise. I knew that God wanted me to name him Elias. (*There Is No Death*, pp. 87–88)

ELANE DURHAM

"I was able to see a number of children that were to be 'mine.'"

I saw that the choice of my mortal family had already been made, and that I was quite anxious to join them. I knew that I would be entering mortality as the oldest of a family of several children, and I knew that our family would have problems, even severe ones. Yet I had agreed to these conditions willingly for the purpose of the soul growth we would all experience. . . .

I was able to see a number of children that were to be "mine." They had helped choose to have me in their world either as a birth mother, grandmother, or foster mother, and I had willingly agreed. (pp. 83–84)

SARAH HINZE

In her book *Coming from the Light*, Sarah Hinze records the stories of many people who saw their children before they were born, and she includes the following account.

Cheryl Cayer

Cheryl Cayer writes of the events that led to their adoption of an infant:

"Mommy."

I raised my head, listening to hear the voice again, thinking one of my daughters needed something.

"Mommy."

The voice was unfamiliar. I sat up, and to my surprise, saw a figure at the end of my bed. The figure was like a shadow, but all in white, with dark hair and a dark complexion. I shook my head and

Keith A. Haslem

thought I must be dreaming, but his arms were outstretched, reaching for me.

I thought, "This can't be for real." I reached for my glasses, thinking my eyes were playing tricks on me. Still, there was a child at the end of my bed. I thought, "What do you want?" He spoke to me in a voice that I could hear, but cannot describe.

"Mommy, it's time for me to come."

That's when I realized he was the fourth child I had been promised. Excitement filled my soul, and then he disappeared.

I could not wait to share my great joy with my husband, Ray, who was up early studying for exams. When I shared the news, Ray said, "Cheryl, you just want another child. Don't get your hopes up. There is no way we can adopt a child. We have three girls. And medically, we know you can't have another child."

A short time afterward, Ray was working and had his music playing when he saw a light on in the corridor down the hall. As he walked toward the light, the music stopped and an overwhelming peace came over him. He was reassured that our fourth child was coming.

We began to prepare ourselves and submitted our forms for adoption of a native child. We had applied before in Wetaskiwin and were turned down. We felt there was no point in trying there again, but then my husband felt that we must move to Leduc and try again. This time, to our surprise, everything went quickly and within no time there was a call from Calgary. They had a child and wanted us to come down the following day.

With great excitement, I drove to the school to tell Ray our baby had arrived. When he opened the door, he was not surprised at all. He just smiled and said, "I know."

As we traveled on our way, I felt very impressed that our son should be named Matthew. When we arrived, the social worker met us and made it very clear that this child was a native, that he was very different from us. None of this mattered. All we wanted was the child we already knew.

When the social worker placed him in Ray's arms, I quickly unwrapped the small infant and knew he was our son, Matthew. A shining beam came forth from his beautiful, dark eyes as if to say, "Mommy, I am here. I am here."

My heart swelled, just as it did after giving birth to my daughters.

When the social worker later came to our home to see how we all were doing, she remarked, "You really shouldn't be getting this child. You haven't waited very long, but for some reason your file kept coming to the top each morning. At first I thought it was a mistake, but when it happened again, I felt impressed to call you."

The unknowing social worker simply reconfirmed what we already knew—some things are meant to be. Our family was now complete and united. (*Coming from the Light*, pp. 27–29)

DR. WAYNE W. DYER and DEE GARNES

Dr. Wayne W. Dyer and Dee Garnes published a book titled *Memories of Heaven* in 2015 in which they share vignettes written by individuals who have had experiences with their children or other very young people who apparently remembered scenes from their premortal existence. These vignettes include the children choosing their parents and associating with other family members that had already lived and died.

AUTHOR'S PERSPECTIVE

Would God send His spirit children to earth randomly?

Can you imagine God sending an exceptional, highly intelligent and advanced spirit into the primitive Pantanal of Brazil where they would have virtually no opportunity to progress, saying, "Well, it's your turn to go down, and the next delivery is in the Pantanal. Tough break for you. Well, off you go."

If God is perfect in every way, then He is a perfect planner. This would suggest that He planned, or allowed to be planned, family relationships in the premortal realm in order to accommodate premortal friends wanting to share their mortal lives, or to place individuals in family situations that would be the most compatible with their specific needs, abilities, and best interests.

I find it interesting that adoptions seem to be a not uncommon mechanism to unite intended families.

However, I suspect that, being perfect, God likely has a "Plan B," "Plan C," etc., in case couples that were intended to be together, in the exercise of their agency, did not end up together.

63

WILL I BE REUNITED WITH THE CHILD I LOST?

SYNOPSIS

If we are to enjoy an eventual reunion with our family members it can be assumed that we will also be reunited with a son or daughter who was lost during mortality. But if that child has the spirit of an adult, the natural question might be: "At the Resurrection, will the child I lost be an adult or will they be the same age they were when they died?"

Although none of the Witnesses addressed this question specifically, it is of sufficient import to so many parents that I will include the The Church of Jesus Christ of Latter-day Saints Perspective for the comfort and consolation it may offer. According to the The Church of Jesus Christ of Latter-day Saints Perspective, those who die young will be resurrected at the same age that they died, and their parents may have the opportunity to raise them to physical maturity.

THE CHURCH OF JESUS CHRIST OF LATTER-DAY SAINTS PERSPECTIVE

JOSEPH F. SMITH
(sixth prophet and president of the Church of Jesus Christ of Latter-day Saints)

Resurrected at the age when their death occurred.

Going Home

Joseph F. Smith reiterates the teachings of Joseph Smith Jr. (first prophet and president of the Church of Jesus Christ of Latter-day Saints) who taught that it may be possible for parents who have lost a child to one day resume the privilege of raising that child.

"The mother who laid down her little child . . . [will] after the resurrection . . . have all the joy . . . in seeing her child grow to the full measure of the stature of its spirit."

Our beloved friends who are now deprived of their little one, have great cause for joy and rejoicing, even in the midst of the deep sorrow that they feel at the loss of their little one for a time. They know that he is all right; they have the assurance that their little one has passed away without sin. Such children are in the bosom of the Father. They will inherit their glory and their exultation, and they will not be deprived of the blessings that belong to them. . . .

Joseph Smith Jr. declared that the mother who laid down her little child, being deprived of the privilege, the joy, and the satisfaction of bringing it up to manhood or womanhood in this world, would, after the resurrection, have all the joy, satisfaction and pleasure, and even more than it would have been possible to have had in mortality, in seeing her child grow to the full measure of the stature of its spirit. . . .

It matters not whether these tabernacles mature in this world, or have to wait and mature in the world to come, according to the word of the Prophet Joseph Smith, the body will develop, either in time or in eternity, to the full stature of the spirit, and when the mother is deprived of the pleasure and joy of rearing her babe to manhood or womanhood in this life, through the hand of death, that privilege will be renewed to her hereafter, and she will enjoy it to a fuller fruition than it would be possible for her to do here. When she does it there, it will be with the certain knowledge that the results will be without failure; whereas here, the results are unknown until after we have passed the test.

With these thoughts in my mind, I take consolation in the fact that I shall meet my children who have passed behind the veil; I have lost a number, and I have felt all that a parent can feel, I think, in the loss of my children. I have felt it keenly, for I love children, and I am particularly fond of the little ones, but I feel thankful to God for the knowledge of these principles, because now I have every confidence in his word and in his promise that I will possess in the future all that

Keith A. Haslem

belongs to me, and my joy will be full. I will not be deprived of any privilege or any blessing that I am worthy of and that may be properly entrusted to me. But every gift, and every blessing, that is possible for me to become of I shall possess, either in time or in eternity, and it will not matter, so that I acknowledge the hand of God in all these things, and say in my heart, "The Lord giveth and the Lord taketh away, blessed be the name of the Lord." This is the way we should feel with regard to our children, or our relatives, or friends, or whatever vicissitudes we may be called to pass through. (*Gospel Doctrine*, pp. 452–54)

WILFORD WOODRUFF
(fourth prophet and president of the Church of Jesus Christ of Latter-day Saints)

President Woodruff taught:

"Our children will be restored to us as they are laid down."

"Children are taken way in their infancy, and they go to the spirit world. . . . Our children will be restored to us as they are laid down if we, their parents, keep the faith and prove ourselves worthy to obtain eternal life" (*For They Shall Be Comforted*, Burton, p. 60).

To summarize the basic doctrine of the Church of Jesus Christ of Latter-day Saints on this issue:

Members of the Church of Jesus Christ of Latter-day Saints believe that the first and most important purpose for coming to earth is to gain a physical body—an essential step in our eternal progression. This is accomplished even though a baby may live only a matter of moments after birth.

Another important reason to come to earth is to prove our worthiness to inherit the kingdom of God after we are resurrected. Some spirits come to earth but they have already done so much to prove themselves in the premortal realm that they do not need to be tested as mortals.

Members of the Church of Jesus Christ of Latter-day Saints believe that any child who dies before the age of eight will automatically inherit heaven.

If parents who have lost babies or young children comply with the requisite laws and ordinances of God, Members of the Church of Jesus Christ of Latter-day Saints believe that the children lost to them will be reunited with them in the Resurrection—at the same age that they were lost. Those parents will then have the privilege to raise them up in an existence that is devoid of evil influences; and therefore, an existence that is much happier than our present existence.

AUTHOR'S PERSPECTIVE

If the doctrine of the Church of Jesus Christ of Latter-day Saints is true, then parents who have lost children on earth have the comfort of knowing that their child's salvation in heaven is ensured, and the joys of raising them may not be lost but are merely postponed until after the Second Coming of Jesus Christ and the resurrection of the righteous.

64

ARE THERE CHILD SPIRITS IN THE SPIRIT WORLD?

If we lived before coming to earth for perhaps eons of time, then it is logical that our spirits would have been mature at the time of our earthly birth.

SYNOPSIS

Betty J. Eadie, RaNelle Wallace, and other Witnesses seem to confirm that there are no child spirits in the spirit world.

BETTY J. EADIE

"I saw no child spirits."

"My escorts . . . took me to a place where many spirits prepared for life on earth. They were mature spirits—I saw no children spirits during my entire experience" (*Embraced by the Light*, p. 89).

RANELLE WALLACE

RaNelle sees her son as an adult, moments before he is born.

During her near-death experience, RaNelle met a young man who she understood was intended to be her future son. Almost seven years after her experience, as RaNelle struggled through a difficult childbirth, she recounted seeing her son's mature, adult spirit standing next to her. (See Chapter 62.)

RAYMOND A. MOODY JR.

Dr. Moody talked to child NDErs who said that they were adults during their NDE.

"Over the last couple of years, I've started asking children how old they are during the NDE. In other words, is their spirit body one of a child or an adult? A surprising number of them say that they are adults during the episode, although they can't say how they know this" (*The Light Beyond*, p. 74).

JEFFREY LONG

Dr. Long talks about NDErs encountering family members during their experience. He also noted: "Those [family members] who died as very young children may appear older. But even if the deceased appear to be a very different age than when they died, the NDEr still recognizes them" (*Evidence of the Afterlife*, p. 129).

DUANE S. CROWTHER

Duane's wife sees their deceased child as an adult spirit.

In Duane Crowther's book *Life Everlasting*, he describes how his daughter, who died as a young girl, was seen by his wife on the day that their daughter died. But his wife said that she had the appearance of a young woman who appeared to be about twenty years of age.

Later, she was seen again, as an adult spirit, by members of an audience that Duane Crowther was addressing—regarding the topic of life after death—and she appeared to be there to protect him from spirits that were hostile to his purpose (*Life Everlasting*, see pp. 255–57).

Duane also quotes from the account of Henry Zollinger, who had a near-death experience after being crushed by a hay derrick in August 1920:

"My spirit left my body and I could see it lying under the derrick and at that moment my guardian angel, my mother and my sister Ann were beside me. My mother died Jan. 31, 1918 and *my sister at the age of four years. I saw that her spirit was full grown* in stature and also seemed very intelligent" (*Life Everlasting*, p. 25).

Keith A. Haslem

THE CHURCH OF JESUS CHRIST OF LATTER-DAY SAINTS PERSPECTIVE

JOSEPH F. SMITH
(sixth prophet and president of the Church of Jesus Christ of Latter-day Saints)

"**Our children were full grown . . . before they entered mortality.**"

> The spirits of our children are immortal before they came to us, and their spirits, after bodily death, are like they were before they came. They are as they would have appeared if they had lived in the flesh, to grow to maturity, or to develop their physical bodies to the full stature of their spirits. If you see one of your children that has passed away it may appear to you in the form in which you would recognize it, the form of childhood; but if it came to you as a messenger bearing some important truth, it would perhaps come as the spirit of Bishop Edward Hunter's son (who died when a little child) came to him, in the stature of full-grown manhood, and revealed himself to his father, and said, "I am your son."
>
> Bishop Hunter did not understand it. He went to his father and said: "Hyrum, what does it mean?"
>
> Father [Hyrum Smith, brother of Joseph Smith Jr.] told him that the Spirit of Jesus Christ was full-grown before he was born into the world; and so our children were full-grown and possessed their full stature in the spirit, before they entered mortality, the same stature that they will possess after they have passed away from mortality, and as they will also appear after the resurrection, when they shall have completed their mission. (*Gospel Doctrine*, p. 455)

AUTHOR'S PERSPECTIVE

When a young child, in protest, tells a parent, "I'm not little, I'm big!" are those the words of a wishful child or the words of a mature adult spirit frustrated by their physical immaturity?

Going Home

Could it be the only immaturity of young children is their inability to verbalize and sound like an adult? Is their naivety only based upon a lack of mortal experience? In reality, our children may have greater basic intelligence than we do—based upon their comparative progress in the premortal world—and that superiority will only become manifest after a few years of physical maturation, education, and experience.

WHAT IS THE ROLE OF WOMANHOOD?

In the age of women's liberation and the drive for female success in the professional world, the esteem given to stay-at-home moms has seemingly declined.

SYNOPSIS

Elane Durham and RaNelle Wallace gained a heightened appreciation for the role of women, as bearers and nurturers of the spirit offspring of heavenly parents—a role for which women are generally better suited.

ELANE DURHAM

During her experience, Elane came to an understanding of her role as a woman in bearing and nurturing children.

"Nothing in a woman's life can be more important."

> I understood perfectly my role and position as a woman, and felt absolutely comfortable with it. I was given to understand that men and women are co-creators with God, and that part of the role of women is to bear the mortal bodies of the premortal spirit children of our heavenly parents. But our divine role goes much farther than that, for I was shown how we were given the sacred gift of nurturing. It is no accident that women are more inclined to nurture others than are men, for this was a part of our premortal heritage.
>
> I was also shown how vital a woman's role is, to the exaltation of our heavenly family. It is absolutely essential, and I sensed that

nothing in a woman's life can be more important. As my grandmother used to tell my mother, the hand that rocks the cradle rules the world. This is more true than she could have known.

... Men and women are meant to compliment rather than compete with each other. (*I Stand All Amazed*, pp. 41–42)

RANELLE WALLACE

RaNelle also came to a better understanding of the importance of womanhood.

"Now I love and honor what I can do as a woman."

> We continued on and Grandma showed me the importance of being a mother and the value of the things I did for my children. I saw that my sacrifices for them had not been in vain. Although I had considered myself an unsuccessful mother, in reality I had helped my children more than I realized. I was shown the difference between men's and women's roles, both on earth and hereafter, and I saw things that changed my views on equality and fairness. I have always loved my womanhood, but now I love and honor what I can do as a woman. I don't need to do what a man does to have meaning in life. Womanhood gives me the same eternal significance as manhood gives to men. By fulfilling and magnifying my roles as mother, wife, daughter, sister, friend, I will gain the most glorious rewards possible. For both genders, loving and helping people is the key. (*The Burning Within*, p. 113)

THE CHURCH OF JESUS CHRIST OF LATTER-DAY SAINTS PERSPECTIVE

It should be noted that many women do not have an opportunity to get married and become a mother during mortality. Members of the Church of Jesus Christ of Latter-day Saints believe that no blessing will be denied to women who live worthy of such blessings, whether in mortality or afterward.

Keith A. Haslem

AUTHOR'S PERSPECTIVE

In my forty plus years as an adult, it has been easy to observe that women are superior to men in many ways. They are generally more valiant in their faith and their nurturing abilities with children are clearly superior. They are the "weaker sex" only in terms of their physical capacities, which is of negligible importance.

A devoted and loving mother will be revered by her posterity for the eternities. The same may not be true for a successful woman in the business world.

WHY DID EVE PARTAKE OF THE FORBIDDEN FRUIT?

Some Christians believe that Eve partook of the forbidden fruit because she was foolish enough to be deceived by Satan. God told Adam and Eve that they die if they partook of the fruit. Satan told Eve, "Ye shall not surely die . . . [but] shall be as gods, knowing good and evil." Eve saw that the fruit was "to be desired to make one wise" (Genesis 3:1–6).

Eve likely did want to have the opportunity to gain wisdom. But she may have also had another motivation.

SYNOPSIS

During her experience, Betty J. Eadie gained a new perspective about Eve's motivation to partake of the forbidden fruit. She learned that, in addition to Eve's desire to learn the difference between good and evil, Eve also yearned for the experience of motherhood; an experience which would comply with God's commandment to her and Adam to "multiply, and replenish the earth" (Genesis 1:28).

BETTY J. EADIE

"Eve . . . wanted to become a mother desperately."

> I was shown that Adam was more satisfied with his condition in the Garden and that Eve was more restless. I was shown that she wanted to become a mother desperately enough that she was willing to risk death to obtain it. Eve did not "fall" to temptation as much as she made a conscious decision to bring about the conditions necessary for her progression, and her initiative was used to finally get Adam to

> partake of the fruit. In their partaking of the fruit, then, they brought mankind to mortality, which gave us conditions necessary for having children—but also to die. (*Embraced by the Light*, p. 109)

Essentially, Eve's maternal instincts were at least partial motivation for partaking of the fruit. She wanted to obey another of God's commandments—to "multiply and replenish the earth"—and she knew that couldn't happen within the conditions of the Garden of Eden.

Satan attacks women "through their restlessness."

Betty also offers the additional insight that women are, by nature, "more restless" than men, and that Satan uses this restlessness in his efforts to destroy families.

> I also understood the peril women faced from Satan. I saw that he would use the same process of temptation in the world that had been used in the Garden. He would try to destroy families, and therefore humanity, by tempting women. . . . He would attack women through their restlessness, using the strength of their emotions—the same emotions that gave Eve power to move when Adam was too satisfied with his situation. I understood that he would attack the relationship between husband and wife, distancing them from each other, using the attractions of sex and greed to destroy their home. (*Embraced by the Light*, pp. 109–11)

EVIDENCE OF "FEMININE RESTLESSNESS"?

Is there statistical evidence of this "feminine restlessness" with respect to the disintegration of marriages? The National Center for Health Statistics reports that approximately 50 percent of all marriages end in divorce and approximately 80 percent of divorces are initiated by the wife. This means that approximately 40 percent of all marriages will be ended by the wife ("Why Women File 80 Percent of Divorces," *divorcesource.com*, posted January 20, 2016, www.divorcesource.com/blog/why-women-file-80-percent-of-divorces/).

Of course, this could be a function of factors, from my perception, such as, men are more likely to be abusive, have extra-marital affairs, or be remiss in their duties as a husband, father, and provider.

AUTHOR'S PERSPECTIVE

Mother Eve should be honored, never denigrated. She had the courage and selflessness to lead out—to leave the comforts of the Garden of Eden in order to obey God's commandment to begin the mortal experience of the human family.

67

DO WE HAVE A MOTHER IN HEAVEN?

For those who believe that we have a Father in Heaven, that faith then begs the question: do we also have a Mother in Heaven?

SYNOPSIS

According to Elane Durham and the theology of the Church of Jesus Christ of Latter-day Saints, the answer is "Yes, we do have a Mother in Heaven."

ELANE DURHAM

During her experience, Elaine Durham remembered having family relationships, including a mother, prior to coming to earth.

"I had a Father in heaven [and] a Mother as well."

> In connection with my memory of a premortal life I realized that I was part of a "family" that had been around when this earth was formed from matter in the heavens, and I understood how this family had been organized. I knew not only that I had a Father in heaven but a Mother as well, and that every living soul, including Christ, was the offspring of eternal parents. It was time I had spent living with these parents, prior to my mortal birth, that I was now being allowed to remember. (*I Stand All Amazed*, p. 40)

BIBLICAL PERSPECTIVE

Paul the Apostle, in Acts 17:29, taught that "we are the offspring of God." It is generally understood that offspring are born of two parents: both a father and a mother.

THE CHURCH OF JESUS CHRIST OF LATTER-DAY SAINTS PERSPECTIVE

In order to reinforce the importance of the family unit in a society where it's definition and importance are becoming ambiguous, the Church of Jesus Christ of Latter-day Saints issued an official declaration to the world in 1995. Part of that proclamation states:

"Each is a beloved spirit son or daughter of heavenly parents."

"ALL HUMAN BEINGS—male and female—are created in the image of God. Each is a beloved spirit son or daughter of heavenly parents, and, as such, each has a divine nature and destiny" ("The Family: A Proclamation to the World").

"Our heavenly parents work together for the salvation of the human family."

In October 2015, the Church of Jesus Christ of Latter-day Saints released an article—titled "Mother in Heaven" that offers addition information about our heavenly mother. The article can be accessed with the following URL: www.lds.org/topics/mother-in-heaven

ELIZA R. SNOW

Eliza R. Snow was a prominent woman in the early history of the Church of Jesus Christ of Latter-day Saints, and wrote the hymn, "O My Father." Part of the second verse in this hymn reads as follows:

> In the heav'ns are parents single?
> No, the thought makes reason stare!
> Truth is reason; truth eternal
> Tells me I've a mother there.

(The Mormon Tabernacle Choir sings a rendition of this hymn that you can watch on YouTube.)

Keith A. Haslem

AUTHOR'S PERSPECTIVE

One might wonder why this maternal relationship is not mentioned in the Bible.

Consider how frequently God's name is taken in vain. If it were common knowledge that we have a Mother in Heaven then Her name would also likely be profaned. Given His love for Her, and His desire to protect Her—I wonder if God prevented that from happening by simply not making Her existence common knowledge.

68

WHY IS IT IMPORTANT TO LOVE YOURSELF?

SYNOPSIS

Both Betty J. Eadie and RaNelle Wallace learned that before you can truly love others you must learn to love yourself. Otherwise, it is difficult to truly love others.

BETTY J. EADIE

"Without feelings of self-love . . . the love we feel for others is counterfeit."

> I understood that love is supreme. . . . First, we must love the Creator. This is the greatest love we can have (although we may not know this until we meet him). Then we must love ourselves. I knew that without feelings of self-love that the love we feel for others is counterfeit. Then, we must love all others as ourselves. As we see the light of Christ in ourselves, we will see it in others too, and it will become impossible not to love that part of God in them.
>
> The most important thing I could do in life was to love others as myself. But to love others as myself, I first had to really love myself. The beauty and light of Christ were within me—he saw it!—and now I had to search within myself to find it as well. (*Embraced by the Light*, p. 59–60, 117)

RANELLE WALLACE

RaNelle learned an important lesson from her grandmother.

"You must love yourself before you can love others."

>Grandmother then showed me much of my past again, this time focusing on my poor self-esteem. I hadn't loved myself, and this affected the way I had treated others. "You must love yourself before you can love others," she said. I viewed mistakes I had made as a mother due to my lack of self-esteem. I had lost my temper and hurt my children unjustly. I wanted to hurt myself but instead had hurt them. "Remember," she said, "that each child is a child of God. They are your spiritual equals. They have a life on earth as precious as yours, and they need your help. It's your obligation to give them as much knowledge as you can. Feed them truth. Give them experiences for their growth. Learn to love yourself, RaNelle, and you will love your children more."
>
>Then she showed me how to love myself more. I needed to feed myself knowledge and truth, to study in my fields of interest, even going back to school if necessary. I also needed to pray more, and I was surprised when I saw just how little I had prayed in life.
>
>"Pray as a mother," she said. "Pray to know how to raise your children, and your prayers will be answered. Read the scriptures. They are filled with truth. Study them, and you too will be filled. Answers will come. Wisdom will be added to you. You will feel the Spirit and come closer to the Lord." (*The Burning Within*, pp. 113–14)

NICK VUJICIC

Nick Vujicic, born without arms or legs, travels the world speaking to people about pursuing their dreams. He offers the following advice with regard to learning to love yourself.

"You don't have to live up to anyone else's expectations."

>Loving yourself is not about being selfish, self-satisfied, or self-centered; it's about accepting your life as a gift to be nurtured and shared as a blessing to others.
>
>Instead of dwelling on your imperfections, your failings, or your mistakes, focus on your blessings and the contribution you can make, whether it's a talent, knowledge, wisdom, creativity, hard work, or a

nurturing soul. You don't have to live up to anyone else's expectations. You can define your own version of perfection. (*Life Without Limits*, p. 77)

AUTHOR'S PERSPECTIVE

Don't be so hard on yourself.

It is unlikely that a person could think badly of themselves and well of another. It's more likely that they would feel jealousy. Jealousy seems to be an unlikely motivator of noble behavior.

We are all prone, by our basic natures, to make mistakes. Consequently, in order to love ourselves we must also be willing to admit our own fallibility and be self-forgiving.

As we forgive ourselves we also become better able to forgive others, which is a prerequisite for obtaining forgiveness from God.

69

WHY IS IT IMPORTANT TO FORGIVE YOURSELF AND OTHERS?

SYNOPSIS

Betty J. Eadie learned that if you want to gain forgiveness, you must first give forgiveness.

Elane Durham learned that sometimes those who need our forgiveness were led to their transgressions against us because of adverse conditions in their own background.

Sarah LaNelle Menet came to understand that our personal progress suffers if we are unwilling to forgive.

BETTY J. EADIE

"If I am unable to forgive myself, it is impossible for me to truly forgive others."

"And I must forgive others. What I give out is what I receive. If I want forgiveness, I have to give forgiveness" (*Embraced by the Light*, p. 116).

ELANE DURHAM

After experiencing her Life Review in the presence of Jesus Christ, and feeling assurance from Him that she had been forgiven of the sins that

Going Home

she had repented of, Elane Durham come to understand the importance of also being able to forgive herself.

> Being encircled within His love I was able, for the first time in my life, to completely forgive myself. I had to, for I could not in any way oppose how Christ felt about me. Unconditionally I was loved, completely had I been forgiven, and perfectly was I understood. And because His thought and understanding and love had somehow become my own, I was able to feel the same way about myself as He did. (*I Stand All Amazed*, p. 33)

Elane was abused as a child by her father. During her near-death experience, she was given insight with regard to her father and other family members.

The backgrounds of some people may influence why they wrong us.

> I was also allowed to feel His [Christ's] unconditional love for my father, which gave me great peace.
>
> I do not mean to imply that my father's actions toward me were excused, for I knew they were not. In fact they were terrible sins for which he was absolutely accountable. . . . But still Christ loved him perfectly, and I knew that through the power of that love my dad, if he chose, could one day be redeemed.
>
> In connection with that, for years I had felt tremendous guilt over my inability to get along with my mother. . . . I was shown how my mother had been raised under the firm, Victorian hand of my Grandmother, who had never taught her how to show or give love. I also saw how Mom, who had been two years old when her own father had died, had been pretty much fed and clothed and "cared for" by her older siblings, and that two of them—brothers—had molested her. Thus she, like myself, had gone through abuse that was not of her own making, and had carried great shame and guilt though her own life. And oh, how my heart went out to her when I was given the knowledge of that. . . . She nevertheless carried the burden of her own choices, her own actions, just as I had done. . . .
>
> I had also felt like a failure because of the breakup of my marriage to my abusive first husband. But now, encircled in Christ's love, I saw this man in a whole new light, and my guilt was erased as I came to realize that nothing I could have done would have saved that marriage. The man himself, I saw, had been severely abused by his

alcoholic father. Thus, in his adulthood he was re-enacting the same sorts of things his father had done to him, seeking always the control that had been denied him as a child. And no matter what I would have done, or how I might have behaved would not have stopped his own headlong rush toward destruction. (*I Stand All Amazed*, pp. 34–35)

SARAH LANELLE MENET

"Without forgiveness [we will be] dragged down in a spiritual sense . . . unable to progress."

Many times we feel justified in taking revenge on those who hurt us by cheating us in business, personal relationships, or otherwise. We want assurance that they understand how much they have wronged us. The time will come when they will have a perfect knowledge of how we were affected by what they did. It is our responsibility to forgive them and let natural processes be the teacher. Also, we do not have the ability to accurately judge another's motives. We need to allow God to make those judgments. (*There Is No Death*, pp. 58–59)

We need to also understand the responsibility that we have in the forgiveness process. There is a connection between people who have hurt others and those who have been hurt. The way to break that connection is for the injured person to forgive. We must forgive those who have injured us emotionally or physically to free ourselves from that connection and to make ourselves acceptable to the Lord. . . . Also, when we forgive, the Lord blesses us in special ways. (*There Is No Death*, p. 104)

BIBLICAL PERSPECTIVE

"Therefore thou art inexcusable, O man, whosoever thou art that judgest: for wherein thou judgest another, thou condemnest thyself" (Romans 2:1).

Then Peter came to him, and said, Lord, how oft shall my brother sin against me, and I forgive him? till seven times?

Jesus saith unto him, I say not unto thee, Until seven times: but, Until seventy times seven. (Matthew 18:21–22)

THE CHURCH OF JESUS CHRIST OF LATTER-DAY SAINTS PERSPECTIVE

Wherefore, I say unto you, that ye ought to forgive one another; for he that forgiveth not his brother his trespasses standeth condemned before the Lord; for there remaineth in him the greater sin.

I, the Lord, will forgive whom I will forgive, but of you it is required to forgive all men (Doctrine and Covenants 64:9–10).

JEFFREY R. HOLLAND
(an apostle for the Church of Jesus Christ of Latter-day Saints, 1994–)

Elder Holland taught that to not forgive one's self is "not Christian."

"There is something in many of us that particularly fails to forgive and forget earlier mistakes in life. . . . It is not good. It is not Christian. It stands in terrible opposition to the grandeur and majesty of the Atonement of Christ. To be tied to earlier mistakes is the worst kind of wallowing in the past from which we are called to cease and desist" ("The Best Is Yet to Be," *Ensign,* January 2010).

AUTHOR'S PERSPECTIVE

Intentionally, or perhaps unintentionally, we all transgress against others. If we hope for forgiveness for our own offenses, would it not be hypocritical to withhold it from those who trespass against us, be it intentional or unintentional?

70

IS REPENTANCE POSSIBLE IN THE SPIRIT WORLD?

SYNOPSIS

The concept that repentance is possible in the spirit world may be foreign to most of the Christian world. However, Sarah Lanelle Menet learned that it is possible.

The theology of the Church of Jesus Christ of Latter-day Saints also asserts that repentance is possible in the spirit world.

SARAH LANELLE MENET

"It is far easier to repent or change our lives while in the mortal world."

> Another concept I understood was that it is far easier to repent or change our lives while in the mortal world than it is after passing into the spirit world. When we make the transition we call death, which is referred to there as the "new birth," we take with us our attitudes, passions, desires, habits, qualities, and character. We really don't change at all. Everything that makes us who we are comes with us as part of our soul essence or spiritual DNA. Included in our soul is this recording of all of our words and actions and experiences from the very beginning since that is part of who we really are.
>
> However, once we are in the spirit world, all of our emotions and attitudes become *greatly intensified*, thereby increasing the difficulty involved in changing them. (*There Is No Death*, pp. 42–43; emphasis added)

THE CHURCH OF JESUS CHRIST OF LATTER-DAY SAINTS PERSPECTIVE

Members of the Church of Jesus Christ of Latter-day Saints believe that every individual must have the opportunity to accept or reject the gospel of Jesus Christ if they are to have the opportunity to live with Him one day. Obviously, billions of inhabitants of the earth will not have that opportunity, due to the time they lived in or the place they lived in while on earth. Therefore, members of the Church of Jesus Christ of Latter-day Saints believe that a great missionary effort will take place in the spirit world to ensure that all people have the opportunity to accept the gospel, which involves repentance for sins.

JOSEPH F. SMITH
(sixth prophet and president of the Church of Jesus Christ of Latter-day Saints)

The gospel of Jesus Christ is taught in the spirit world.

Joseph F. Smith received a vision on October 3, 1918. As a result of his vision, he taught:

"The dead who repent will be redeemed."

> I beheld that the faithful elders of this dispensation, when they depart from mortal life, continue their labors in the preaching of the gospel of repentance and redemption, through the sacrifice of the Only Begotten Son of God, among those who are in darkness and under the bondage of sin in the great world of the spirits of the dead.
>
> The dead who repent will be redeemed, through obedience to the ordinances of the house of God,
>
> And after they have paid the penalty of their transgressions, and are washed clean, shall receive a reward according to their works, for they are heirs of salvation.
>
> Thus was the vision of the redemption of the dead revealed to me, and I bear record, and I know that this record is true, through

Keith A. Haslem

the blessing of our Lord and Savior, Jesus Christ, even so. Amen. (Doctrine and Covenants 138:57–60)

MELVIN J. BALLARD
(an apostle for the Church of Jesus Christ of Latter-day Saints, 1919–1939)

Melvin J. Ballard taught that repentance in the spirit world is more difficult than it is while on earth

"It will take them a thousand years to do what would have taken but three score years to accomplish in this life."

> It is my judgment that any man or woman can do more to conform to the laws of God in one year in this life than they could in ten years when they are dead. The spirit only can repent and change, and then the battle has to go forward with the flesh afterwards. It is much easier to overcome and serve the Lord when both the flesh and the spirit are combined as one. This is the time when men are more pliable and susceptible. We will find when we are dead every desire, every feeling will be *greatly intensified*. . . .
>
> This life is the time to repent. That is why I presume it will take a thousand years after the first resurrection until the last group will be prepared to come forth. It will take them a thousand years to do what it would have taken but three score years to accomplish in this life. . . .
>
> Then, every man and woman who is putting off until the next life the task of correcting and overcoming the weakness of the flesh are sentencing themselves to years of bondage. (Lundall, *The Vision*, pp. 46–47; emphasis added)

BRUCE R. MCCONKIE
(an apostle for the Church of Jesus Christ of Latter-day Saints, 1972–1985)

Elder Bruce R. McConkie taught that we retain the same attitudes and inclinations when we go to the spirit world.

"They continue to walk the same path."

Going Home

"Life and work and activity all continue in the spirit world. Men have the same talents and intelligence there which they had in this life. They possess the same attitudes, inclinations, and feelings there which they had in this life. They believe the same things, as far as eternal truths are concerned; they continue to walk in the same path they were following in this life" (*Mormon Doctrine*, p. 762).

BOOK OF MORMON

The Prophet Alma taught:

"Ye cannot say, when ye are brought to that awful crisis, that I will repent."

> Yea, I would that ye would come forth and harden not your hearts any longer; for behold, now is the time and the day of your salvation; and therefore, if ye will repent and harden not your hearts, immediately shall the great plan of redemption be brought about unto you.
>
> For behold, this life is the time for men to prepare to meet God; yea, behold the day of this life is the day for men to perform their labors.
>
> And now, as I said unto you before, as ye have had so many witnesses, therefore, I beseech of you that ye do not procrastinate the day of your repentance until the end; for after this day of life, which is given us to prepare for eternity, behold, if we do not improve our time while in this life, then cometh the night of darkness wherein there can be no labor performed.
>
> Ye cannot say, when ye are brought to that awful crisis, that I will repent, that I will return to my God. Nay, ye cannot say this; for that same spirit which doth possess your bodies at the time that ye go out of this life, that same spirit will have power to possess your body in that eternal world.
>
> For behold, if ye have procrastinated the day of your repentance even until death, behold, ye have become subjected to the spirit of the devil, and he doth seal you his; therefore the Spirit of the Lord hath withdrawn from you, and hath no place in you, and the devil hath all power over you; and this is the final state of the wicked. (Alma 34:31–35)

Keith A. Haslem

AUTHOR'S PERSPECTIVE

While it may be of some comfort to know that repentance is possible in the spirit world, it appears that the incremental difficulty of it argues strongly that repentance should not be procrastinated.

71

WHY SHOULD WE LEARN TO LOVE UNCONDITIONALLY?

The reoccurring message from individuals who have had near-death experiences is that the most important purpose for our existence on earth is to learn how to love as God does: universally and unconditionally.

SYNOPSIS

Betty J. Eadie learned that "without love we are nothing." This echoes the teaching of the Apostle Paul who taught the Corinthians, "[If I] have not charity, I am nothing" (1 Corinthians 13:2).

She also learned that love can be expressed through acts of kindness as simple as a smile or through a small act of sacrifice. She came to the conclusion that being kind to others will bring joy to ourselves and will become a goodness that goes with us to the next life.

RaNelle Wallace was emphatically taught by her grandmother that "The key is love."

Elane Durham learned that we should feel a responsibility to help everyone—our spiritual siblings.

Other Witnesses also learned about the importance of loving unconditionally.

Keith A. Haslem

BETTY J. EADIE

"Our strength will be found in our charity. . . . Our good deeds and kind words will come back to bless us a hundred fold after this life."

> Above all, I was shown that love is supreme. I saw that truly without love we are nothing. We are here to help each other, to care for each other, to understand, forgive, and serve one another. We are here to have love for every person born on earth. Their earthly form might be black, yellow, brown, handsome, ugly, thin, fat, wealthy, poor, intelligent, or ignorant, but we are not to judge by these appearances. . . .
>
> I knew that anything we do to show love is worthwhile: a smile, a word of encouragement, a small act of sacrifice. . . . I learned that we must love our enemies—let go of anger, hate, envy, bitterness, and the refusal to forgive. These things destroy the spirit. We will have to account for how we treat others. (*Embraced by the Light*, pp. 51–52)

We must be willing to help each other. We must be willing to see that the poor are as worthy of our esteem as the rich. We must be willing to accept all others, even those different from us. All are worthy of our love and kindness. . . . The only thing we can take with us from this life is the good that we have done to others. I saw that all our good deeds and kind words will come back to bless us a hundred fold after this life. Our strength will be found in our charity. . . . Oh, that I could be a blessing to others in my life. My soul reverberated with the final fact: Our strength will be found in our charity. (*Embraced by the Light*, pp. 101–2)

"If we're kind, we'll have joy."

During Betty's Life Review,

> The Savior stepped toward me, full of concern and love. His spirit gave me strength, and he said that I was judging myself too critically. "You're being too harsh on yourself," he said. Then he showed me the reverse side of the ripple effect. I saw myself perform an act of kindness, just a simple act of unselfishness, and I saw the ripples go out again. The friend I had been kind to was kind in turn to one her friends, and the chain repeated itself. I saw love and happiness increase in others' lives because of that one simple act on my part. I saw their happiness grow and affect their lives in positive ways, some

> significantly. My pain was replaced with joy. I felt the love they felt, I felt their joy. And this from one simple act of kindness. A powerful thought hit me, and I repeated it over and over in my mind: "Love is really the only thing that matters. Love is really the only thing that matters, and love is joy!" . . .
>
> It all seemed so simple. *If we're kind, we'll have joy.* (*Embraced by the Light*, pp. 113–14)

RANELLE WALLACE

Just before returning to her body, RaNelle Wallace's grandmother gave her a final bit of wisdom.

"The key is love . . . the key is love . . . the key is love."

> "RaNelle," Grandmother said, "there is one more thing I need to say to you. Tell everyone that the key is love."
>
> "The key is love," she repeated.
>
> "The key is love," she said a third time.
>
> Then she let go of my hand, and the word love reverberated in my mind as I left her and fell into a deep blackness. I was crying as I left the world of light and glory and love.
>
> The last thing I saw was her outstretched hand. (*The Burning Within*, p. 116)

"Love is a power."

RaNelle Wallace learned another profound lesson while in the company of her grandmother.

> As we stood on the bluff overlooking a small valley, I saw a scene that changed me forever. The scene was sacred beyond words, beyond expression, and those who have witnessed it keep it hidden in their hearts. I saw that I had indeed lacked faith, that love isn't simply a word or an emotion; love is a power that gives action to all around it. Love is the power of life. This was a turning point for me, something that allowed all of my understanding and love to magnify, but I can never share the details here except to say that I know that love between people here can be eternal. (*The Burning Within*, p. 105)

Keith A. Haslem

ELANE DURHAM

Elane Durham, after meeting Christ, learned the importance of loving others.

"Especially when it was hard for me to love them."

"I knew then that the Savior wanted me to understand that His question [which was, "What have you done for your fellow man?"] had to do, not with worldly things, but with how much honest and sincere love I had given to others, especially when it was hard for me to love them" (*I Stand All Amazed*, p. 36).

She also learned:

We have "a responsibility for everyone."

"I came to understand that we are all children of our Father in Heaven, sisters and brothers, and because of that relationship I hold a responsibility for everyone else" (*I Stand All Amazed*, p. 46).

SARAH LANELLE MENET

As she talked about the importance of learning how to give unconditional love, Sarah told the following story:

Kindness can be lifesaving.

> I recently heard a story about a young man who performed a simple act of service that saved someone's life. A boy who was considered a "geek" at school dropped a large pile of books while on his way home from school. Another young man, who was one of the most popular boys at school, was right there and asked if he needed help and then helped the "geek" to his feet and picked up all of the spilled books. They gradually became friends.
>
> Years later, the boy who had fallen down and dropped his books was giving a lecture and divulged that when this incident took place back in high school, he was about to do something drastic. He had been so completely discouraged that he had cleaned out his locker so that no one would have to deal with the mess, and then he planned to commit suicide later that day. The kindly lift he was given in his time of need turned him around in his thoughts and stopped him from acting out his intention. We do not realize how many times simple

acts of kindness, a reassuring word, or a smile can give another courage to go on. (*There Is No Death*, pp. 97–98)

GEORGE G. RITCHIE JR.

After his near-death experience, and during the course of the war, Dr. Ritchie met a man—Bill Cody—who exemplified loving unconditionally.

> I never heard him curse the Germans or talk badly about them. . . .
> Bill and I had grown to be close friends and I asked him one day, "How is it you do not hate the Germans after all they have done to you and your family?" [Bill Cody had to watch German SS troops murder his wife and five sons.] He turned and looked at me and said, "Did not our Lord teach us to love our enemies and those who spitefully use us? If I had not tried to follow Him, I could not have lived through what I have come through." (*My Life After Dying*, p. 49)

Bill's example helped George Ritchie finally forgive the dean who had kicked him out of medical school and back into the army.

RAYMOND A. MOODY JR.

In his book *The Light Beyond*, Dr. Moody records that NDEers all come back from their experience with a new appreciation of the importance of learning to love others.

"Have you learned to love?"

> "Have you learned to love?" is a question faced in the course of the episode by almost all NDEers. Upon their return, almost all of them say that love is the most important thing in life. Many say it is why we are here. Most find it the hallmark of happiness and fulfillment, with other values paling beside it. . . .
> As one NDEer told me:
> "You know, this experience has a hold on your everyday life, from then on. Walking down the street is a different experience entirely, believe you me. I used to walk down the street in my own little world, with my mind on a dozen different little problems. Now I walk down the street and I feel I am in an ocean of humanity. *Each*

Keith A. Haslem

> *person I see, I want to get to know*, and I am certain that if I really knew them I would love them.
>
> A man who works in the office with me asked why I always had a smile on my face. He didn't know about my experience, so I told him that because I almost died, I was happy to be alive and let it pass. Someday, he'll find out for himself." (*The Light Beyond*, pp. 41–42)

Dr. Moody noted that people who have had an NDE have a new "profound appreciation of life." After their NDE, people tend to declare that life is precious, that it's the "little things" that count, and that life is to be lived to its fullest.

He cites the experience of a woman NDEer.

"The simple acts of kindness . . . are the most important."

> One woman told me that the life review doesn't show just the big events of one's life, as you might think. She said that it shows the little things, too. For instance, one of the incidents that came across very powerfully in her review was a time when she found a little girl lost in a department store. The girl was crying, and the woman set her up on a counter and talked to her until her mother arrived.
>
> It was those kinds of things—the little things you do while not even thinking—that come up most importantly in the review.
>
> Many people are asked by the being, "What was in your heart while this was going on?" It's as though he's telling the NDEer that the simple acts of kindness that come from the heart are the most important because they are most sincere. (*Life After Life*, p. 48)

"Everyone has stressed the importance in this life of trying to cultivate love for others."

> There is remarkable agreement in the "lessons," as it were, which have been brought back from these close encounters with death. Almost everyone has stressed the importance in this life of trying to cultivate love for others, a love of a unique and profound kind. One man who met the being of light felt totally loved and accepted, even while his whole life was displayed in a panorama for the being to see. He felt that the "question" that the being was asking him was whether he was able to love others in the same way. He now feels that it is his commission while on earth to try to learn to be able to do so. (*Life After Life*, pp. 92–93)

NICK VUJICIC

During his speeches, Nick—who was born without arms or legs—makes a point of telling his audiences that,

"I love you just as you are. You are beautiful to me" (*Life Without Limits*, p. 81).

After his speeches, people may wait for hours to meet him and give him a hug. Nick offers an explanation for their behavior.

"Now I'm a handsome enough bloke, but people don't stand in lines for hours to hug me because I'm dashing. What really seems to be drawing them is that I unleash a pair of powerful forces that so many are lacking in their lives: *unconditional love and self-acceptance*" (*Life Without Limits*, p. 81).

AUTHOR'S PERSPECTIVE

Take an interest in other people

The virtue of loving universally is obvious. But how exactly do we go about that? If you go around hugging everyone you meet, you might get arrested!

From my viewpoint, I would capsulize the concept in three words: take an interest. Show the people you come in contact with that you are interested in them. This can be done as easily as asking, "So how is your day going?" or even just offering a smile and a "Hello" to a complete stranger. And, of course, we should *always* be kind and never judgmental.

72

HOW CAN WE LEARN TO LOVE THROUGH SERVICE?

SYNOPSIS

Knowing that loving others unconditionally is one of the most important things we can do in this life, how can we do so? In a word: service.

Elane Durham learned that, "love is service and service is love. The one cannot truly exist without the other."

Betty J. Eadie learned that, "Service is a balm to both the spirit and the body."

During her near-death experience, Sarah LaNelle Menet learned a term used in the spirit world, pronounced *xoi-coi*, that refers to a person who is only interested in themselves.

ELANE DURHAM

"I learn to love others through serving them. . . . Love is service and service is love. The one cannot truly exist without the other."

> I realized that I learn to love others through serving them, and the more willing and joyful I am about it, the faster I develop love. That is why Christ could love me so perfectly. He had served me perfectly by willingly and even joyfully giving His own life in my behalf. . . .
>
> Love is service and service is love. The one cannot truly exist without the other. (*I Stand All Amazed*, p. 40)

Elane's observation brings to mind the indictment pronounced by William Shakespeare:

"They do not love that do not show their love" (*The Two Gentlemen of Verona*, Act 1, scene 2, line 31).

Elane also observed:

"Wealth lies not in what I own . . . but rather in what I give away."

> I was told, I need to learn that true wealth lies not in what I own or have, but rather in what I give away. For instance, I was informed that the rich man has a responsibility to enrich the lives of the less fortunate, and the poor man has no less a responsibility in his own sphere of influence. Even the gift of seemingly insignificant things, like a smile, or listening ear or especially a fervent, silent prayer, helps fulfill this responsibility. (*I Stand All Amazed*, p. 60)

BETTY J. EADIE

"Our gifts and talents are given to us to help us serve."

"Whatever we become here in mortality is meaningless unless it is done for the benefit of others. Our gifts and talents are given to us to help us serve. And in serving others we grow spiritually" (*Embraced by the Light*, p. 50).

"Service is a balm to both the spirit and body."

> The spirit has power to control the mind, and the mind controls the body. . . .
>
> I understood that we are at our most self-centered state when we are depressed. Nothing can sap our natural strength and health as much as prolonged depression. But when we make the effort to move ourselves away from self and begin to concentrate on the needs of others and how to serve them, we begin to heal. Service is a balm to both the spirit and body. (*Embraced by the Light*, pp. 62–63)

SARAH LANELLE MENET

"Mother Theresa said, 'Love is service to others.'"

> In this growing process called life we can't, and we're not intended, to "go it alone." Nor were we intended to go through these experiences

just to benefit ourselves. We are here to travel this life together, learning and growing from each other and thereby succeeding together in the end. We are all connected to and have known each other in a very real way for eons. *The person we bump into on the street may have been our best friend before coming to this earth.*

Without exception, all of those living upon the earth at the present time knew and loved each other before being born. We don't remember this because shortly after we are born, a block is put on a part of our "spiritual DNA" to prevent us from remembering our lives before coming to earth. However, every once in a while some small memory will leak through the block, and we will have a vague recognition of people or places. That is why many of us may have at some time in our lives met someone that we immediately "clicked" with, someone that we felt we had known "forever." Indeed it may be so.

. . . Another truth is that we cannot go to Heaven alone. If a major part of this life's existence is to learn to help and love others, then we cannot live like hermits and expect to go to heaven. I once read that Mother Theresa said, "Love is service to others." I think that is it exactly. It is by serving others, helping them to become better people and loving them, that we learn the true principle of love. We grow and progress by doing for and giving to others in need, as Mother Theresa said, by service. (*There Is No Death*, pp. 96–97; emphasis added)

Xoi-coi: spirit world term for someone interested only in themselves.

I also learned a word that is used in the spirit world for which an equivalent in our language does not exist. The word is xoi-coi. Though I'm not sure of the spelling, it is pronounced "x-oy koy." This word means "someone who doesn't do anything meaningful while on earth." This person doesn't progress, help others, or care. In a way, he or she just takes up space, doing nothing worthwhile. Unfortunately, I learned there are a lot of spirits who come to earth and become xoi-cois. They live to "party" and spend countless hours trying only to entertain themselves and satisfy their wants, which they will never fill because these pleasures are empty and have no lasting or eternal value. They do nothing to elevate mankind or contribute to the improvement of the world. Such positive contribution may be large or small because all do not have the same power to make a difference, but the important thing is to try. Even very small acts of kindness can make a big difference. I believe that many souls in the world to come will thank us for what we assumed was unappreciated or insignificant. (*There Is No Death*, pp. 98–99)

THE CHURCH OF JESUS CHRIST OF LATTER-DAY SAINTS PERSPECTIVE

DIETER F. UCHDORF
(an apostle for the Church of Jesus Christ of Latter-day Saints, 2004–)

Dieter F. Uchdorf taught:

Serve others and help yourself.

On your journey back to Heavenly Father you will soon realize that this journey isn't just about focusing on your own life. No, this path inevitably leads you to become a blessing in the lives of God's other children—your brothers and sisters. And the interesting thing about the journey is that as you serve God, and as you care for and help your fellowmen, you will see great progress in your own life, in ways you could never imagine. ("A Yearning for Home," *Ensign*, November 2017)

THOMAS S. MONSON
(sixteenth prophet and president of the Church of Jesus Christ of Latter-day Saints)

Using a scripture from the New Testament, Thomas S. Monson taught about service:

The Savior taught His disciples, "For whosoever will save his life shall lose it: but whosoever will lose his life for my sake, the same shall save it" (Luke 9:24).

I believe the Savior is telling us that unless we lose ourselves in service to others, there is little purpose to our own lives. Those who live

Keith A. Haslem

only for themselves eventually shrivel up and figuratively lose their lives, while those who lose themselves in service to others grow and flourish and in effect save their lives. ("What Have I Done for Someone Today?," *Ensign*, November 2009, 85)

JOSÉ L. ALONSO
(a General Authority for the Church of Jesus Christ of Latter-day Saints, 2011–)

Elder Alonso taught:

"Love without service is like faith without works; it's dead indeed."

In today's world of so much suffering because of different circumstances, sending a text message with a funny emoji or posting a nice picture with the words "I love you" is good and valuable. But what many of us need to do is leave our mobile devices behind and, with our hands and our feet, help others in great need. Love without service is like faith without works; it's dead indeed. ("Love One Another as He Has Loved Us," *Ensign*, November 2017, 120)

Facilitation from the Church of Jesus Christ of Latter-day Saints for giving service.

- www.justserve.org
    - The Church of Jesus Christ of Latter-day Saints sponsors the website *www.justserve.org*, where you can log in and review the opportunities to give service in your own community.
- Tithes and fast-offerings
    - In addition to offering tithing—ten percent of their income—to fund the growth of the Church of Jesus Christ of Latter-day Saints, faithful members also contribute fast-offerings to help other members who are struggling financially. They can also designate amounts to be allocated to "Humanitarian Aid," which is used

to help the poor throughout the world—regardless of their denomination. Unlike many other charities, there are no administrative costs taken out. People who are not members are also welcome to contribute.

AUTHOR'S PERSPECTIVE

The message of our resources is clear. If you want to develop a love for someone, find ways to serve them. And when you serve someone else it somehow "boomerangs" back to you, allowing you to feel a new compassion for them.

People who volunteer for community service out of an initial sense of duty often become passionate about their cause because they develop intense feelings of compassion for those they are helping.

73

WHY DO WE NEED HUMILITY?

SYNOPSIS

While being escorted by her grandmother, RaNelle Wallace met a woman who had been prominent—even commanding "obeisance"—during her mortal life. Her vanity became delusions of self-importance—even in the spirit world—blocking her progress.

RANELLE WALLACE

"In love with herself . . . queen to nothing but her own vanity"

> Then she [RaNelle's grandmother] said, "Come. You must learn humility." And we came to a strange building below us. It had four walls, but no floor or ceiling. We could see partway down into it, then the room's light seemed to fade where the floor should have been. The walls were solid but translucent, as if they could be penetrated by light—or, rather, by beings of light. This seemed important.
>
> I saw stairs leading down into a dark area. My grandmother told me to follow the stairs down into the room.
>
> Somehow I sensed a deeper darkness. "No, Grandma, I don't want to."
>
> "You need to," she said. "This is important."
>
> "Can't you come with me?"
>
> "I cannot."
>
> I realized that there are laws in that world, just as there are laws here. This was a law she could not break: I had to go alone.

Going Home

I started down, and the stairs seemed to disappear so that I gradually descended, or floated, into the room. The light was much dimmer, and I became frightened, though I knew that the light in that room was brighter than sunlight. At first I thought the room was empty, then I saw her.

A beautiful woman lay on her side on an altar. Behind her and to the sides hung broad scallops of fine scarlet fabric. Her head was propped on one hand, and her thick dazzling black hair fell across the front of her neck. She had an olive complexion, smoother than cream, lips full and exquisitely formed. Her eyes, a stunning blue, were set in a flawless face that looked as if it had never seen a harsh moment. Her fingernails were long and delicate, appearing to have never experienced work. Even her feet were beautiful—slender and soft; and I noticed that her toenails were perfectly groomed.

Gold and brass bracelets adorned her ankles and wrists in the style of her time on earth. A necklace of gold and brass hung about her neck, with a large ruby just above her breasts. Her blouse was crimson and partially sheer. It hung loosely from her shoulders and tucked into her waist. The front of it was open, slightly exposing her breasts and midriff. Her legs were draped in the same fashion. She looked about the room with an air of supremacy. Even in this realm of absolute beauty she was stunning.

I understood that she had been a queen, a woman of power and title who had lived before Christ and had reigned over many people. In life she had done as she had pleased, commanded populations, granting and taking life, enjoying every whim. She had cultivated her beauty artfully and had used it to increase her power.

She looked at me and I knew that she expected me to bow, to honor her, but I refused; something told me not to. Her air of dignity unruffled, she looked about the room again as if expecting others to show obeisance, to show me how to reverence her beauty and power.

She was caught in a delusion. The room was deserted—there were no others—yet she believed there were multitudes surrounding her, bowing and giving her glory. I began looking at her with pity and sadness. Then I was shown that she had lived her life in selfishness and greed, that she had never given kindness for the sake of being kind. She had never given anything of herself, and now she was caught in eternity, in love with herself, smiling benevolently upon her invisible subjects, basking in honor and adulation that didn't exist. She was queen to nothing but her own vanity.

Keith A. Haslem

Her self-delusion was so complete that I began to fear being in her presence. I feared her sickness, the smugness, the self-glory, the darkness of her deception—and I cried out for my grandmother.

"Come, RaNelle," I heard her say, and I glided up out of the roofless room and back to the garden. My grandmother took my hand. Her touch and the beauty of the garden were like spiritual balm.

"Did you see?" she asked. "Did you learn?"

"Yes," I said, grateful to be out of the room, but aware also that I had seen a potential for delusion in my own soul.

"Thank you."

We didn't speak of it again. There was no need. The image of the woman, once a queen on earth, now a figment of vanity, was seared into my soul. Even now when I see vanity, I feel a sadness for the person displaying it. I want to wake them up to what's real about themselves—their inner beauty, light, and love. My grandmother saw the impact of the lesson upon me, and we moved on. (*The Burning Within*, pp. 110–12)

AUTHOR'S PERSPECTIVE

Vanity is repulsive.

It is remarkable that arrogant people seem oblivious to the fact that their demeanor is repulsive to most people.

I wonder how many people, accustomed to the "limelight" won't know what to do with themselves when they go to the spirit world and find no adoring audiences. How long will they be kings and queens to nothing but their own vanity?

74

HOW CAN FEAR STOP OUR PROGRESS?

SYNOPSIS

RaNelle Wallace learned that the biggest roadblock in her life so far had been fear.

Betty J. Eadie learned that a fear of God made it difficult to love Him, herself, and other people.

Elisabeth Kübler-Ross suggested that we need to "learn not be afraid."

RANELLE WALLACE

During her NDE, RaNelle gained an important understanding regarding fear when she became intimidated by the volume of knowledge and truth that was pouring into her.

"The greatest block to my growth in life: fear"

> Then I understood what had become the greatest block to my growth in life: fear. It had plagued me all my years, had stopped my progress, cut short my attempts at working through problems. Fear had limited my enjoyment of life and it was blocking me now. When I feared, my powers of travel, understanding, and progression became paralyzed. "Don't fear this," I said to myself. "Let go." And we were traveling again, knowledge pouring into me faster than ever. (*The Burning Within*, p. 106)

Keith A. Haslem

BETTY J. EADIE

"Since I feared God, I could not truly love him [or] myself . . . [or] others."

As I remained in the Savior's glow, in his absolute love, I realized that when I had feared him as a child I had actually moved myself further from him. When I thought he didn't love me, I was moving my love from him. . . .

I understood how others had been instrumental in distancing me from him. . . . Because of their own fears, they were using fear to control others. They intimidated those under them to believe in God, to "fear God or go to hell." This prevented me from really loving God. I understood again that fear is the opposite of love and is Satan's greatest tool. Since I feared God, I could not truly love him, and in not loving him, I couldn't love myself or others purely either. The law of love had been broken. (*Embraced by the Light*, pp. 60–61)

ELISABETH KÜBLER-ROSS

"Learn not to be afraid"

"Get in touch with your own inner self and learn not to be afraid. One way to not be afraid is to know that death does not exist, that everything in this life has a positive purpose. Get rid of all your negativity and begin to view life as a challenge, a testing ground of your own inner resources and strength" (*On Life After Death*, p. 34).

BIBLICAL PERSPECTIVE

"There is no fear in love, but perfect love casteth out fear: because fear hath torment. He that feareth is not made perfect in love" (1 John 4:18).

AUTHOR'S PERSPECTIVE

If God can do anything (see Mark 10:27), and He loves us and is able and willing to help us succeed, then what do we have to fear?

75

WHAT ARE THE DANGERS OF FEELING DEPRESSION AND ANGER?

SYNOPSIS

Sarah LaNelle Menet learned that people who are depressed or allow themselves to become angry are more susceptible to the influence of evil spirits and more prone to make poor choices.

Elder Jeffrey R. Holland, an apostle in the Church of Jesus Christ of Latter-day Saints, counsels people suffering from mental or emotional disorders to seek the advice of trained professionals who may be able to help—similarly as people with physical disorders seek help from a medical doctor.

SARAH LANELLE MENET

"Many of the depressed people on the earth today are under the influence of Satan."

> There are many evil spirits here on earth. They are all around us and have the ability to roam where they will in this world. . . . Often we can feel the presence or influence of these evil spirits. Their primary attitude is one of hate, anger, or depression; and so if we let ourselves go and become uncontrollably angry or hateful we can be fairly sure of their presence and attempts to influence us for bad. Many of the depressed people on the earth today are under the influence of Satan and his evil spirits. Their desire is to cause us to feel downhearted and

Keith A. Haslem

despondent and to believe that our situation is completely hopeless and beyond our power to change or control. When we are like that, it is much easier for them to influence us to make bad choices. (*There Is No Death*, p. 101)

THE CHURCH OF JESUS CHRIST OF LATTER-DAY SAINTS PERSPECTIVE

Although susceptibility to evil spirits may be common to both anger and depression, members of the Church of Jesus Christ of Latter-day Saints believe that depression is a mental condition that should be treated like a physical malady is treated. Below are some excerpts from an address—"Like a Broken Vessel"—given to the membership of the Church of Jesus Christ of Latter-day Saints in October 2013.

JEFFREY R. HOLLAND
(an apostle for the Church of Jesus Christ of Latter-day Saints, 1994–)

I wish to speak to those who suffer from some form of mental illness or emotional disorder, whether those afflictions be slight or severe, of brief duration or persistent over a lifetime. We sense the complexity of such matters when we hear professionals speak of neuroses and psychoses, of genetic predispositions and chromosome defects, of bipolarity, paranoia, and schizophrenia. However bewildering this all may be, these afflictions are some of the realities of mortal life, and there should be no more shame in acknowledging them than in acknowledging a battle with high blood pressure or the sudden appearance of a malignant tumor. . . .

. . . Seek the advice of reputable people with certified training, professional skills, and good values. Be honest with them about your history and your struggles. Prayerfully and responsibly consider the counsel they give and the solutions they prescribe. If you had appendicitis, God would expect you to seek a priesthood blessing and get the best medical care available. So too with emotional disorders. Our Father in Heaven expects us to use all of the marvelous gifts He has provided in this glorious dispensation. ("Like a Broken Vessel," *Ensign*, November 2013)

AUTHOR'S PERSPECTIVE

Satan has no compassion for anyone. He will happily take advantage of depression and other mental illnesses to advance his goals.

Medications prescribed by medical professionals can be an appropriate way to reduce risks and make progress toward a healthy mental state.

In addition, many people actively involved in rendering service in their communities will tell you that such activities help with their depression. For a list of service opportunities in your community go to, *www.justserve.org*—a site sponsored by the Church of Jesus Christ of Latter-day Saints.

76

WHY IS MATERIALISM AN INSIGNIFICANT PURSUIT?

Many people focus on the acquisition of wealth and material possessions, thinking it will improve the quality of their lives. Yet, it is common for individuals, after near-death experiences, to regard material possessions as unimportant.

SYNOPSIS

Sarah LaNelle Menet gained the understanding that focusing on material things was a waste of time.

Many of NDErs interviewed in the studies made by Dr. Maurice Rawlings and Dr. Kenneth Ring echoed Sarah's sentiment.

SARAH LANELLE MENET

"An unbelievable waste of time"

> We spent thousands of years as spirits before coming to earth, and we will spend millions more in the spirit world and beyond after we leave this existence. We are only here on earth for a relatively short span, which seems like a few minutes to everyone in the spirit world. Spending so much of our lives focusing and concentrating all of our efforts on things like the attainment of wealth, beauty, and material possessions is an unbelievable waste of time. Our probation on earth is a time of teaching, learning, overcoming, improving, and preparing for what follows. (*There Is No Death*, p. 96)

MAURICE RAWLINGS

In his book *Beyond Death's Door*, Dr. Rawlings quotes an individual who had a near-death experience.

"The material things don't count."

"I always thought about social status and wealth symbols as the most important things in life until life was suddenly taken from me. Now I know that none of these are important. Only the love you show others will endure or be remembered. The material things don't count" (*Beyond Death's Door*, p. 90).

KENNETH RING

In his book *Heading Toward Omega*, Dr. Ring studied individuals who had been through a near-death experience and the impact it had in their lives during the subsequent years. One of the foremost impacts was the subjects' reduced interest in materialism. The following quotes come from some of his research subjects.

"I know the Lord will take care of me."

A female interviewee said: "Before I was living for material things. . . . Before I was conscious of only me, what I had, what I wanted. . . . I have gradually sloughed off the desire to have and to hold earthly possessions, material possessions to any great degree. I don't worry about tomorrow . . . because I know that the Lord will take care of me" (*Heading Toward Omega*, p. 132).

Another female interviewee explained: "Material things . . . have completely faded into the background; material things aren't important" (*Heading Toward Omega*, p. 133).

Another of Dr. Ring's subjects said: "My interest in material wealth and greed for possession was replaced by a thirst for spiritual understanding and a passionate desire to see world conditions improve" (*Heading Toward Omega*, p. 133).

Dr. Ring suggests that NDErs are less materialistic because their experience gives them a better understanding of who they are and what is most valuable beyond this mortal life. He observes:

"However 'much' one has, it is never enough to allay the desire for more. . . . Ambitions are fueled by personal insecurity."

Keith A. Haslem

> One wants to acquire either the good opinion of others or material goods. In either case, such ambitions are fueled by personal insecurity, and however "much" one has, it is never enough to allay the desire for more.
>
> As we have already seen, because of what NDErs experience while close to death, they return to life by and large bereft of the kind of insecurity that motivates most of the rest of us. (*Heading Toward Omega*, p. 131)

Dr. Ring concludes his discussion of materialism by observing that, "matter is not what matters" (*Heading Toward Omega*, p. 133).

AUTHOR'S PERSPECTIVE

If we are going to live for "millions of years" after this mortal life, then it makes sense that we should do what we can now to optimize the conditions of our future existence. Obviously, with regard to material possessions, "you can't take it with you."

What you *can* take with you is the knowledge you've acquired and the positive relationships you've developed with those who are important to you.

DID WE HELP WITH THE CREATION OF THE EARTH?

SYNOPSIS

The creation of the earth and all the various forms of life was obviously a huge job. Betty J. Eadie came to understand that God had help.

BETTY J. EADIE

"We all assisted in creating our conditions here."

> I remembered the creation of the earth. I actually experienced it as if it were being reenacted before my eyes. . . .
>
> All people as spirits in the pre-mortal world took part in the creation of the earth. We were thrilled to be part of it. . . .
>
> We assisted God in the development of plants and animal life that would be here. Everything was created of spirit matter before it was created physically—solar systems, suns, moons, stars, plants, life upon the planets, mountains, rivers, seas, etc. I saw this process, and then to further understand it, I was told by the Savior that the spirit creation could be compared to one of our photographic prints: the spirit creation would be like a sharp, brilliant print, and the earth would be like its dark negative. This earth is only a shadow of the beauty and glory of its spirit creation, but it is what we needed for our growth. It was important that I understand that we all assisted in creating our conditions here. (*Embraced by the Light*, pp. 47–48)

All created elements have a degree of intelligence and a capacity to experience joy.

Keith A. Haslem

"I saw that all things were created by spiritual power. Each element, each particle of creation, has intelligence in it, which intelligence is filled with spirit and life, and thus has the capacity for experiencing joy . . . when God speaks to these elements, they respond, and they have joy in obeying his word" (*Embraced by the Light*, p. 55).

THE CHURCH OF JESUS CHRIST OF LATTER-DAY SAINTS PERSPECTIVE

Members of the Church of Jesus Christ of Latter-day Saints believe that all living things were created spiritually first, before they were created physically.

> And every plant of the field before it was in the earth, and every herb of the field before it grew. For I, the Lord God, created all things, of which I have spoken, spiritually, before they were naturally upon the face of the earth. . . . And I, the Lord God, had created all the children of men; and not yet a man to till the ground; for in heaven created I them; and there was not yet flesh upon the earth, neither in the water, neither in the air. (Moses 3:5)

AUTHOR'S PERSPECTIVE

The logic of a group effort.

If God is perfect then He is the perfect administrator and delegator. Allowing His children to exercise their creative abilities and assist Him in the work of creation seems only generous. With an estimated *8.7 million species* of plant and animal life on Earth, a "group effort" would also be more efficient.

78

ARE THERE OTHER WORLDS IN THE UNIVERSE?

SYNOPSIS

Several of the Witnesses talk about the existence of other worlds inhabited by humans.

In their NDEs, Betty J. Eadie and Sarah LaNelle Menet traveled to other worlds inhabited by "our spiritual brothers and sisters."

Elane Durham saw millions of other worlds and learned that we might have gone to one of them. But this earth, because of its adversities, was the place to learn the fastest.

Astronomers have discovered—so far—seven earth-size planets that they believe could support life. Astronomer Carl Sagan believes there are a million planets *in our galaxy* that are inhabited by advanced civilizations. And there are *billions of galaxies* in the universe.

Members of the Church of Jesus Christ of Latter-day Saints believe that God has created "worlds without number."

BETTY J. EADIE

Betty J. Eadie recounts:

"I saw galaxies and traveled to them with . . . almost instantaneous speed . . . meeting our spiritual brothers and sisters."

Keith A. Haslem

I remembered that God was the creator of many worlds, galaxies, and realms beyond our understanding, and I wanted to see them. . . . I entered the vastness of space and learned that it is not a void; it was full of love and light—the tangible presence of the Spirit of God. . . .

I traveled tremendous distances, knowing that the stars I saw were not visible from the earth. I saw galaxies and traveled to them with ease and almost instantaneous speed, visiting their worlds and meeting more children of our God, all of them our spiritual brothers and sisters. . . .

I saw worlds that our most powerful telescopes could never see, and I know the love that exists there. . . .

Much later, when I returned to my mortal body, I felt cheated when I was unable to remember the details of this experience, but with the passage of time I have learned that I needed this forgetfulness for my own good. If I could remember the glorious and perfect worlds I had seen, I would live a constantly frustrated life and mar my own God-given mission. (*Embraced by the Light*, pp. 86–88)

SARAH LANELLE MENET

"Many planets in the universe . . . are inhabited with beings just like us."

Spirits are also able to travel to different worlds and planets if they desire, and it all happens at the speed of a thought. . . .

. . . There are many planets in the universe that are inhabited with beings just like us, because they also are made in the image of God, but we need not be concerned with what is going on elsewhere. They are not a threat to us as many suppose. (*There Is No Death*, p. 109)

ELANE DURHAM

"Innumerable earths that were inhabited with others of God's children."

As I understood what the angel was explaining to me, I became aware that I had knowledge or memory of millions and millions of other planets or earths. . . . In fact, there were more earths out there in the void of space than I could possibly imagine, including innumerable earths that were inhabited with others of God's children. As the angel pointed outward I even saw new earths being created or put together, or "born." (*I Stand All Amazed*, p. 62)

Elane learned that we might have gone to other earths instead of this one:

The being with me let me know that earth was the most dreaded place to go, but it was also the place to learn the fastest—because of the adversities. Earth was put here for us to learn, and we are here for that purpose. . . .

In a global sense I knew that there were other galaxies and other worlds. There were other places to live, to learn lessons from. Earth was not the only place where lessons could be learned. *In fact, I could have stayed where I was and continued to learn, but not as fast as if I returned to earth.* The hardships and adversities of earth accelerate the learning experience, and those lessons help us to reach a more perfected state. (Crowther, quoted in *Life Everlasting*, p. 120)

SCIENTIFIC PERSPECTIVE

The following is an article appearing in the *Deseret News*, titled, "7 Earth-size worlds found orbiting star; could hold life":

For the first time, astronomers have discovered seven Earth-size planets orbiting a single nearby star—and these new worlds could hold life.

This cluster of planets is less than 40 light-years away in the constellation Aquarius, according to NASA and the Belgian-led research team who announced the discovery Wednesday. . . .

"We've made a crucial step toward finding if there is life out there," said the University of Cambridge's Amaury Triaud, one of the researchers. . . .

NASA's Thomas Zurbuchen, associate administrator for the science mission, said the discovery "gives us a hint that finding a second Earth is not just a matter of if, but when." ("7 Earth-size worlds found orbiting star; could hold life," *Deseret News*)

STEPHAN DOLE
(astronomer)

"1,000,000 [worlds that] support advanced civilizations"

Keith A. Haslem

Stephan Dole has noted that this planet travels in a galaxy that probably contains more than 600,000,000 other earthlike life-bearing planets. One of Dole's colleagues, Carl Sagan, estimates that at least 1,000,000 of these bear intelligent life and support advanced civilizations. (Sagan, The Cosmic Connection, 1973). And, as Isaac Asimov reminds us, there are billions of other galaxies (Elmer and Alyce Green, *Beyond Biofeedback*, p. 335)

THE CHURCH OF JESUS CHRIST OF LATTER-DAY SAINTS PERSPECTIVE

Members of the Church of Jesus Christ of Latter-day Saints believe that God has created "worlds without number" that are inhabited like this earth. They point to "an extract from the translation of the Bible as revealed to Joseph Smith the Prophet, June 1830–February 1831," called the book of Moses which is contained in the Pearl of Great Price, and is accepted as part of the scriptural canon in the Church of Jesus Christ of Latter-day Saints.

"Worlds without number have I created."

> And behold, the glory of the Lord was upon Moses, so that Moses stood in the presence of God, and talked with him face to face. And the Lord God said unto Moses: For mine own purposes have I made these things. Here is wisdom and it remaineth in me.
>
> And by the word of my power, have I created them, which is mine Only Begotten Son, who is full of grace and truth.
>
> And worlds without number have I created; and I also created them for mine own purpose; and by the Son I created them, which is mine Only Begotten.
>
> And the first man of all men have I called Adam, which is many.
>
> But only an account of this earth, and the inhabitants thereof, give I unto you. For behold, there are many worlds that have passed away by the word of my power. And there are many that now stand, and innumerable are they unto man; but all things are numbered unto me, for they are mine and I know them. (Moses 1:31–35)

AUTHOR'S PERSPECTIVE

In the fourth century BC, the earth was thought to be the center of the universe. By the sixteenth century, that theory changed and the sun was thought to be the center of the universe.

As science continues to advance, it is coming ever closer to the truth. This truth is that we are not alone in the universe. To think otherwise is akin to the enlightenment of the fourth century.

PART IV
HELL AND EVIL SPIRITS

Hell 367
Evil Spirits 382

79

WHAT IS HELL LIKE?

I am somewhat reluctant to include this chapter, because I don't a believe fear of hell is an effective motivator of good character. Yet, perhaps it might be a starting place.

SYNOPSIS

Several of the witnesses had glimpses of hellish regions.

Dr. George G. Ritchie Jr. was given a view of miserable spirits engaging in acts of hate, anger, and attempted sexual perversions.

Sarah LaNelle Menet viewed a place of darkness where the inhabitants' anguish was an "inner, self-inflicted torment." However, she did learn that "hell" is not an eternal abode.

Dr. Maurice Rawlings believes that NDErs who get a glimpse of the dreadful region of the spirit world have that memory blocked out after their return. He estimates that the number of such bad experiences are as frequent as the number of pleasant experiences.

Members of the Church of Jesus Christ of Latter-day Saints believe the inhabitants of "hell" will be released at the time of their physical resurrection.

GEORGE G. RITCHIE JR.

"Hoards of . . . the most frustrated, the angriest, the most completely miserable beings."

> Now however, although we were apparently still somewhere on the surface of the earth, I could see no living man or woman. The plain was crowded, even jammed with hordes of ghostly discarnate

beings . . . and they were the most frustrated, the angriest, the most completely miserable beings I had ever laid eyes on. . . .

. . . Everywhere people were locked in what looked like fights to the death, writhing, punching, gouging . . . and then I noticed that no one was apparently being injured. There was no blood, no bodies strewn the ground; a blow that ought to have eliminated an opponent would leave him exactly as before.

Although they appeared to be literally on top of each other, it was as though each man was boxing the air; at last I realized that of course, having no substance, they could not actually touch one another. They could not kill, though they clearly wanted to, because their intended victims were already dead, and so they hurled themselves at each other in a frenzy of impotent rage.

If I suspected before that I was seeing hell, now I was sure of it. . . . These creatures seemed locked into habits of mind and emotion, into hatred, lust, destructive thought-patterns.

Even more hideous than the bites and kicks they exchanged, were the sexual abuses many were performing in feverish pantomime. Perversions I had never dreamed of were being vainly attempted all around us.

. . . Once again, however, no condemnation came from the Presence [Jesus] at my side, only a compassion for these unhappy creatures that was breaking His heart. Clearly it was not His will that any one of them should be in this place. (*Return from Tomorrow*, pp. 63–64)

"There was no 'alone' in this realm. . . . A kind of consolation in finding others as loathsome as one's self."

Then—what was keeping them here? Why didn't each one just get up and leave? I could see no reason why the person being screamed at by that man with the contorted face didn't simply walk away. Or why that young woman didn't put a thousand miles between herself and the other one who was so furiously beating her with insubstantial fists? They couldn't actually hold onto their victims, any of these insanely angry beings. There were no fences. Nothing apparently prevented them from simply going off alone.

Unless . . . unless there was no "alone" in this realm of disembodied spirits. No private corners in a universe where there were no walls. No place that was not inhabited by other beings to whom one was totally exposed at all times. What was it going to be like, I thought with sudden panic, to live forever where my most private thoughts were not private at all. No disguising them, no covering them up, no way to pretend I was anything but what I actually was. How unbearable. Unless of course everyone around me had the same kind of thoughts. . . . Unless there was a kind of consolation in finding others as loathsome as one's self, even if all we could do was hurl our venom at each other. Perhaps this was the explanation for this hideous plain. Perhaps in the course of eons or of seconds, each creature here had sought out the company of others as pride-and-hate filled as himself, until together they formed this society of the damned.

Perhaps it was not Jesus who had abandoned them, but they who had fled from the Light that showed up their darkness. (*Return from Tomorrow*, pp. 63–65)

Ministering spirits even in hell

Yet, even in hell, George witnessed that the inhabitants were all attended by ministering spirits.

Or . . . were they as alone as at first it appeared? Gradually I was becoming aware that there was something else on that plain of grappling forms. Almost from the beginning I had sensed it, but for a long time I could not locate it. When I did it was with a shock that left me stunned.

That entire unhappy plain was hovered over by beings seemingly made of light. It was their very size and blinding brightness that had prevented me at first from seeing them. Now that I had, now that I adjusted my eyes to take them in, I could see that that these immense presences were bending over the little creatures on the plain. Perhaps even conversing with them.

Were these bright beings angels? . . . All I clearly saw was that not one of these bickering beings on the plain had been abandoned. They were being attended, watched over, ministered to. And the equally observable fact was that not one of them knew it. If Jesus or His angels were speaking to them, they certainly did not hear. (*Return from Tomorrow*, p. 66)

"The failure to see Jesus"

"And suddenly I realized that there was a common denominator to all these scenes so far. It was the failure to see Jesus. Whether it

Keith A. Haslem

was a physical appetite, an earthly concern, an absorption with self—whatever got in the way of His light created the separation into which we stepped at death" (*Return from Tomorrow*, p. 67).

"No fire and brimstone . . . a place totally devoid of love"

> What I saw horrified me more than anything I have ever seen in life. Since you could tell what the beings of this place thought, you knew they were filled with hate, deceit, lies, self-righteousness bordering on megalomania, and lewd sexual aggressiveness that were causing them to carry out all kind of abominable acts on each other.
>
> This was breaking the heart of the Son of God standing beside me. Even here were angels trying get them to change their thoughts. Since they could not admit there were beings greater than themselves, they could not see or hear them. There was no fire and brimstone here; no boxed-in canyons, but something a thousand times worse from my point of view. Here was a place totally devoid of love. This was HELL. (*My Life After Dying*, p. 27)

SARAH LANELLE MENET

"Anguish not caused by physical pain, but by an inner, self-inflicted torment. . . . A place of near-total darkness."

> The following descriptions of my death experience are without a doubt the most significant to me. Though I saw wondrous things, experiencing the amazing abilities of the spirit body, and viewed future world events, the singular, life-changing event in all of this was the time I spent in a place we on earth commonly refer to as "hell."
>
> In a moment I once again changed locations. This time I was transported to a place of near-total darkness with shades of gray and black. Several things hit me all at once, and the total impact of it all was almost ferocious in its intensity. All of my newly discovered senses were bombarded with a heavy, overwhelming fear.
>
> . . . [I] found myself surrounded by almost complete darkness. But it was more and much worse than mere darkness. It was an oppressive physical weight that I could feel pressing upon all of my body.
>
> The cries around me were something I felt with my whole being rather than just heard. They were awful and reached into my core, filling me with a sense of fear and horror. At first I thought the sounds

were those of tortured animals wailing in pain, but I quickly realized almost in shock that these unbelievable sounds were coming from people. Many were sobbing hysterically. Still others were wailing and grinding their teeth in terrible anguish that was caused not by physical pain, but by an inner, self-inflicted torment because of the weight of their sins.

... As I moved about, I could actually feel the "air" surrounding my body as it relentlessly clung around me like thick whipped cream. I started to feel claustrophobic, like a person drowning in thick, heavy goo. Into my mind it came that the "air" I was feeling was actually some kind of a tangible substance that locked these spirits into this place and did not allow them to cross over into the beautiful part of the spirit world where I had previously been.

... I asked in my mind, Am I in Hell?

The answer came quickly. No, this is not Hell, exactly. This was a place of temporary confinement for those spirits who had committed acts of evil during their lives on earth and, having not repented of them, had to suffer for their choices. Here they suffered a penalty for their sins that would help them understand the broad consequences of sin. People on earth referred to this place as hell because it is so horrifying, but here they call it *the spirit prison*. I understood that there were several areas to this spirit prison, and I was in the worst part of this place of sorrow. ...

People who had committed heinous, horrible crimes against other human beings were locked into this terrible place where they would for a period of time feel the pain they had inflicted on others, but that pain was enormously multiplied. They were in agony beyond mortal comprehension. I also understood that many of those held there were still filled with the hate and anger that had consumed them while upon the earth. I was somehow permitted to feel a small part of their emotions. The desires to murder, inflict pain, and destroy that they felt in their earth lives had remained with them, but they were now prevented from committing those sins because of their spiritual nature. I understood that you could not physically hurt a spirit, good or evil.

I asked, How could a loving God put any of His children in a place like this no matter what they had done? (*There Is No Death*, p. 56; emphasis added)

"God did not put them in this place."

Keith A. Haslem

The answer came immediately to me: God did not put them in this place. Their own actions drew them here. I then understood that somehow their evil deeds and desires while in mortality caused them to be attracted and pulled to this dreadful fate. I didn't exactly understand how that worked, but the answer satisfied me.

The reason it was so dark was because the people who were here, which included murderers, adulterers, rapists, and child molesters along with many others, had no light coming from their bodies. In the spirit world where I just came from, the plants, animals, buildings, and especially the people all had light coming from them. That is why they didn't need to have a sun or a star to give them light. They produced their own by means of their goodness. . . . Here in the spirit prison it was so dark because the people were dark. They had rejected the light of God and turned against it and therefore it wasn't in them. (*There Is No Death*, p. 56)

Those in hell feel the pain they inflicted on others.

"Once again I realized that we not only feel the pain of what we have personally done in our lives, but we also feel the pain that we have inflicted upon others—from their perspective. The unspeakable regret and torment these spirits were suffering was because of this ability to feel what others feel" (*There Is No Death*, p. 58).

MAURICE RAWLINGS

Dr. Rawlings, a cardiologist, whose research is detailed in his book *Beyond Death's Door*, believes that although the majority of the NDE accounts are of visits to a paradisaical realm, there are nonetheless many NDErs that visit a very unpleasant realm. But for some reason, the memories of that realm are blocked from their memory shortly after the person returns.

Dr. Rawlings writes of an experience he had with a patient who apparently got a glimpse of hell between Dr. Rawling's repeated attempts to resuscitate him from a heart attack.

"It really may not be safe to die!"

More and more of my patients who are recovering from serious illnesses tell me there is a life after death. There is a heaven and a hell. I had always thought of death as painless extinction. I had bet my

Going Home

> life on it. Now I have to reconsider my own destiny, and what I have found isn't good. I have found it really may not be safe to die!
>
> The turning point of in my own thinking occurred because of the event I alluded to previously. I requested that a patient perform what we call a "stress test" to evaluate complaints about chest pains. . . . [During the stress test, the patient] had a cardiac arrest and dropped dead right in my office. . . .
>
> With my ear to his chest, I could hear no heartbeat at all. . . . I could feel no pulse . . . he quit breathing altogether. . . .
>
> While I started external heart massage, one nurse initiated mouth-to-mouth breathing. (*Beyond Death's Door*, p. 18)

Dr. Rawlings hooked the patient up to some pacemaker equipment, then the patient said:

"I am in hell! . . . Don't stop [trying to resuscitate me]!"

> The patient began "coming to." But whenever I would reach for instruments or otherwise interrupt my compression of his chest, the patient would again lose consciousness, roll his eyes upward, arch his back in mild convulsion, stop breathing, and die once more.
>
> Each time he regained heartbeat and respiration, the patient screamed, "I am in hell!" He was terrified and pleaded with me to help him. I was scared to death. In fact, this episode literally scared the hell out of me! It terrified me enough to write this book.
>
> He then issued a very strange plea: "Don't stop!" You see, the first thing most patients I resuscitate tell me, as soon as they recover consciousness, is "Take your hands off my chest; you're hurting me!" I am big and my method of external heart massage sometimes fractures ribs. But this patient was telling me, "Don't stop!"
>
> Then I noticed a genuinely alarmed look on his face. . . . This patient had a grotesque grimace expressing sheer horror! . . .
>
> Then still another strange thing happened. He said, "Don't you understand? I am in hell. Each time you quit I go back to hell! Don't let me go back to hell!"
>
> Being accustomed to patients under this kind of emotional stress, I dismissed his complaint and told him to keep his "hell" to himself. I remember telling him, "I'm busy. Don't bother me about your hell until I finish getting this pacemaker into place."
>
> But the man was serious, and it finally occurred to me that he was indeed in trouble. He was in a panic like I had never seen before. As a result, I started working feverishly and rapidly. By this time the

patient had experienced three or four episodes of complete unconsciousness and clinical death from cessation of both heartbeat and breathing.

After several episodes he finally asked me, "How do I stay out of hell?" I told him I guessed it was the same principle learned in Sunday school—that I guessed Jesus Christ would be the one whom you would ask to save you.

Then he said, "I don't know how. Pray for me."

Pray for him? What nerve! I told him I was a doctor, not a preacher.

"Pray for me!" he repeated. (*Beyond Death's Door*, pp. 18–20)

Dr. Rawlings did end up offering a brief prayer for the man.

"I don't recall any hell."

The patient's condition finally stabilized, and he was transported to a hospital. I went home, dusted off the Bible, and started reading it. . . . I decided I had better start reading it very closely.

A couple of days later, I approached the patient with pad and pencil in hand for an interview. At his bedside I asked him to recall what he actually saw in hell. Were there any flames? Did the devil have a pitchfork? What did hell look like?

He said, "What hell? I don't recall any hell!" I recounted all of the details he had described two days earlier while he was on the floor next to the treadmill machine being resuscitated. He could recall none of the unpleasant events! *Apparently, the experiences were so frightening, so horrible, that his conscious mind could not cope with them; and they were subsequently suppressed far into his subconscious.*

The man . . . is now a strong Christian, although before his incident he had gone to church only occasionally. . . . He does remember "passing out" once or twice. . . . He still does not recall the experiences that occurred in hell, but he does recall standing in the back of the room and watching us work on his body there on the floor.

He also recalls meeting both his mother and stepmother during one of these subsequent death episodes. The meeting place was a gorge full of beautiful colors. He also saw other relatives who had died before. This experience was very pleasurable, occurring in a narrow valley with very lush vegetation and brilliant illumination by a huge beam of light. He "saw" his mother for the first time. She had died at the age of twenty-one when he was fifteen months old and his father had never remarried. This man had never even seen a picture of his real mother, and yet he was able to pick her picture out of several others a few weeks later when his mother's sister, after hearing of his experience, produced some family pictures for identification. There was no mistake. The same auburn hair, the same eyes and mouth—the face was identical to the lady he saw in his experience. She was still twenty-one years old. He was astounded and so was his father. (*Beyond Death's Door*, pp. 17–22; emphasis added)

Dr. Rawlings also tells of the case of a fourteen-year-old girl who tried to commit suicide.

"Those demons . . . they wouldn't let go of me. . . . It was just awful!"

A fourteen-year-old girl became despondent over a report card from school. Communication with her parents usually centered upon her deficits, and recently upon her inadequacy to measure up to the grades of her sister who was a couple of years older and seemed to be accomplished in nearly everything. Even "looks" were compared. She never seemed to receive any praise, and now she had to confront her parents with her report card. She went up to her room, and thinking the best way to solve the problem, she took a bottle of aspirin from the bathroom. It probably had eighty tablets in it, and she had to take a lot of water to get them down. Her parents found her a couple of hours later in a coma. She had vomited over her own face and onto the pillow. Fortunately, many of the aspirin had not been absorbed and she recovered a couple of hours later in the hospital emergency room after we used a stomach pump with bicarbonate of soda to neutralize acidosis which caused a peculiar, heavy breathing, a characteristic of aspirin coma.

During one of the vomiting episodes she inhaled some of the vomitus, developed spasm of the vocal cords, stopped breathing, and then had a cardiac arrest. She recovered immediately with external heart massage and placement of a breathing tube down her throat into her windpipe. Her recollections during the recovery were poor, but at the time she kept saying, "Mama, help me! Make them let go of me! They're trying to hurt me!" The doctors tried to apologize for hurting her, but she said it wasn't the doctors, but "Them, those demons in hell . . . they wouldn't let go of me . . . they wanted me . . . . I couldn't get back. . . . It was just awful!"

She slept for another day, and her mother hugged her most of that time. After the various tubes were removed, I asked her to recall what had happened. She remembered taking the aspirin, but absolutely nothing else! Somewhere in her mind the events may still be suppressed. . . .

She subsequently became a missionary several years later. . . . I am told that everywhere she goes she brings exuberance—a contagious feeling. (*Beyond Death's Door*, pp. 111–12)

"After many interrogations of patients I have personally resuscitated, I was amazed by the discovery that many have bad experiences. If patients could be immediately interviewed, I believe researchers would find bad experiences to be as frequent as good ones" (*Beyond Death's Door*, p. 66).

C. S. LEWIS

Oxford scholar and one-time atheist, C. S. Lewis, expresses an interesting opinion.

"I willingly believe that the damned are, in one sense, successful, rebels to the end; that the doors of hell are locked from the inside . . . [to] enjoy forever the horrible freedom [from God] they have demanded" (*The Problem of Pain*, p. 130).

THE CHURCH OF JESUS CHRIST OF LATTER-DAY SAINTS PERSPECTIVE

No literal lake of "fire and brimstone."

Members of the Church of Jesus Christ of Latter-day Saints do not believe that the wicked, at their deaths, will be thrown by a loving God into a literal lake of fire and brimstone.

JOSEPH SMITH JR.
(first prophet and president of the Church of Jesus Christ of Latter-day Saints)

Joseph Smith Jr. taught:

"A man is his own tormentor and his own condemner. Hence the saying, They shall go into the lake that burns with fire and brimstone.

The torment of disappointment in the mind of man is as exquisite as a lake burning with fire and brimstone. I say, so is the torment of man" (From "The King Follett Discourse," as quoted by N. B. Lundall, *The Vision*, p. 27).

BOOK OF MORMON

"Cast out into outer darkness."

The Book of Mormon alludes to a place of darkness where the wicked will abide in a hell not constructed by God, but in one that is more of their own making.

> And then it shall come to pass, that the spirits of the wicked, yea, who are evil—for behold, they have no part nor portion of the Spirit of the Lord; for behold, they chose evil works rather than good; therefore the spirit of the devil did enter into them, and take possession of their house—and these shall be cast out into outer darkness; there shall be weeping, and wailing, and gnashing of teeth, and this because of their own iniquity, being led captive by the will of the devil.
>
> Now this is the state of the souls of the wicked, yea, in darkness, and a state of awful, fearful looking for the fiery indignation of the wrath of God upon them; thus they remain in this state, as well as the righteous in paradise, until the time of their resurrection. (Alma 40:13–14)

Most Christian religions believe that the inhabitants of hell will suffer there eternally. Members of the Church of Jesus Christ of Latter-day Saints believe that hell is a temporary abode that will end when the inhabitants are finally resurrected.

AUTHOR'S PERSPECTIVE

It may be that the wicked will never actually *experience* the "fiery indignation" of the wrath of God (Hebrews 10:27) upon them, because God is a God of love, not vengeance. Nevertheless, their ignorance of God's unconditional love for them and their consequent fear of His wrath will nonetheless create a fearful and miserable existence until the day of their resurrection. This hellish abode may extend for a thousand years beyond the day of the Second Coming of Christ, which will be

Keith A. Haslem

discussed further in Chapter 83: What Happens After Jesus's Second Coming?

ASIDE

If you would like to read more accounts about the hellish regions of the spirit world, you can read: *Proof of Heaven: A Neurosurgeon's Journey into the Afterlife*, by Eben Alexander and/or *My Descent into Death: A Second Chance at Life*, by Howard Storm

80

DOES HELL GO ON FOR ETERNITY?

SYNOPSIS

Most Christian churches believe that the unfortunate inhabitants of hell will remain there for eternity. Sarah LaNelle Menet alludes to the concept that the inhabitants of hell *won't* be there for eternity. Members of the Church of Jesus Christ of Latter-day Saints believe the same thing.

SARAH LANELLE MENET

"Over a thousand years . . . perhaps for another thousand years"

> I wondered how long they would have to stay and instantly knew that some of them had already been there for a very long time—over a thousand years as time is measured on earth. Many others would stay perhaps for another thousand years or until they had fully repented of the things they had done. . . . What they had put out on earth was now coming back to them. (*There Is No Death*, pp. 53–57)

THE CHURCH OF JESUS CHRIST OF LATTER-DAY SAINTS PERSPECTIVE

Members of the Church of Jesus Christ of Latter-day Saints also believe that hell will be a temporary abode.

Keith A. Haslem

"Endless punishment" and "eternal punishment" allude to the nature of the punishment, not the duration.

The basis for the theology of the Church of Jesus Christ of Latter-day Saints is a revelation given to Joseph Smith Jr., as recorded in Doctrine and Covenants 19, which reads, in part:

> I am Alpha and Omega, Christ the Lord; yea, even I am he, the beginning and the end, the Redeemer of the world. . . .
>
> And surely every man must repent or suffer, for I, God, am endless.
>
> Wherefore, I revoke not the judgments which I shall pass, but woes shall go forth, weeping, wailing and gnashing of teeth, yea, to those who are found on my left hand.
>
> *Nevertheless, it is not written that there shall be no end to this torment,* but it is written endless torment. . . .
>
> For, behold, the mystery of godliness, how great it is! For, behold, I am endless, and the punishment which is given from my hand is endless punishment, for Endless is my name. Wherefore—
>
> Eternal punishment is God's punishment.
>
> Endless punishment is God's punishment. (Doctrine and Covenants 19:1, 4–6, 10–12; emphasis added)

Therefore, the terms "eternal punishment" and "endless punishment" speak *not* of the *duration* of God's punishment, but rather to the *nature* of the punishment.

BRUCE R. MCCONKIE
(an apostle for the Church of Jesus Christ of Latter-day Saints, 1972–1985)

"Hell will have an end"

Elder McConkie reinforces this concept when he wrote on the topic of hell in his book *Mormon Doctrine*.

> That part of the spirit world inhabited by wicked spirits who are awaiting the eventual day of their resurrection is called hell. Between their death and resurrection, these souls of the wicked are cast out into outer darkness . . . [and] suffer the torments of the damned. . . .
>
> Hell will have an end. Viewing future events, John [the New Testament Apostle] saw that "death and hell delivered up the dead

which were in them: and they were judged every man according to their works" (Rev. 20:13). (*Mormon Doctrine*, p. 349)

Elder McConkie also quotes the Book of Mormon prophet Jacob who discoursed on the Atonement of Jesus Christ.

"Hell must deliver up its captive spirits, and the grave must deliver up its captive bodies, and the bodies and the spirits of men will be restored one to the other" (2 Nephi 9:10–12). It was in keeping with this principle for David to receive the promise: 'Thou wilt not leave my soul in hell' (Ps. 16:10; Acts 2:27) (*Mormon Doctrine*, pp. 349–50).

The duration of hell—more than one thousand years?

Members of the Church of Jesus Christ of Latter-day Saints believe those in hell will be released at the time when the wicked are finally resurrected and stand before God to be judged according to their works—the Final Judgment. The wicked, having already paid the price of their sins during their time in hell, will be judged with regard to their good works on the earth and will then be assigned to an appropriate level of heavenly glory for the balance of eternity.

Members of the Church of Jesus Christ of Latter-day Saints believe the resurrection of the wicked may not happen until the end of the thousand-year period spoken of in Revelation 20:1–5—a period that follows the Second Coming of Christ.

AUTHOR'S PERSPECTIVE

Eternity is a long time. In comparison, our mortal lives are but a moment in time. Would God punish a soul for eternity for the deeds they had done during a relative moment in time? That sounds like neither a loving nor a just God.

DO EVIL SPIRITS EXIST?

SYNOPSIS

Some may find the concept of evil spirits implausible; however, there is evidence that they do exist.

Sarah LaNelle Menet learned that evil spirits do exist, and in the face of their influence, we show our "true colors." They also instigate many of the horrific things that happen on earth.

Members of the Church of Jesus Christ of Latter-day Saints believe that some spirits in the premortal world rebelled against God and were therefore cast out of heaven and denied the opportunity to come to earth. Those spirits are now doing what they can to influence earth's inhabitants to do evil so that they will be unable to return to God's presence.

SARAH LANELLE MENET

Sarah learned that Satan and evil spirits do exist, and they are allowed to tempt people to reveal their "true colors."

"Evil spirits . . . cause or instigate most of the terrible things that happen here on earth."

> As God plans and prepares blessings for us, I learned that there is an evil spirit called Satan who, with the assistance of other spirits like him, orchestrates bad experiences in our lives. Satan, I learned, is a very real spirit person. He was the leader of a group of spirits who

Going Home

rebelled or tried to fight against God a long time ago before we came to earth.

It is these evil spirits who cause or instigate most of the terrible things that happen here on earth. While God and Christ are always in complete control, they do temporarily allow Satan and his evil spirits a certain amount of freedom to influence people for bad and to attempt to draw people away from the right path. In this way God and Jesus allow us to see which way we will choose to go and whom we will follow. (*There Is No Death*, pp. 99–100)

"[Evil spirits'] primary attitude is one of hate, anger, or depression."

There are many evil spirits here on the earth. They are all around us and have the ability to roam where they will in this world. Again, they can't really harm us unless we give them power to do so by making bad choices. Often we can feel the presence or influence of these evil spirits. Their primary attitude is one of hate, anger, or depression; and so if we let ourselves go and become uncontrollably angry or hateful we can be fairly sure of their presence and attempts to influence us for bad. Many of the depressed people on the earth today are under the influence of Satan and his evil spirits. Their desire is to cause us to feel downhearted and despondent and to believe that our situation is completely hopeless and beyond our power to change or control. When we are like that it is much easier for them to influence us to make bad choices.

. . . The evil spirits have an advantage that we do not. Their memories have not been blocked the way ours have, and so they remember the thousands of years we lived together where they knew us very well. They know our weaknesses and try to use them to persuade us to make bad choices. (*There Is No Death*, p. 101)

"There are also a lot of good spirits around us . . . guardian angels."

To counter the influence of those evil spirits, there are also a lot of good spirits around us who whisper to our minds warnings of danger of a physical or spiritual nature and encourage us to make good, positive choices. Usually these good spirits around us are loved ones, family members who have either passed away or who have not yet come to earth. They love us and are constantly looking after us, often speaking peace and hope to our hearts. . . . Good spirits also protect us from crossing over before our time. We call these spirits guardian angels. (*There Is No Death*, pp. 101–2)

THE CHURCH OF JESUS CHRIST OF LATTER-DAY SAINTS PERSPECTIVE

Members of the Church of Jesus Christ of Latter-day Saints believe that in the premortal world of spirits, a great council was held by God and all of His spirit children. Two plans were proposed to bring about the salvation of these spirit children. One was proposed by God and proposed that all men would have their agency to choose as they wanted while on earth. As a part of this plan, Jesus Christ offered to be our Savior. The other plan, proposed by Satan, denied men their free agency. God chose Jesus's plan.

Satan rebelled and one third of the hosts of heaven chose to follow him. Because of their rebellion, Satan and his followers were cast out of heaven and denied the privilege of coming to earth and obtaining physical bodies. They have become the devil and his angels, and they traverse the earth in an effort to persuade those here to make choices that will prevent them from returning to God's presence after their physical death.

BIBLICAL REFERENCE

The Apostle John spoke of these events in the book of Revelation. In these verses, the "great red dragon" is Satan.

> And there appeared another wonder in heaven; and behold a great red dragon. . . .
>
> And his tail drew the third part of the stars of heaven, and did cast them to the earth. . . .
>
> And there was a war in heaven: Michael and his angels fought against the dragon; and the dragon fought and his angels,
>
> And prevailed not; neither was their place found any more in heaven.
>
> And the great dragon was cast out, that old serpent, called the Devil, and Satan, which deceiveth the whole world: he was cast out

into the earth, and his angels were cast out with him. (Revelation 12:3–4, 7–9)

AUTHOR'S PERSPECTIVE

Perhaps the most dangerous attitude a person can have regarding evil spirits is to naively believe they don't exist.

There are individuals who have consciously chosen to become disciples of Satan, and they may tell you that he has appeared to them.

Even the common Ouija board game can offer startling evidence of unseen powers not of this world, and those powers do not arise from good spirits.

82

IS POSSESSION BY EVIL SPIRITS POSSIBLE?

Several accounts of individuals being possessed by evil spirits are recounted in the New Testament, the most familiar of which is the man referred to as Legion, because he was possessed by many evil spirits (see Mark 5:1–13). Jesus cast out the evil spirits, who went into a herd of swine which immediately "ran violently down a steep slope into the sea, (they were about two thousand;) and were choked in the sea" (Mark 5:13).

The concept of possessed people may seem mythical in this day and age. But several of the Witnesses vouch for the concept that possession is possible in our day.

SYNOPSIS

Dr. George G. Ritchie witnessed spirits attempting to possess the bodies of drunken sailors in a bar.

Sarah LaNelle Menet comments that resistance to possessions is reduced when people are under the influence of alcohol or drugs.

Brigham Young taught that evil spirits attempt to inhabit physical bodies.

GEORGE G. RITCHIE JR.

During his experience in the spirit world, Dr. Ritchie observed both mortals and spirits in a bar: "I began to notice something else. All of the living people were surrounded by a faint luminous glow, almost like an electrical field over the surface of their bodies. This luminosity moved as they moved, like a second skin made out of pale, scarcely visible light" (*Return from Tomorrow*, p. 59).

A spirit enters the body of a drunken patron.

> I watched one young sailor rise unsteadily from a stool, take two or three steps, and sag heavily to the floor. Two of his buddies stooped down and started dragging him away from the crush.
>
> But that was not what I was looking at. I was staring in amazement as the bright cocoon around the unconscious sailor simply opened up. It parted at the very crown of his head and began peeling away from his head, his shoulders. Instantly, quicker than I'd ever seen anyone move, one of the insubstantial beings who had been standing near him at the bar was on top of him....
>
> In the next instant, to my utter mystification, the springing figure had vanished....
>
> Twice more, as I stared, stupefied, the identical scene was repeated. A man passed out, a crack swiftly opened in the aureole round him, one of the non-solid people vanished as he hurled himself at that opening, almost is if he had scrambled inside the other man.
>
> Was that covering of light some kind of shield, then? Was it a protection against... against disembodied beings like myself? (*Return from Tomorrow*, pp. 60-61)

Dr. Richie surmises that these spirits, who had "developed a dependence on alcohol" during mortality, sought some type of satisfaction by inserting themselves into a body whose defense was compromised because of excessive consumption of alcohol.

SARAH LANELLE MENET

"When we partake of mind-altering drugs and alcohol... [our] resistance [to possessions] is lowered."

> When an evil spirit enters a human physical body, we call it a "possession." It happens much more frequently than we realize. Possessions can be very mild or extend to complete control. All of us have a natural resistance to such a possession so that evil spirits cannot enter into us. However, when we partake of mind-altering drugs and alcohol, this resistance is lowered. It can happen with the first drink. A hole

opens up at the crown of the head that actually allows an evil spirit to drop down into us. Once inside, they have a greater power over us and can influence our behavior to a great degree. This is why Satan and his evil cohorts encourage the use of alcohol and drugs. It is also why so many heinous crimes are committed under the influence of these substances. We will be held responsible for the acts we commit while under their influence. (*There Is No Death*, p. 111)

THE CHURCH OF JESUS CHRIST OF LATTER-DAY SAINTS PERSPECTIVE

BRIGHAM YOUNG
(second prophet and president of the Church of Jesus Christ of Latter-day Saints)

Brigham Young once remarked:

"[Evil spirits] are continually trying to get into the tabernacles of the human family."

You may now see people with legions of evil spirits in and around them: there are men who walk our streets that have more than a hundred devils in them and round about them, prompting them to do all manner of evil, and some too that profess to be Latter-day Saints.

. . . You can see the acts of these evil spirits in every place, the whole country is full of them, the whole earth is alive with them, and they are continually trying to get into the tabernacles of the human family, and are always on hand to prompt us to depart from the strict line of our duty. (*Journal of Discourses*, 3:369)

AUTHOR'S PERSPECTIVE

Flip Wilson, an African-American comedian of the late 1960s and 1970s coined a humorous, self-rationalizing admission: "The devil made me do it."

In reality, I wonder how many of the heinous acts of men are committed while being possessed with an evil spirit. Consider how many perpetrators assert they have no recollection of crimes they committed. Nevertheless, accountability for such acts cannot be escaped when poor decisions compromise normal sensibilities.

PART V
AFTER JESUS'S SECOND COMING

83

WHAT HAPPENS AFTER JESUS'S SECOND COMING?

SYNOPSIS

Sarah LaNelle Menet and George G. Ritchie allude to a future period of peace on the earth, which aligns with biblical teachings.

Members of the Church of Jesus Christ of Latter-day Saints believe that all wicked people will be destroyed at the Second Coming of Christ, and the remainder will live on a paradisaical earth with Christ for a thousand years. They term this period "the Millennium."

SARAH LANELLE MENET

Sarah LaNelle Menet speaks of the Second Coming of Christ, and her belief that "many of us" will still be on the earth when He comes again.

"This wonderful time of peace and happiness is not very far off."

> Jesus Christ will return to the earth and reward the good people with tremendous blessings, including his presence, once again. It will be a wonderful time, very similar to what it is like in the paradise part of the spirit world. During this time, evil will not be able to have any effect upon us. Through some process, the evil spirits will not be able to influence those who remain. This wonderful time of peace and happiness is not very far off, and I believe that many of us now living

will make it through the bad times that lie ahead to experience the joyous times that follow. (*There Is No Death*, p. 113)

GEORGE G. RITCHIE JR.

A "corridor in time" where "man and nature both were better."

"A second corridor started to open through time. . . . The planet grew more peaceful. Man and nature were both better. Man was not as critical of himself or others. He was not as destructive of nature and he was beginning to understand what love is" (*My Life After Dying*, p. 32).

BIBLICAL PERSPECTIVE

The Apostle John saw a vision of the end of the world. Following the Second Coming of Jesus Christ—which will be preceded by wars and great natural disasters—the Apostle John wrote that

[After Jesus's Second Coming, Satan will be] "bound a thousand years."

> And I saw an angel come down from heaven, having the key of the bottomless pit and a great chain in his hand.
>
> And he laid hold on the dragon, that old serpent, which is the Devil, and Satan, and bound him a thousand years,
>
> And cast him into the bottomless pit, and shut him up, and set a seal upon him, that he should deceive the nations no more, till the thousand years should be fulfilled: and after that he must be loosed a little season. (Revelation 20:1–3)

The concept of nature being more peaceful is reminiscent of a prophecy of the Old Testament Prophet Isaiah.

ISAIAH

"The wolf and the lamb shall feed together, and the lion shall eat straw like the bullock. . . . They shall not hurt nor destroy in all my holy mountain, saith the Lord" (Isaiah 65:25).

Going Home

THE CHURCH OF JESUS CHRIST OF LATTER-DAY SAINTS PERSPECTIVE

During this thousand-year period of peace—the Millennium—members of the Church of Jesus Christ of Latter-day Saints believe that "Christ will reign personally upon the earth; and, that the earth will be renewed and receive its paradisaical glory" (Articles of Faith 1:10).

BRUCE R. MCCONKIE
(an apostle for the Church of Jesus Christ of Latter-day Saints, 1972–1985)

During this millennial period, Elder McConkie taught that Satan will be bound and "corruption, death and disease will cease . . . [and] the kingdom of God on earth will be fully established in all its glory, beauty and perfection" (*Mormon Doctrine*, p. 492).

AUTHOR'S PERSPECTIVE

Who will be on the earth during the Millennium?

My belief, per the doctrine of the Church of Jesus Christ of Latter-day Saints, is that those who were good and honorable during mortality will be resurrected and be inhabitants of the earth during the Millennium.

84

WHO WILL BE RESURRECTED?

Although treatment of this topic by the Witnesses is minimal, I will include this brief discussion because of its universal relevance with regard to life after death.

SYNOPSIS

Elane Durham states that all men will eventually take up their bodies again.

Biblical references also teach this principle.

Members of the Church of Jesus Christ of Latter-day Saints believe that all mankind will eventually be resurrected and possess perfect physical bodies.

ELANE DURHAM

"We will all be empowered to take [our bodies] up again."

> Finally, I knew that though babies and all other mortals lay their bodies down in death, through Christ's resurrection we will all be empowered to take them up again, just as He took up His body from the tomb. Then our physical bodies will be in a glorified state, made of light is the best way I can describe them, and in that glorified state we will all be empowered to continue our spiritual growth to whatever heights we desire. (*I Stand All Amazed*, p. 79)

THE CHURCH OF JESUS CHRIST OF LATTER-DAY SAINTS PERSPECTIVE

The Book of Mormon teaches that all men will be resurrected with perfect bodies.

> The spirit and the body shall be reunited again in its perfect form; both limb and joint shall be restored to its proper frame. . . .
>
> Now, this restoration shall come to all, both old and young, both bond and free, both male and female, both the wicked and the righteous; and even there shall not so much as a hair of their heads be lost; but everything shall be restored to its perfect frame. (Alma 11:43–44)

BIBLICAL PERSPECTIVE

The Apostle Paul taught the Corinthians: "For as in Adam all die, even so in Christ shall all be made alive" (1 Corinthians 15:22).

Job stated his faith in the midst of his trials. "And though after my skin worms destroy this body, yet in my flesh shall I see God" (Job 19:26).

The Apostle John alludes to the reunion of the body, the spirits of those in hell, and the Final Judgment. "And the sea gave up the dead which were in it; and death [the body] and hell [the spirit] delivered up the dead which were in them, and they were judged every man according to their works" (Revelation 20:13).

AUTHOR'S PERSPECTIVE

My perspective, based upon my religious faith, is that all mankind will eventually have a resurrected physical body, and that gives me great hope and comfort. Although I have enjoyed a healthy physical body throughout my life, I find the promise of a perfected physical body after the Resurrection comforting and reassuring, especially with regard to the many who have struggled and suffered with various physical afflictions during mortality.

85

WHAT HAPPENS AFTER THE FINAL JUDGMENT?

SYNOPSIS

Sarah LaNelle Menet learned that the paradisaical region of the spirit world is not heaven, but rather is only a waiting place pending the Final Judgment.

The Bible teaches that the Resurrection and Final Judgment will take place at the end of the thousand-year period of peace.

After the Final Judgment, most of the Christian world believes that we will be assigned to spend eternity in heaven or hell. Members of the Church of Jesus Christ of Latter-day Saints believe that there are three kingdoms to which we may be assigned: the celestial kingdom, the terrestrial kingdom, or the telestial kingdom.

SARAH LANELLE MENET

Paradise is not the same as heaven.

Sarah LaNelle Menet learned that the paradisaical realm she saw during her near-death experience was not heaven.

"This place . . . was not heaven . . . only a waiting place."

> I learned while asking questions on the hill previously that this place, in all its magnificence, was not heaven. This was only a waiting place for the spirits of people who have departed from the earth while waiting for a future time when they would be assigned another place

or kingdom. I understood that these other kingdoms were more splendid than this temporary one.

The spirit world was divided into different levels, and there also came understanding that the kingdoms of glory contained levels, each being more beautiful and glorious than the one before it, until reaching the highest level where God the Father and Jesus Christ actually dwell. When the time of the resurrection and judgment comes, every spirit will be assigned to a level within one of these kingdoms according to the choices they made.

. . . Having seen the beauty of the waiting place for spirits, I cannot imagine the grandeur of the mansions where our Father and Jesus live. I would gladly have stayed in the world I had just encountered forever. I could not dream of a kingdom more glorious than this one. (*There Is No Death*, pp. 37–38)

BIBLICAL PERSPECTIVE

The Final Judgment takes place at the end of the thousand-year period of peace.

The Apostle John writes that Satan will be loosed at the end of the thousand-year period of peace.

> And when the thousand years are expired, Satan shall be loosed out of his prison,
> And shall go out to deceive the nations which are in the four quarters of the earth, Gog and Magog, to gather them together to battle. (Revelation 20:7–8)

Revelation 20:10 indicates that Satan and his forces will be defeated and vanquished, and verse 12 indicates that the Final Judgment will then take place.

"And I saw the dead, small and great, stand before God; and the books were opened: and another book was opened, which is the book of life: and the dead were judged out of those things which were written in the books, according to their works" (Revelation 20:12).

Keith A. Haslem

THE CHURCH OF JESUS CHRIST OF LATTER-DAY SAINTS PERSPECTIVE

Three kingdoms of glory.

The typical Christian belief is that after the Final Judgment all men will be assigned either to heaven or to hell for eternity. Members of the Church of Jesus Christ of Latter-day Saints have an expanded view, which includes three different kingdoms of glory to which we may be assigned.

First, let's consider a hypothetical case of twin brothers, Lestor and Larry.

Both brothers are fundamentally good men; they go to church regularly, pray often, and treat other people well. But Lestor has a particularly good-looking woman living next door. Unfortunately, he breaks the last of the ten commandments, and covets his neighbor's wife. Let's assume that this sin is sufficient to disqualify him from heaven. So, despite being basically the same in all other facets of worthiness, Lestor is doomed to be "cast into a lake of fire and brimstone" (see Revelation 20:10), where he will be continually burning but never consumed for all eternity. But his brother, Larry, revels in the magnificence of heaven. A fair judgment by a just God?

Members of the Church of Jesus Christ of Latter-day Saints believe that all men will be assigned to one of three kingdoms of glory: the celestial kingdom, the terrestrial kingdom, or the telestial kingdom. Two of these kingdoms, or degrees of glory, are mentioned by the Apostle Paul as he teaches the Corinthians about the Resurrection.

> There are also celestial bodies, and bodies terrestrial: but the glory of the celestial is one, and the glory of the terrestrial is another.
>
> There is one glory of the sun, and another glory of the moon, and another glory of the stars: for one star differeth from another star in glory.
>
> So also is the resurrection of the dead. (1 Corinthians 15:40–42)

In 2 Corinthians 12:2, Paul makes another allusion to three postmortal realms: "I knew a man in Christ above fourteen years ago, (whether in the body, I cannot tell; or whether out of the body, I cannot tell: God knoweth;) such an one was caught up to the third heaven."

The celestial kingdom—the highest kingdom.

Heaven as it is commonly perceived, is termed the celestial kingdom in the theology of the Church of Jesus Christ of Latter-day Saints. This is where God the Father dwells. The inhabitants of the celestial kingdom will be those who applied the Atonement of Jesus Christ in their lives (through faith and repentance) and kept all the laws and ordinances of the gospel. Their potential is to become like God—perfect—as Christ commanded His disciples to be in Matthew 5:48.

"Be ye therefore perfect, even as your Father which is in heaven is perfect."

Inhabitants of this kingdom will be able to enjoy family relationships, including spousal relationships, for all eternity.

The terrestrial kingdom—the middle kingdom.

The inhabitants of the terrestrial kingdom, will enjoy the presence of Jesus Christ. Those assigned to this kingdom will include "they who are honorable men of the earth, who were blinded by the craftiness of men," or who were "not valiant in the testimony of Jesus" (Doctrine and Covenants 76:75, 79). It will be a kingdom of glory likely more blissful than anything we can possibly imagine.

The telestial kingdom—the lowest kingdom.

Those who were previously residents of hell will likely be assigned to the telestial kingdom, the lowest of the three kingdoms. However, members of the Church of Jesus Christ of Latter-day Saints believe that the conditions of this kingdom will be far better even than the conditions we now experience on earth. The inhabitants, having previously paid the price of their sins while in hell, are now appropriately rewarded for whatever good deeds they did while on the earth.

Keith A. Haslem

AUTHOR'S PERSPECTIVE

My personal opinion is that the vast majority of the inhabitants of the earth will end up in the middle kingdom—the terrestrial kingdom. They will enjoy presence of Jesus Christ, and say to themselves, "I did it! I made it to Heaven! And it's so much better than I ever dreamt it would be!"

PART VI
PARTING THOUGHTS

86

PARTING THOUGHTS FROM THE RESEARCHERS

As they conclude their books, the NDE researchers I have quoted summarize their work with their most significant observations.

SYNOPSIS

As a result of his extensive study of NDEs, Dr. Moody feels the need to express his love to those he loves.

Dr. Kübler-Ross recommends that we "pass on . . . a little more love."

Dr. Kenneth Ring suggests that death is not something to be dreaded. He also constructed the equation: Death = God = Love.

Dr. Michael B. Sabom agrees with Albert Einstein, who says, "[he is] convinced that a Spirit is manifest in the Laws of the Universe."

As a result of his studies, Dr. Jeffrey Long writes that, "I'm showing more love to others now than before."

Dr. Melvin Morse has concluded that "death is not to be feared."

Dr. Osis and Dr. Haraldsson recommend that we should be attentive to the "central theme" of those that have experienced near-death experiences—which seems to be the importance of learning how to love others unconditionally.

RAYMOND A. MOODY JR.

In *Reflections on Life After Life,* Dr. Moody was asked: "What is your own personal attitude toward this research? Has it affected your life in any way?"

Keith A. Haslem

"More than ever now I am very careful to let each person I love know how I feel."

> I have come to accept as a matter of religious faith that there is a life after death, and I believe that the phenomenon we have been examining is a manifestation of that life.
>
> However, far from being obsessed with death, I want to live. The persons I have interviewed would agree. The focus of their attention, as a result of having been through this experience, is on living. For we are all in this life now. At the same time, I hope to be able to apply what I have learned in this study to my life. I want to go on developing, as far as I can, in the areas of loving others and acquiring knowledge and wisdom. . . .
>
> . . . I have begun to realize how near to death we all are in our daily lives. More than ever now I am very careful to let each person I love know how I feel. (*Reflections on Life After Life*, pp. 111–12)

In the concluding chapter of *The Light Beyond*, Dr. Moody observed:

Almost every NDE researcher in the world believes in life after death.

> I have talked to almost every NDE researcher in the world about his or her work. I know that most of them believe in their hearts that NDEs are a glimpse of life after life. But as scientists and people of medicine, they still haven't come up with "scientific proof" that a part of us goes on living after our physical being is dead. This lack of proof keeps them from going public with their true feelings. . . .
>
> After twenty-two years of looking at the near-death experience, I think there isn't enough scientific proof to show conclusively that there is life after death. But that means scientific proof.
>
> Matters of the heart are different. They are open to judgments that don't require a strictly scientific view of the world. But with researchers like myself, they do call for educated analysis.
>
> Based upon such examination, I am convinced that NDEers do get a glimpse of the beyond, a brief passage into a whole other reality.
>
> The psychotherapist C. G. Jung summed up my feeling on life after life in a letter he wrote in 1944. This letter is especially significant

since Jung himself had an NDE during a heart attack just a few months before he wrote it:

"What happens after death is so unspeakably glorious that our imaginations and our feelings do not suffice to form even an approximate conception of it." (*The Light Beyond*, pp. 193, 197–98)

ELISABETH KÜBLER-ROSS

"Start looking at life differently"

"We are created for a very simple, beautiful, and wonderful life. My greatest wish is that you will start looking at life differently" (*On Life After Death*, p. 12).

"Pass on . . . a little more love"

"My wish is that you pass on to many people a little more love. . . . There are twenty million children in the world dying of starvation. Adopt one of those children, and start buying smaller presents" (*On Life After Death*, p.14).

As she concludes her book, Dr. Kübler-Ross speaks of dealing with the death of a parent.

Love your parents . . . despite their imperfections.

> Death is but a transition from this life to another existence where there is no more pain and anguish. All the bitterness and disagreements will vanish, and the only thing that lives forever is LOVE. So love each other NOW, for we never know how long we will be blessed with the presence of those who gave us LIFE—no matter how imperfect many a parent has been. (*On Life After Death*, p. 84)

KENNETH RING

As he concludes his book *Heading Toward Omega*, Dr. Ring proffers a simple equation.

"Death = God = Love"

> From the study of the NDE, we have learned to see death in a new way, not as something to be dreaded but, on the contrary, as an encounter with the Beloved. Those who can come to understand death in this

Keith A. Haslem

way, as the NDErs are compelled to, need never fear death again. And liberated from this primary fear, they too, like NDErs, become free to experienced life as the gift it is and to live naturally, as a child does, with delight. Not everyone can have or needs to have an NDE, but everyone can learn to assimilate these lessons of the NDE into his own life if he chooses to. . . .

And beyond all this, there is still the profound *evolutionary* meaning of NDE—that NDErs and others who have had similar awakenings may in some way prefigure our own planetary destiny, the next stage of human evolution, the dazzling ascent toward Omega and the conscious reunion with the Divine. (*Heading Toward Omega*, p. 268–69; emphasis in original)

For NDErs, the equations Death=God=Love are obvious (*Heading Toward Omega*, p. 85).

MICHAEL B. SABOM

On the last page of his book, *Recollections of Death*, Dr. Sabom, a cardiologist, summarizes his feelings after his five-year study of patients who had near-death experiences.

"My involvement in the lives and deaths of the people in this book has made me humble to the ways of the universe."

I have been deeply touched by the testimonies of those whose stories fill this book. As a physician, I have evaluated the medical circumstances and have been utterly amazed at the survival of many of these people whose physical condition plainly seemed to rule against their continuing to live. I have been equally fascinated by the descriptions of their journeys while unconscious and near death. My personal reaction to these events is not so much a "scientifically weighted" response as it is a keenly felt identification with the tears of joy and sorrow that have accompanied the unfolding of many of these stories. In short, my involvement in the lives and deaths of the people in this book has made me humble to the ways of the universe, much like Albert Einstein, who once wrote:

"Everyone who is seriously involved in the pursuit of science becomes convinced that a Spirit is manifest in the Laws of the Universe—a spirit vastly superior to that of man, and one in the face of which we, with our modest powers, must feel humble." (*Recollections of Death*, p. 186)

Going Home

JEFFREY LONG

"Absolutely convinced that an afterlife exists"

"After considering the strength of the evidence, I am absolutely convinced that an afterlife exists. I encourage each reader to consider the evidence and come to your own conclusion" (*Evidence of the Afterlife*, p. 199).

In the final paragraph of his book, Dr. Long considers the personal effect of his research.

"I'm showing more love to others now than before."

For me personally, I'm showing more love to others now than before I started my near-death-experiences studies. My understanding of near-death experiences has made me a better doctor. I face life with more courage and confidence. I believe NDErs really do bring back a piece of the afterlife. When NDErs share their remarkable experiences, I believe a piece of the afterlife, in some mysterious way, becomes available to us all. (*Evidence of the Afterlife*, pp. 199–202)

MELVIN MORSE

"Death is not to be feared."

When I accepted Dr. Raymond Moody's challenge to study NDEs scientifically, I felt certain that science would explain them.

All these years later, I accept what the ancients knew: All men must die and death is not to be feared. There is a light that we will all experience after death, and that Light represents joy, peace, and unconditional love. . . . I also believe in the reality of the near-death experience. The effects that such events have on the lives (and deaths) of those who have them are "proof enough" for me. (*Closer to the Light*, pp. 197, 203)

KARLIS OSIS and ERLENDUR HARALDSSON

The vast majority of Osis and Haraldsson's book, *At the Hour of Death*, uses the language and jargon of scientific research. Their personal perspective is perhaps best represented by the book's epilogue, where they

Keith A. Haslem

adopt layman's language and make the analogy of a "modern Lazarus" who counsels us regarding what to expect when we die.

"Pay attention [to those who have had near-death experiences]."

"Lazarus and a thousand others have spoken. In our judgment, it would be prudent to pay attention to the central message whispered by them at the hour of death" (*At the Hour of Death*, pp. 209–10).

AUTHOR'S PERSPECTIVE

Why risk your professional credibility?

It is easier to be skeptical of life after death than to be a believer, particularly if you are a scientist or an "intellectual." So the fact that these scientists and professionals were willing to sacrifice, if necessary, their professional credibility at the altar of enlightenment, argues that they must have been very sure of their assertions that life does continue after death.

87

PARTING THOUGHTS FROM THE WITNESSES

The Witnesses reserved, perhaps, their most significant observations regarding their near-death experiences for the conclusion of their accounts. The predominant theme is obvious: the importance of learning to love unconditionally, as God loves us.

SYNOPSIS

Dr. Ritchie suggests that our happiness in the next world will be a function of how well we learn to love in this world.

RaNelle Wallace's grandmother made this point emphatically to RaNelle: "The key is love."

Betty J. Eadie suggests that the best way to experience joy is to express love.

Sarah LaNelle Menet writes that to learn to love is to accomplish a primary reason for living.

Elane Durham writes that although she is "homesick" she knows she has "work" to do, which includes "loving and serving others without judgment."

Captain Dale Black assures us that although the ride through life may be bumpy, "it will be *so* worth it."

GEORGE G. RITCHIE JR.

In the last paragraph of his book *Return from Tomorrow*, Dr. Ritchie draws a conclusion.

Keith A. Haslem

The quality of our lives in the next world will depend on how we get on with the "business of loving" in this world.

"God is busy building a race of men who know how to love. I believe that the fate of the earth itself depends on the progress we make—and that the time now is very short. As for what we'll find in the next world, here too I believe that what we'll discover there depends on how well we get on with the business of loving, here and now" (*Return from Tomorrow*, p. 124).

In the last chapter of *My Life After Dying*, Dr. Ritchie contemplates what he regards as his mission.

"I have a commission to pass on what I have seen and learned."

> Is it accidental that I and others had these near-death experiences? Or did we die, or come close to dying . . . because a great and loving God was trying not only to save us, but to bring us back in order to tell and show in our living a better way of life for our world?
>
> . . . I have been living with this stupendous sense of destiny and the realization that I was given orders to return to his realm not because I had any desire to, but because I have a commission to pass on what I have seen and learned. My writing this book, particularly this last chapter, is an attempt to help show a way to reach the highest realm, heaven—not when we die but while we are alive. (*My Life After Dying*, pp. 157–58)

RANELLE WALLACE

On the last page of her book, RaNelle writes:

"God never falls short. . . . His love never left."

> I learned that God never falls short. And just as important, I learned that He will do all in His power to protect us from our own shortcomings. He had warned me a dozen times not to go on that flight, but I had not heeded the voice. Then, after the crash, it was only a few hours later that I was given the greatest gift imaginable [her experience in the spirit world] in the fullness of his matchless love.
>
> His love never left. (*The Burning Within*, p. 218)

Just prior to her return to her body, RaNelle's grandmother gave her some profound counsel:

Going Home

"The key is love. . . . The key is love. . . . The key is love."

"RaNelle," Grandmother said, "there is one more thing I need to say to you. Tell everyone that the key is love."

"The key is love," she repeated.

"The key is love," she said a third time. (*The Burning Within*, p. 116)

BETTY J. EADIE

"We must eventually accept [Jesus] and surrender to his love."

"Of all knowledge, however, there is none more essential than knowing Jesus Christ. I was told that he is the door through which we will all return. He is the only door through which we can return. Whether we learn of Jesus Christ here or while in the spirit, we must eventually accept him and surrender to his love" (*Embraced by the Light*, p. 85).

In the last paragraph of her book, Betty writes:

"Greater joy will come to us through love than in any other way."

We are to love one another. I know that. We are to be kind, to be tolerant, to give generous service. I know that greater joy will come to us through love than in any other way. I have seen its wonderful, glorious rewards. The details of my experience are important only to the point that they help us to love. All else is an appendage to that. It is a simple matter of following the Savior's message which he most clearly expressed to me: "Above all else, love one another."

I will continue to try. (*Embraced by the Light*, p. 147)

SARAH LANELLE MENET

"One of the main reasons we come to earth is to learn to develop . . . unconditional love for others."

I believe that the most important concept I learned while standing upon the hill [in the spirit world] was just how very much we are loved and the importance of loving and caring for each other in our individual lives. My entire experience was permeated with a feeling of the importance of love.

One of the main reasons we come to earth is to learn to develop this same kind of pure, unconditional love for others. (*There Is No Death*, p. 94)

The last paragraph of Sarah's book reads

"The Savior will always be in complete control, and good will triumph over evil."

I hope that everyone who has read this book will come away with the understanding that God does live and loves each one of us. He wants His people who are worthy and prepared to survive the calamities that are ahead of us. I know the Lord will be there to help us do so.

We need to be assured that even at a time when the world seems to be completely out of control the Savior will always be in complete control, and good will triumph over evil. We have no need to fear because the King of our universe will make all wrongs right. (*There Is No Death*, p. 131)

ELANE DURHAM

"I know that the best is yet to come."

As she concludes her book, Elane Durham reminisces on her very difficult life, and rather than wish that it could have been different, she says:

No, I think I'd keep everything just as it happened in my life, and I'll spend the rest of it trying to make it better. I've learned that the riches of this world aren't in what I own, but rather in who I am and what I give away. The question I've learned to ask myself, then, is what makes me most happy? I guess I'll know if I've answered it correctly when I go home for good—and I'm looking forward to that day.

More than the pages of this book can convey, I've had a glimpse of what's beyond this life, and it was great!

... I'm "homesick" and anxious to return home, but I also know I have "work" to do before I can—work that, now that ordinances have been performed and laws accepted and woven into the fabric of my life, has to do with loving and serving others without judgment. . . .

. . . I know that the best is yet to come. (*I Stand All Amazed*, pp. 165–66)

CAPTAIN DALE BLACK

The last paragraph of Captain Black's book reads:

"[Life is] *so* worth it."

This is your captain speaking: Before I sign off, I want to thank you for taking this trip with me. May the Lord's protection be upon you wherever you go. Wherever it is, may God go with you. May *He* be your Captain, and *you* the copilot. And when at last your journey is over and it's time for your wings to be folded, know this: Your homecoming will be worth the trip it took to get you there, however bumpy the ride, whatever "crashes" you experience along the way.

Yes, it will be *so* worth it.

You can trust me on that! (*Flight to Heaven*, p. 181)

AUTHOR'S PERSPECTIVE

I wonder how many personal acquaintances of these Witnesses cornered them and asked, "So, you went to heaven then came back. Come on. Really?"

I'm sure these Witnesses knew beforehand that they would be doubted and ridiculed. They must have known that their personal and professional credibility would be put at risk. To make a few bucks selling a book seems like inadequate compensation for that.

It seems obvious that they recorded their accounts because they felt they had an *obligation* to do so; that it was part of their mission in life. They wanted to *do a generous thing* and impart a message that could offer comfort and peace for many individuals in need.

I have nothing but respect and appreciation for these Witnesses. Their accounts are fascinating and inspiring. I highly recommend that you read their books in their entirety.

88

PARTING THOUGHTS FROM THE AUTHOR

In the Preface of this book, I posed some fundamental questions asked by deep-thinkers.

Based upon the resources we have drawn from in this book, and in part from my own personal faith, the following are brief answers to some of those questions.

WHERE DID I COME FROM?

Prior to our birth, we lived in a world of spirits—the offspring of heavenly parents. We progressed to a point where we desired to come to earth to have the experiences that can only be had with a physical body.

WHY AM I HERE ON EARTH?

To prepare to die

The way I see it, the purpose of our lives is to prepare to go home, and hopefully not be too embarrassed when we get there and see our Life Review. That review will go better if we have learned to show love unconditionally, which can be done by taking an interest in peoples' lives and being willing to make some sacrifices on their behalf.

To learn to love God and all men

We are on earth to find God and Jesus Christ. We are here to learn to trust them and learn to love them. We need to learn to obey their commandments and learn to love our spiritual siblings unconditionally—the same way God loves us.

To seek knowledge and development

Finally, we are earth to have instructive experiences and to obtain knowledge and understanding. Even if we have to learn it from "the school of hard knocks, where the school colors are black and blue and the school yell is 'Ouch!'" (An idiomatic phrase coined by Elbert Hubbard in a piece he wrote for *Cosmopolitan* in 1902. See also Wikipedia, "School of Hard Knocks," last updated 9 December 2017, en.wikipedia.org/wiki/School_of_Hard_Knocks.)

WHY DOES LIFE HAVE TO BE SO DIFFICULT?

The greatest growth and learning is typically achieved during a time of struggle, not ease.

Struggle gracefully

The challenge is to *struggle gracefully* through the trials of life, to learn to trust that God will help us through our trials, and to focus on being grateful for all the good things in our lives.

Fortunately, we don't have to struggle alone. God, the perfect administrator, has authorized and delegated authority to spirit beings to guide and inspire us in every aspect of our lives.

Life is like a university.

Earth is like a great university, and the most important courses are CDFR courses (Child Development and Family Relations).

The first commandment given by God to Adam and Eve was "Be fruitful, and multiply, and replenish the earth" (Genesis 1:28). He gave that commandment because He knows that the family unit yields the greatest source of happiness.

After that, you have the challenge of developing good family relationships, because those relationships can potentially provide an eternity of happiness. And let's not forget that everyone on the earth is part of the same spirit family.

In addition to the CDFR courses, we should seek truth and knowledge energetically, inasmuch as that is something we can take with us and give us advantage in the next world.

Keith A. Haslem

WHAT WILL HAPPEN TO ME AFTER I DIE?

When God decides that we have done enough to "graduate" from mortality, we die and go back into a world of spirits where we will be surrounded by people who are *like us*. Hopefully these will be people with whom we developed mutually loving relationships on earth, not miserable self-absorbed individuals incapable of loving anyone but themselves.

The optimal realm will be the one in which the inhabitants enjoy the presence of God and His Son, Jesus Christ. Their love for us is, by all accounts, wonderful beyond description.

No fear of death

I have no fear of death. I look forward to going home!

No more financial worries. A nice home with *no mortgage*. No health problems. No dieting. A beautiful living environment. Fantastic, free, and convenient vacations. Incredible abilities to acquire knowledge. A reunion with earthly family and friends *and* the spiritual friends I had for eons of time before coming to earth.

Looking forward to a reunion with my elder brother

What I look forward to most—the most thrilling part of graduating—is my reunion with the Prince of Peace, our elder brother, the Son of God—Jesus Christ. He loves *everyone* unconditionally. So, he must love me. And you too.

APPENDICES

APPENDIX A

MEMORABLE QUOTES

BETTY J. EADIE

In her book *Embraced by the Light*, Betty said:

- Regarding the creation of the earth: "We all assisted in creating our conditions here" (p. 47).
- Without feelings of self-love . . . the love we feel for others is counterfeit (p. 60).
- God wants us to become as he is (p. 61).
- Service is a balm to both the spirit and body (p. 63).
- [In the premortal world] we were very willing, even anxious . . . to accept all of our ailments, illnesses [that we would endure in mortality] (p. 67).
- I saw galaxies and traveled to them with . . . almost instantaneous speed . . . meeting our spiritual brothers and sisters (p. 88).
- Our good deeds and kind words will come back to bless us a hundred fold after this life (p. 101).
- Our strength will be found in our charity (p. 102).
- Eve . . . wanted to become a mother desperately (p. 109).
- If we're kind, we'll have joy (p. 114).
- If I am unable to forgive myself, it is impossible for me to truly forgive others (p. 116).

Alluding to guardian angels:

- We are all precious and carefully watched over (p. 121).
- Every unhappy experience had allowed me to obtain greater

Appendix A

understanding. . . . I saw that the guardian angels remained with me through my trials (p. 115).
- Greater joy will come to us through love than in any other way (p. 147).

SARAH LANELLE MENET

In her book *There Is No Death*, Sarah said:

- On the feeling of well-being that exists in the spirit world; it is "like being wrapped in a blanket of love" (p. 32).
- No righteous person in this world dies before his or her time (p. 51).
- One of the main reasons we come to earth is to learn to develop . . . unconditional love for others (p. 94).
- [In the premortal world,] we formed groups . . . with those spirits we wanted to have as part of our earthly family (p. 105).
- Very little [of what happens in our lives] is by accident (p. 115).

RANELLE WALLACE

In her book *The Burning Within*, RaNelle said:

- We simply don't have the language [to describe] the beauty of [the spirit] world (p. 102).
- You must love yourself before you can love others (p. 114).
- Told by her grandmother: "The key is love. . . . The key is love. . . . The key is love" (p. 116).

ELANE DURHAM

In *I Stand All Amazed*, Elane said:

- I learn to love others through serving them (p. 39).
- I had a Father in heaven [and] a Mother as well (p. 40).
- Wealth lies not in what I own . . . but rather what I give away (p. 60).

- Suffering becomes a soul-building experience (p. 79).
- Earth life [is] only scant seconds in the eternal scheme of things (p. 82).
- I know that the best is yet to come (p. 166).

CAPTAIN DALE BLACK

In his book *Flight to Heaven*, Captain Black said:

- Yes, [life] will be so worth it (p. 181).

GEORGE G. RITCHIE JR.

In his book *Return from Tomorrow*, Dr. Ritchie said:

- On the love he sensed from Jesus: "An astonishing love. A love beyond my wildest imagining" (p. 49).
- [Those who commit suicide are] chained to every consequence of their act (p. 59).
- [Dr. Ritchie saw spirits who had developed in mortality with] a dependence on alcohol that went beyond physical.... That became mental ... spiritual (p. 61).
- The quality of our lives in the next world will depend on how we get on with the "business of loving" ... in this world (p. 124).

RAYMOND A. MOODY JR.

In his book *Life After Life*, Dr. Moody said:

- There will always be a quest for knowledge ... it goes on after death (p. 68).
- On what death is: "You just graduate from one thing to another" (p. 97).

In his book *Reflections on Life After Death*, Dr. Moody said:

- More than ever now I am very careful to let each person I love know how I feel. (p. 112).

Appendix A

ELISABETH KÜBLER-ROSS

In her book *On Life After Death*, Dr. Kübler-Ross said:

- Nobody will die alone (p. 9).
- Life on earth was nothing but a school. . . . As soon as you have finished this school and mastered your lessons, you are allowed to go home, to graduate! (p. 11).
- My wish is that you pass on to many people a little more love. . . . There are twenty million children in the world dying of starvation. Adopt one of those children, and start buying smaller presents (p. 14).

KENNETH RING

In his book *Heading Toward Omega*, Dr. Ring said:

- For NDErs, the equations Death=God=Love are obvious (p. 85).

MELVIN MORSE

In his book *Closer to the Light*, Dr. Morse said:

- All men must die and death is not to be feared (p. 197).

BRIGHAM YOUNG

- We have more friends behind the veil than on this side (*Discourses of Brigham Young*, p. 379).

JOSEPH SMITH JR.

On children who die:

- They were too pure, too lovely, to live on this earth (*History of the Church*, 4:553–54).
- The mother who laid down her little child . . . [will] after the resurrection . . . have all the joy . . . in seeing her child grow to the full measure of the stature of its spirit (*Gospel Doctrine*, p. 453).

Appendix A

BRUCE R. MCCONKIE

- Hell will have an end (*Mormon Doctrine*, p. 349).

JEFFREY R. HOLLAND

- [Angels] are always near. . . . God never leaves us alone, never leaves us unaided ("The Ministry of Angels," *Ensign*, November 2008).

GORDON B. HINCKLEY

- It isn't as bad as you sometimes think it is. It all works out. Don't worry. . . . Put your trust in God, and move forward with faith and confidence in the future (Jordan Utah South regional conference, priesthood session, March 1, 1997).

MARK TWAIN

As quoted in *Memories of Heaven*:
- It ain't what you don't know that gets you into trouble. It's what you know for sure that just ain't so (Dyer, p. 32).

MOTHER THERESA

As quoted in *There Is No Death*:
- Love is service to others (Menet, p. 97).

APPENDIX B

INSPIRING BOOKS

Chapter 41 addresses the purpose of trials and hardships in life. The following books detail the tremendous challenges endured by their authors and illustrate the strength of the human spirit to endure difficult times.

BOOK	AUTHOR
Alicia: My Story	Alicia Appleman-Jurman
Burned Alive: A Victim of the Law of Men	Souad
Dancing Under the Red Star: The Extraordinary Story of Margaret Werner, the Only American Woman to Survive Stalin's Gulag	Karl Tobien
Fifty Russian Winters: An American Woman's Life in the Soviet Union	Margaret Wettlin
First They Killed My Father: A Daughter of Cambodia Remembers	Loung Ung
In My Hands: Memories of a Holocaust Rescuer	Irene Gut Opdyke
Indestructible: One Man's Rescue Mission That Changed the Course of WWII	John R. Bruning
Life Without Limits: Inspiration for a Ridiculously Good Life	Nick Vujicic
The Long Walk: The True Story of a Trek to Freedom	Slavomir Rawicz
Long Walk to Freedom: The Autobiography of Nelson Mandela	Nelson Mandela
Man's Search for Meaning	Viktor E. Frankl

Appendix B

BOOK	AUTHOR
Notes from the Gallows	Julius Fuchik
A Single Tear: A Family's Persecution, Love, and Endurance in Communist China	Ningkun Wu
Still Me	Christopher Reeve
Unbroken: A World War II Story of Survival, Resilience, and Redemption	Laura Hillenbrand

APPENDIX C

BIBLIOGRAPHY

Alexander, Eben. *Proof of Heaven: A Neurosurgeon's Journey into the Afterlife.* New York: Simon & Schuster Paperbacks, 2012.

Alonso, Jose L. "Love One Another as He Has Loved Us." *Ensign.* November 2017.

Benson, Ezra Taft. "Life Is Eternal." *Ensign.* June 1971.

Black, Dale. *Flight to Heaven: A Plane Crash . . . A Lone Survivor . . . A Journey to Heaven—and Back.* Bloomington, MN: Bethany House, 2010.

Bradley, James *Flyboys: A True Story of Courage.* New York: Back Bay Books, 2003.

Brinkley, Dannion, and Paul Perry. *Saved by the Light: The True Story of a Man Who Died Twice and the Profound Revelations He Received.* New York: HarperCollins, 2008.

Brown, Joyce H. *God's Heavenly Answers: Near-Death Experiences Revealed.* Mesquite, NV: Davidson Press, 2014.

Bruning, John R. *Indestructible: One Man's Rescue Mission That Changed the Course of WWII.* Hachette Books, 2017.

Burpo, Todd, and Lynn Vincent. *Heaven Is for Real: A Little Boy's Astounding Story of His Trip to Heaven and Back.* Nashville: HIFR Ministries, 2010.

Burton, Alma, and Clea Burton. *For They Shall Be Comforted.* Springville, UT: Cedar Fort, 1995.

Children's Songbook. Salt Lake City: The Church of Jesus Christ of Latter-day Saints, 1989.

Crowther, Duane S. *Life Everlasting: A Definitive Study of Life After Death.* Springville, UT: Horizon Publishers, 2005.

Discourses of Brigham Young. Compiled by John A. Widtsoe. 1954.

Appendix C

Dougherty, Ned. *Fast Lane to Heaven: A Life-After-Death Journey.* Charlottesville, VA: Hampton Roads, 2001.

Dunn, Marcia. "7 Earth-size worlds found orbiting star; could hold life." *Deseret News.* February 22, 2017.

Durham, Elane. *I Stand All Amazed: Love and Healing from Higher Realms.* Granite Publishing, 1998.

Dyer, Wayne W., and Dee Garnes. *Memories of Heaven: Children's Astounding Recollections of the Time Before They Came to Earth.* Hay House, 2015.

Eadie, Betty J. *Embraced by the Light: The Most Profound and Complete Near-Death Experience Ever.* Gold Leaf Press, 1992.

Eby, Richard E., *Caught Up into Paradise.* Revell, 1978.

Evans, Richard L. *Richard Evans' Quote Book.* Publishers Press, 1971.

"The Family: A Proclamation to the World." *Ensign.* November 2010.

Gallup, George. *Adventures in Immortality: A Look Beyond the Threshold of Death.* McGraw Hill, 1982.

Green, Elmer and Alyce Green. *Beyond Biofeedback.* Delacorte Press, 1977.

Habib, Samaa, and Bodie Thoene. *Face to Face with Jesus: A Former Muslim's Extraordinary Journey to Heaven and Encounter with the God of Love.* Bloomington, MN: Chosen Books, 2014.

Harris, Barbara, and Lionel C. Bascom. *Full Circle: The Near-Death Experience and Beyond.* Pocket Books, 1990.

Hinze, Sarah. *Coming from the Light: Spiritual Accounts of Life Before Life.* Springville, UT: Cedar Fort, 1994.

Holland, Jeffrey R. "Like a Broken Vessel." *Ensign.* November 2013.

———. "The Ministry of Angels." *Ensign.* November 2008.

Hymns of the Church of Jesus Christ of Latter-day Saints. Salt Lake City: The Church of Jesus Christ of Latter-day Saints, 1985.

Journal of Discourses. 26 vols. 1854–1886.

Kimball, Spencer W. *Teachings of Presidents of the Church: Spencer W. Kimball.* Salt Lake City: The Church of Jesus Christ of Latter-day Saints, 2006.

King James Bible. Latter-day Saint ed. 2013.

Kramarik, Akiane, and Foreli Kramarik. *Akiane: Her Life, Her Art, Her Poetry.* Nashville: W. Publishing, 2006.

Kübler-Ross, Elisabeth. *On Life After Death.* Berkeley, CA: Celestial Arts, 1991.

Appendix C

Lewis, C. S. *The Problem of Pain*. New York: HarperCollins, 1996.

Long, Jeffrey, and Paul Perry. *Evidence of the Afterlife: The Science of Near-Death Experiences*. New York: HarperCollins, 2010.

Lundwall, N. B. *The Vision*. Bookcraft, 1946.

Malz, Betty. *My Glimpse of Eternity*. Bloomington, MN: Chosen Books, 1977.

Mandela, Nelson. *Long Walk to Freedom: The Autobiography of Nelson Mandela*. Little, Brown, 1994.

McConkie, Bruce R. *Mormon Doctrine*. Salt Lake City: Deseret Book, 1958.

McKay, David O. Conference Report. October 1966.

Menet, LaNelle Sarah. *There Is No Death: The Extraordinary True Experience of Sarah LaNelle Menet*. Mountain Top, 2002.

Monson, Thomas S. "What Have I Done for Someone Today?" *Ensign*. November 2009.

Moody, Raymond A., Jr. *Life After Life: The Bestselling Original Investigation That Revealed "Near-Death Experiences."* Mockingbird, 1975.

Moody, Raymond A., Jr. *The Light Beyond: New Explorations by the Author of* Life After Life. Bantam, 1989.

Moody, Raymond A., Jr. *Reflections on Life After Life*. Bantam, 1977.

Morse, Melvin, and Paul Perry. *Closer to the Light: Learning from the Near-Death Experiences of Children*. New York: Random House, 1990.

"Mother in Heaven." *LDS.org*. Accessed March 30, 2018. www.lds.org/topics/mother-in-heaven?lang=eng.

Neal, Mary C. *To Heaven and Back: A Doctor's Extraordinary Account of Her Death, Heaven, Angels, and Life Again*. New York: Random House, 2011.

Nelson, Russell M. "Doors of Death." *Ensign*. May 1992.

Ningkun, Wu, and Yikai Li. *A Single Tear: A Family's Persecution, Love, and Endurance in Communist China*. Little, Brown, 1993.

Oaks, Dallin H. "The Aaronic Priesthood and the Sacrament." *Ensign*. November 1998.

Osis, Karlis, and Erlendur Haraldsson. *At the Hour of Death: The Results of Research on Over 1,000 Afterlife Experiences*. Avon, 1977.

Peck, M. Scott. *The Road Less Traveled: A New Psychology of Love, Traditional Values, and Spiritual Growth*. Simon & Schuster, 1978.

Appendix C

Piper, Don, and Cecil Murphey. *90 Minutes in Heaven: A True Story of Death and Life*. Revell, 2014.

Pontius, John. *Visions of Glory: One Man's Astonishing Account of the Last Days*. Springville, UT: Cedar Fort, 2012.

Pratt, Parley P. *Key to the Science of Theology*. Salt Lake City: Deseret Book, 1973.

Rawlings, Maurice. *Beyond Death's Door*. Thomas Nelson, 1978.

Richardson, Lance. *The Message*. American Family Publishing, 2000.

Ring, Kenneth. *Heading Toward Omega: In Search of the Meaning of the Near-Death Experience*. William Morrow, 1984.

Ring, Kenneth. *Life at Death: A Scientific Investigation of the Near-Death Experience*. William Morrow, 1982.

Ritchie, George G., Jr. *My Life After Dying: How 9 Minutes in Heaven Taught Me How to Live on Earth*. Charlottesville, VA: Hampton Roads, 1991.

Ritchie, George G., Jr., and Elizabeth Sherrill. *Return from Tomorrow*. Grand Rapids, MI: Chosen Books, 1978.

Romano, David A. "When Tomorrow Starts Without Me," In *Chicken Soup for the Teenage Soul on Tough Stuff: Stories of Tough Times and Lessons Learned*. Edited by Jack Canfield, Mark Victor Hansen, and Kimberly Kirkberger. Chicken Soup for the Soul Publishing, 2012.

Sabom, Michael B. *Recollections of Death: A Medical Investigation*. HarperCollins, 1981.

Scott, Elwood. *40 Days in Heaven: The True Testimony of Seneca Sodi's Visitation to Paradise, the Holy City and the Glory of God's Throne*. King Edward, 2010.

Shakespeare, William. *Two Gentlemen of Verona*. Folger Shakespeare Library, 1999.

Sharkey, Jenny. *A Glimpse of Eternity: One Man's Story of Life Beyond Death*. Arun Books, 2008.

Sill, Sterling W. "To Die Well." *Ensign*. November 1976.

Smith, Joseph. *History of the Church*. 7 vols. Salt Lake City: Deseret Book, 1991.

Smith, Joseph F. *Gospel Doctrine: Sermons and Writings of President Joseph F. Smith*. Deseret Book, 2002.

Smith, Joseph Fielding. *Teachings of the Prophet Joseph Smith*. Deseret Book, 1976.

Appendix C

Sorensen, Michele R., and David R. Willmore. *The Journey Beyond Life.* Sounds of Zion, 1988.

Springer, Rebecca Ruter. *My Dream of Heaven.* Harrison House, 2002.

Storm, Howard. *My Descent into Death: A Second Chance at Life.* Doubleday, 2005.

Strohm, Barry R. *Afterlife: What Really Happens on the Other Side.* Schiffer, 2015.

Sullivan, Marlene Bateman *Gaze into Heaven: Near-Death Experiences in Early Church History.* Springville, UT: Cedar Fort, 2013.

Tooley, Lawrence E. *I Saw Heaven: A Remarkable Visit to the Spirit World.* Horizon Publishers, 1997.

Top, Brent L. *What's on the Other Side?: What the Gospel Teaches Us about the Spirit World.* Salt Lake City: Deseret Book, 2012.

Uchtdorf, Dieter F. "A Yearning for Home." *Ensign.* November 2017.

Vujicic, Nick. *Life Without Limits: Inspiration for a Ridiculously Good Life.* Colorado Springs, CO: WaterBrook, 2010.

Wallace, RaNelle, and Curtis Taylor. *The Burning Within.* Gold Leaf, 1994.

Wixom, Hartt, and Judene Wixom. *Trial by Terror: Crisis in Cokeville, Wyoming.* Horizon Publishers, 1987.

Wood, Gary L. *A Place Called Heaven.* Tate Publishing, 2008.

APPENDIX D

PERMISSIONS

Excerpts from *Return from Tomorrow* by George G. Ritchie, copyright 1977. Used by permission of Chosen, a division of Baker Publishing Group.

Excerpts from *Flight to Heaven* by Captain Dale Black and Ken Gire, copyright 2010. Used by permission of Bethany House, a division of Baker Publishing Group.

Excerpts from *I Stand All Amazed* by Elane Durham, copyright 1998. Used by permission of Elane Durham.

Excerpts from *Embraced by the Light* by Betty J. Eadie, copyright 1992. Used by permission of Betty J. Eadie

Excerpts from *The Burning Within* by RaNelle Wallace with Curtis Taylor, copyright 1994. Used by permission of RaNelle Wallace.

Excerpts from *There Is No Death* by Sarah LaNelle Menet, copyright 2002. Used by permission of Sarah LaNelle Menet.

Excerpts from *Chicken Soup for the Teenage Soul on Tough Stuff* by Jack Canfield, Mark Victor Hansen, and Kimberly Kirberger, copyright 2012. Reprinted by permission. All rights reserved.

Excerpts from *Gaze into Heaven: Near-Death Experiences in Early Church History* by Marlene Bateman Sullican, copyright 2013. Used by permission of Cedar Fort, Inc.

Excerpts from *Coming from the Light: Powerful, Tender Accounts of Life Before Life* by Sarah Hinze, copyright 1994. Used by permission of Cedar Fort, Inc.

INDEX

A

addictions 211–12
age (in the spirit world) 50, 96–97, 101, 141
    of children who have died 304, 306–7
agency 31, 197, 223, 234, 242–43, 284, 303, 384
angel 51, 82, 103, 110, 150, 192, 195, 205–6, 209, 214, 217, 221, 227, 230, 251, 266, 297, 299, 309, 360, 392. *See also* being of light, guardian angel, and heavenly being
anger 270, 334, 351–52, 367, 371, 383

B

being of light 13, 56, 58, 61, 85–86, 111, 138, 175, 182, 338. *See also* being of light, guardian angel, and heavenly being
Black, Dale 6, 11, 13, 42, 49, 79, 85, 104–5, 150, 153, 158, 257, 409. *See also Flight to Heaven*
buildings 108, 120–22, 148–49, 372
Burning Within, the 6, 9, 30, 49, 56, 64, 75–76, 84, 96–97, 106, 110, 114, 119, 123, 140, 182, 243, 249, 294–96, 313, 322, 335,

Burning Withing, the (continued)
348–49, 410–11, 420, 430–31. *See also* Wallace, RaNelle

C

celestial kingdom 240, 396, 398, 399
Church of Jesus Christ of Latter-day Saints, the 2, 6–7, 20–21, 28–29, 32, 34 36, 39–40, 71–72, 82, 86, 89, 100, 103, 115, 123, 126, 143, 146, 149, 181, 184–85, 188, 200–1, 212, 219–20, 223, 234, 236–37, 239–40, 267, 273–74, 282, 285, 290, 304–7, 310, 313, 318–19, 327–29, 343–44, 351–53, 358–59, 362, 367, 376–77, 379, 380–82, 384, 388, 391, 393–96, 398–99
clothing (in the spirit world) 100, 106–8, 121
Creation, the 114, 162, 357, 419

D

death 16, 25, 28, 32, 37–41, 52, 111, 114, 185, 204, 229–56, 257–58, 260, 271, 279–81, 286–87, 304–5, 328, 338, 370, 374, 376, 403–8, 416, 421, 423
depression 282–83, 341, 351–53, 383

433

Index

disabilities 190–91, 203
dreams 171, 266–67, 289–90, 292, 322
Durham, Elane 6, 10, 13, 29, 52, 65, 102, 104–5, 110, 139, 163, 181, 190, 203, 209, 213, 225, 236, 269, 275, 278, 312, 318, 324–25, 333, 336, 340, 359, 394, 409, 412. *See also I Stand All Amazed*

E

Eadie, Betty J. 5, 7, 13, 52, 117, 129, 181, 190, 203, 213, 222, 225, 229, 236, 254, 260, 269, 275, 284, 293, 308, 315, 321, 324, 333, 340, 349, 357, 359, 409. *See also Embraced by the Light*
Earth 29–34, 62, 68, 71–72, 74, 76, 78, 88, 92, 96, 106–7, 114–15, 118, 120–21, 123–24, 125–26, 131–32, 135–36, 141–42, 145–46, 156, 162–63, 181–82, 184, 190–98, 203–5, 209–10, 213–14, 220, 225, 229–30, 235–36, 238, 260, 266, 270–73, 294–97, 306, 315–16, 333–34, 342, 351, 354, 357–58, 359–63, 382–85, 391, 393, 399–400, 414–16, 419–20, 422
earthbound spirits 269, 270, 274
Embraced by the Light 5, 8, 29, 37, 38, 47–48, 55, 76, 93, 107, 113, 118, 121, 129, 136, 148, 154–55, 163, 177, 182, 187, 190, 194–95, 203–4, 214, 222–23, 226, 230, 236, 255, 260, 270, 278, 284, 296–97, 299, 308,

Embraced by the Light (continued) 316, 321, 324, 334–35, 341, 350, 357–58, 360, 411, 419. *See also* Eadie, Betty J.
escort 45–47, 63, 65, 142, 206
Eve 315–17
evil spirits 197, 289–90, 351–52, 382–88, 391

F

family 30–31, 32–33, 36, 44–46, 50, 52, 104, 120–21, 124, 141–42, 250, 289, 291, 296–98, 300–1, 304, 309, 318–19, 383, 388, 399, 415–16, 420
fear 39, 218, 255–56, 349–50, 370, 403, 406–7, 416
Final Judgment 381, 395–98
Flight to Heaven 6, 12, 43, 49, 66, 81–82, 85, 91, 94, 97, 105, 153, 158, 286, 413, 421. *See also* Black, Dale
flowers 75, 78, 90, 117–18, 198
food 133–34, 198, 263
forgiveness 54, 277, 323–24, 326–27
fragrances 74, 78, 81, 90

G

Garden of Eden 316–17
gender 32
graduation 37–38, 40, 244
guardian angels 51, 217, 221, 266, 309. *See also* angel

Index

H

heaven 31, 34, 81, 85, 90–91, 94, 120, 124, 147, 227, 240, 269, 306, 372, 384, 396, 398, 400
heavenly being 58. *See also* angel
heavenly city 79, 85, 105, 150, 153
hell 62, 83–84, 212, 269, 273, 282, 350, 367–77, 379–81, 395–96, 398–99
houses 158–59
humility 163, 240, 346, 406

I

I Stand All Amazed 6, 10–11, 30, 35, 37–38, 42, 48, 54, 65–66, 77, 92, 102, 104–5, 107, 110, 140, 163, 166, 181, 191–92, 195–96, 205–6, 209, 214, 237, 270, 279, 313, 318, 325–26, 336, 340–41, 361, 394, 413, 420. *See also* Durham, Elane

J

Jesus Christ 7, 11, 35, 39, 46–48, 53, 69, 150, 160, 162–63, 202, 285, 310, 324, 330, 374, 381, 384, 391–92, 397, 399, 400, 411, 414, 416

K

knowledge 60–61, 112–16, 120–21, 124, 131, 154–57, 163, 181–85, 225–26, 269–70, 322, 326, 349, 356, 360, 404, 411, 415–16, 421

Kramarik, Akiane 133, 134, 168–74, 427

L

language 39, 64, 74–75, 111, 114, 342, 407–8, 420
libraries 113, 120, 154–56
Life After Life 16–17, 26, 37–38, 51, 59–61, 66–67, 86, 97–99, 110–12, 156, 188, 280–81, 338, 403–4, 421, 428. *See also* Moody, Raymond A., Jr.
Life Review 53, 58, 60, 186, 324, 334, 414
location of the spirit world 72, 77, 125
love 27, 46–49, 52, 55, 60–61, 64–65, 74, 76, 78–79, 84–87, 90, 104–5, 140, 145–46, 153, 160–64, 181, 185, 188, 190–91, 201–2, 204, 210, 214, 224, 227, 245, 251, 254, 258–59, 281, 296, 321–23, 325, 333–39, 340–45, 350–57, 403–5, 407, 409–411, 414, 416, 419–23

M

materialism 355–56
Menet, Sarah LaNelle 6, 13, 29, 71, 133, 139, 145, 158, 190, 203, 209, 229, 236, 275, 289, 324, 340, 351, 354, 359, 367, 379, 382, 386, 391, 396, 409. *See also There Is No Death*
Millennium 391, 393
Moody, Raymond A., Jr. 16, 26, 38, 43, 51, 58, 66, 85, 97, 110–11, 114, 137, 182, 187, 259, 272,

435

Index

Moody, Raymond A., Jr. *(continued)* 279, 309, 337, 403, 421. See also *Life After Life*
Mother in Heaven 318–20
music 27, 74–75, 77, 80–81, 92–94, 117–18, 120, 122, 150, 153, 158, 188, 295, 302
My Life After Dying 7, 72, 130–32, 165, 215, 337, 370, 392, 410. See also Ritchie, George G.

N

NDE 2, 5, 8, 11, 13, 16–17, 26, 63, 83, 108, 119, 137, 226, 241, 297, 309, 338, 349, 372, 403–6. See also near-death experience
near-death experience 2, 5, 7–8, 10, 17, 27, 44, 61, 111, 130, 140, 150, 168, 198, 206, 230, 248, 250, 262, 273, 275, 279–80, 287, 295, 297, 300, 308–9, 325, 337, 340, 355, 396, 404, 407. See also NDE
nights 8, 71, 82, 88, 169, 198, 239, 245, 267, 285, 290, 298, 331

O

OBE 2, 5. See also out-of-body experience
other worlds 124, 196, 278, 359–63
out-of-body experience 2, 5, 11–12, 25, 44, 99, 257–59, 292

P

paradise 19, 82–83, 84–85, 159, 301, 391, 396, 427, 429
pets 145–47

possession 377, 386–88. See also evil spirits
prayer 172, 222–24, 285, 322, 374
predeath visions 244, 246
premortal existence 29, 31–32, 34, 140, 190, 206, 303. See also heaven

R

racial differences 104–5
repentance 54, 194, 240, 328–32, 399
Return from Tomorrow 5, 7, 42, 47, 56–57, 108, 122–23, 131, 149, 151, 156, 161, 176, 211–12, 272, 276, 368–70, 387, 409–10, 421, 429, 431. See also Ritchie, George G.
Ritchie, George G. 5, 7, 13, 41, 52, 129, 150, 211, 213, 269, 367, 386, 391. See also *Return from Tomorrow*

S

Second Coming 212, 307, 378, 381, 391, 392
service 181, 190–91, 193, 278, 336, 340–45, 353, 411, 423
spirit body 50, 95, 101, 109, 116, 127, 191, 309, 370
spirit children 157, 303, 312, 384
spiritual abilities 83, 109–10, 114–16, 127, 191, 197, 213, 224, 282, 303, 314, 358, 370, 416
spiritual activities 20, 94, 120–22, 141, 232, 353
spirit world 9, 13, 29, 31, 45–47, 50, 57–58, 63, 71–72, 74, 76,

Index

spirit world *(continued)* 83–84, 87–90, 92–95, 104, 106–7, 111, 113–14, 116–18, 120–21, 123, 125, 127, 129, 132, 134–35, 137, 139, 141–42, 145–46, 148, 150, 154–55, 157–58, 160, 164, 174, 194, 204, 210, 240, 246–48, 250, 257, 266, 268–70, 273, 278–79, 287–88, 290, 292–93, 296, 298–300, 306, 308, 328–32, 340, 342, 346, 348, 354, 367, 371–72, 378, 380, 386, 391, 396–97, 410–11, 420. *See also* heaven

suicide 13, 275–83, 421

T

telestial kingdom 396, 398–99
terrestrial kingdom 396, 398–400
There Is No Death 6, 13, 31, 35, 37–38, 50, 58, 71, 77–79, 88, 90, 94, 96–97, 107–9, 125, 127, 134, 137, 141–42, 146, 149, 155, 159, 164, 166–67, 191, 197, 205, 210, 230, 237, 254, 266, 279, 287, 290, 300–301, 326, 328, 337, 342–43, 352, 354, 360, 371–72, 379, 383–84, 388, 392, 397, 412, 420, 423. *See also* Menet, Sarah LaNelle

travel 63–68, 116, 121, 125–26 127–28, 359–60, 419
trials 30–31, 193–202, 203–8, 395, 415, 420, 424

V

vision (eyesight) 49, 71, 78, 82, 109–10, 117, 177

W

Wallace, RaNelle 8, 30, 48, 55, 63, 74, 84, 95, 97, 106, 110, 113, 118, 123, 136, 140, 182, 241, 249, 284, 293, 308, 313, 322, 335, 346, 349, 410, 420. *See also Burning Within, the*
wings (angel) 102–3
womanhood 312–14

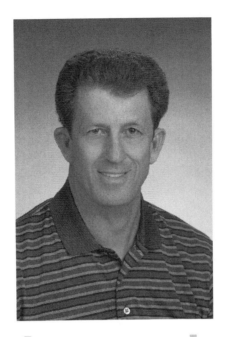

About the Author

Keith A. Haslem

Keith A. Haslem was born and raised in Orem, Utah, and still lives there with his wife, Sydney. They are the parents of five sons and the grandparents of twenty-seven grandchildren.

Haslem graduated from Brigham Young University with a bachelor's degree in accounting, and later received a master of business administration from Utah State University. He has practiced as a certified public accountant and is currently the owner and manager of Professional Employer Benefits, which provides payroll and benefits administration for small businesses.